African American Patients in Psychotherapy

African American Patients in Psychotherapy integrates history, current events, arts, psychoanalytic thinking, and case studies to provide a model for understanding the social and historical dimensions of psychological development across African American communities. Among the topics included are psychological consequences of slavery and Jim Crow, the black patient and the white therapist, the toll of even "small" racist enactments, the black patient's uneasy relationship with health care providers, and a revisiting of the idea of "black rage." Author Ruth Fallenbaum also examines the psychological potential of reparation for centuries of slave labor and legalized wage and property theft.

Ruth Fallenbaum, PhD, is a psychoanalytically oriented clinical psychologist in private practice in Berkeley, California.

African American Patients in Psychotherapy
Understanding the Psychological Effects of Racism and Oppression

Ruth Fallenbaum

NEW YORK AND LONDON

First published 2018
by Routledge
711 Third Avenue, New York, NY 10017

and by Routledge
2 Park Square, Milton Park, Abingdon, Oxon OX14 4RN

Routledge is an imprint of the Taylor & Francis Group, an informa business

© 2018 Ruth Fallenbaum

The right of Ruth Fallenbaum to be identified as author of this work has been asserted by her in accordance with sections 77 and 78 of the Copyright, Designs and Patents Act 1988.

All rights reserved. No part of this book may be reprinted or reproduced or utilized in any form or by any electronic, mechanical, or other means, now known or hereafter invented, including photocopying and recording, or in any information storage or retrieval system, without permission in writing from the publishers.

Trademark notice: Product or corporate names may be trademarks or registered trademarks, and are used only for identification and explanation without intent to infringe.

Library of Congress Cataloging-in-Publication Data
Names: Fallenbaum, Ruth, author.
Title: African American patients in psychotherapy : understanding the psychological effects of racism and oppression / Ruth Fallenbaum.
Description: New York, NY : Routledge, 2018. | Includes bibliographical references.
Identifiers: LCCN 2017045343 | ISBN 9780815371373 (hardcover : alk. paper) | ISBN 9780815371380 (pbk. : alk. paper) | ISBN 9781351181365 (e-book)
Subjects: | MESH: Psychotherapy | African Americans—psychology | Stress, Psychological—ethnology | Racism—psychology | Social Identification | Anger | United States
Classification: LCC RC480.5 | NLM WM 420 | DDC 616.89/14008996073—dc23
LC record available at https://lccn.loc.gov/2017045343

ISBN: 978-0-8153-7137-3 (hbk)
ISBN: 978-0-8153-7138-0 (pbk)
ISBN: 978-1-351-18136-5 (ebk)

Typeset in Goudy
by Keystroke, Neville Lodge, Tettenhall, Wolverhampton

To all my patients, with gratitude and respect.

Contents

	Acknowledgments	ix
1	The Psyche in History	1
	Dramatis Personae	19
2	Chains	21
3	From Lash to Backlash: Invisible Chains	46
4	Identity and the Discovery of "Race"	73
5	"Black Rage" Revisited	98
6	The Color of Psychotherapy	126
7	In Session	151
8	Reparations	177
	Index	192

Acknowledgments

From start to finish, I have been exceptionally fortunate to have had the best kind of assistance and support one could hope for. My patients have guided me to work to understand them, and each one has taught me valuable lessons about life, history, and how to practice clinical psychology. Two talented and generous friends and colleagues, Ghislaine Boulanger and Diane Ehrensaft, have put extraordinary time and thought into helping this project become a book that can hopefully be of use to fellow mental health professionals. They have read every word and provided invaluable feedback, and have helped me negotiate the publishing world with a tenacity that has made my head spin. I cannot thank them enough. I am indebted as well to two non-psychotherapist friends. Bill Issel, professor emeritus of U.S. social and cultural history at San Francisco State University, provided me with a superb reading list to better acquaint me with the historical realities of slavery and Reconstruction. Likewise, Rodger Birt, professor emeritus of humanities at San Francisco State University, gave me a very thoughtful list of readings in black literature that I doubt I would have happened upon without his help. Thank you also to consultants Laura Mason and Nadine Tang for their willingness to share their thoughts about cross-cultural research, and to Jessica Benjamin for her ideas that helped to inform the final chapter.

The warmth and enthusiasm of friends has been sustaining. They cannot imagine how important they have been to me throughout this process: Julia Gresser, Rachael Peltz, Susan Kolodny, Jackie Brookman, Jeanne Wolff Bernstein, Cynthia Carmichael, Sandra Seidlitz, Gale Bell, Kathleen Weaver, Bob Baldock, and my cousin, Julie Moskowitz. Thanks also to Tony Papanikolas for steering me towards some readings that turned out to be important in my thinking about racism in this country, and I am grateful to my long-time friend and colleague, Philip Coleman, for his insights on biracial psychotherapy.

And finally there is my husband, Zeese Papanikolas, loyal supporter and careful reader, who had a wonderful knack of dropping books on my desk that "you might want to look at," and which inevitably enriched this book in so many subtle ways.

I would also like to thank Alfred Music and Hal Leonard LLC for giving me permission to reprint lyrics from the song "(What Did I Do To Be So) Black And Blue":

To the Agreement dated September 15, 2017 between ALFRED PUBLISHING LLC and Ruth Fallenbaum:

(WHAT DID I DO TO BE SO) BLACK AND BLUE

Music by THOMAS "FATS" WALLER and HARRY BROOKS

Words by ANDY RAZAF

Copyright © 1929 (Renewed) EMI MILLS MUSIC, INC., CHAPPELL & CO., INC. and RAZAF MUSIC CO.

All Rights Reserved

Used By Permission of ALFRED MUSIC

FOR OUR 33.34% CONTROL IN THE UNITED STATES and EUROPE

FOR OUR 100% CONTROL IN THE REST OF THE WORLD – EXCLUDING AUSTRALIA

(What Did I Do To Be So) Black And Blue

Words by Andy Razaf
Music by Harry Brooks and Fats Waller
Copyright (c) 1929 by Chappell & Co., EMI Mills Music Inc. and Razaf Music
Copyright Renewed
All Rights for Razaf Music Administered by BMG Rights Management (US) LLC All Rights Reserved Used by Permission
Reprinted by Permission of Hal Leonard LLC

1 The Psyche in History

America has not been kind to its citizens of African descent. Ever. Although adaptability, resilience, and creativity have enabled African Americans to survive the abusive and exploitive American experience into which they were forced, it is no secret that since August 1619, when the first slaves stepped ashore in Virginia, for most black Americans equal access to the success, satisfaction, or even physical safety that their country seems to offer others has been held tantalizingly out of reach. Yet through it all, African Americans persisted and contributed to every aspect of American life. The music that came out of slavery survived the Klan and the indignities of racial prejudice and has become the heart and soul, the very rhythm, of our national culture. Righting the racial injustices has been a persistent challenge for black Americans, and their struggles for liberation, along with the support at times of sympathetic whites, have provided some of U.S. history's most powerful and moving moments. Occasionally, government policy has aligned with these movements, whether for Emancipation or through the Voting Rights Act of 1964, affirmative action, or the desegregation of public schools. These policies and others represent attempts at repairing the wounds of racism as they have presented themselves in their respective eras.

But what of the accumulation of psychological injuries done to those subjected to these injustices along the way? What role can psychotherapy play in addressing the effects of racism and the challenges of "living in America while black"? Are there things that a therapist of another racial background needs to consider that are different when treating an African American client from those that need to be considered when treating non-black clients? For that matter, can white psychotherapists offer meaningful treatment to their black clients at all? In this book, I take up these questions, reflecting on and sharing lessons learned in my work as a white clinical psychologist with a history of working with African American patients.

You may wonder at the value of a book about working with African Americans written by someone who is not. Don't think I have not wondered the same thing. Race—and particularly the black/white divide—is such a powerful signifier in our culture that a writer's racial and ethnic identification feels significant in a way that it might not be were she writing about almost any other subject in psychology. This awkwardness among those of us living with the fabrication we call race complicates to one degree or another all biracial relationships, including the psychotherapeutic relationship. While I bring my own experience and perspective to this subject, I want to acknowledge some of the important books by psychologists and other mental health professionals on the African American experience and psychotherapy: Akhtar's *The African American Experience: Psychoanalytic Perspectives*, Carter's *The Influence of Race and Racial Identity in Psychotherapy*, De Gruy's *Post Traumatic Slave Syndrome*, Grier and Cobbs's *Black Rage*, Jackson and Greene's *Psychotherapy with African American Women*, Vaughans' and Spielberg's *The Psychology of Black Boys and Adolescents*, and White's *Unmasking Race, Culture, and Attachment in the Psychoanalytic Space*. Throughout the book my debt to many others as well, whose articles about race and psychotherapy are cited, will be evident.

In this chapter, I hope to provide an orientation to my approach to the material that will follow. Chapter 2 will focus on how echoes of the experience of slavery continue in the psyches of the descendants of slaves, and takes a look at the continuation of modes of resistance and creativity given birth during its brutality. The following chapter picks up the survey of African American life from Emancipation to the present, and how the cycle of progress and backlash has been processed psychologically through generations of black families. Chapter 4 takes up questions of identity and the personal meanings of race for African Americans in response to white racist mythology, considering issues including microaggressions, the role of skin hue in self-image and family relationships, and ideas about "becoming black." Chapter 5 takes up the relationship between injustice, anger, and trauma—what happens when anger is suppressed, and what happens when it runs amok? Chapter 6 looks at the impact of the therapist's whiteness on the experiences of African American patients in treatment, and looks more broadly at black experience with health care professionals and how that experience affects feelings an African American may have about seeking help. In that chapter, I also look briefly at the mythology of whiteness. In Chapter 7, thoughts about and experiences of racism as brought into session by patients, and areas of confusion and ambiguity around these experiences, will be discussed, as well as countertransference challenges. Throughout all of these chapters, the emphasis will be on the clients, whom you will meet shortly, and how these various topics manifest themselves in their treatments. The final chapter, however, will be different. Here I will look at the word "reparation" in its psychoanalytic incarnation and as a political movement of black Americans seeking acknowledgment of and concrete compensation for the costs they have borne for slavery and subsequent generations of discrimination. How might the success of the reparations movement contribute to the mental health of African American individuals, not to mention their white fellow Americans?

History, Justice, and Psychotherapy

Over the course of 30 years as a clinical psychologist, at least half of my caseload of both short-term and long-term psychodynamic therapy patients has been

African American. What I have come to believe through my work with all of my clients, and through my own analysis and psychotherapy over the years, is the critical role that historical context, including the intergenerational transmission of trauma, plays in psychological development. Nowhere has this fact been driven home as clearly as in my work with the African American men and women who have sat in my consulting room. They have enabled me to learn with them how the injuries, past and present, inflicted by centuries of racism infuse the psychic conflicts of familial relationships and the internal worlds of those who live with these injuries. Furthermore, as my patients deal with continued experiences of racism in their daily interactions with the wider world, I am witness to the emotional processes generated by those current, real-world experiences. My learning has been a slow process in some cases, and that slowness, in turn, has given me a particular sense of urgency to pass on what I have learned.

One of the guiding principles of this book is the affirmation of the vital role of history, in its broadest sense, in the human psyche. An essential goal of psychoanalytically oriented clinical work is to help clients discover and respect their own depths and complexities as psychosocial individuals, to see themselves as whole persons. Often, however, what is explored in the course of psychodynamic psychotherapy is limited to what happens in the consulting room, within the patient's family past and present, and possibly also at the patient's workplace or with friends. Although all of that material is terribly important, to understand a whole person we must acknowledge that the family into which a person has been born has been created, and is currently immersed, in a particular place and moment with roots in history, and that this context is not separable from other psychological experiences in the person's life. In other words, the history and the social environment are not to be considered *in addition* to familial and object relations; they must be recognized as *part of* those formative relationships.

As it happens, psychoanalytically oriented therapy is uniquely suited to this approach. The leisure of having time to allow to unfold, within the relationship between patient and therapist, the elaboration of the patient's memories, thoughts, feelings, and actions can generate the kind of curiosity and imaginative space needed to develop a "thick description" of the patient's being, to adapt anthropologist Clifford Geertz's term, and the richer understanding so critical to psychoanalytically informed work. As I hope to demonstrate, historical realities permeate the consciousnesses of the people whom you will be meeting throughout the book. Sadly, because the history of African Americans in this country is so exceptionally rife with terrorism and violence, from slavery to lynching to yesterday's shooting by a police officer of another unarmed African American, the traumatic nature of much of that history remains embedded in the psychological histories of black survivors, often unprocessed and thus ripe for unconscious transmission from parent to child.

Appreciation of the role of history in people's psyches is not a new idea within psychoanalytic writing. In the decades following World War II, pioneers in the field began to report and reflect upon their observations of survivors of both Nazi concentration camps and the unprecedented destruction of the nuclear bombings of Hiroshima and Nagasaki. Their work bears witness to the long-term psychological effects on the millions of ordinary people who are victims of the events that scream out from newspaper headlines and are subsequently reconstituted into chapters in history books. Henry Krystal's 1968 book, *Massive Psychic Trauma*, broke ground in documenting his and others' work with survivors of the Nazi camps who had been resettled in the U.S. The book is a moving collection of papers and discussions by psychotherapists struggling to determine how to treat the emotional suffering of men, women, and children in the decades following their liberation from the camps, and is in many ways a fascinating historical document. Robert Jay Lifton's *Death in Life: Survivors of Hiroshima* (1968/1991), based on interviews with survivors 17 years after the dropping of the atomic bomb, likewise confirms the profound effects on the psyche caused by the traumatic events that persist long after those events have receded from immediate view.

With the next generation of analysts who came of age after World War II, and who began to reflect on the impact the survivors of the Shoah had on the psychological developments of their descendants, the intergenerational transmission of trauma emerged as a field of study. Faimberg (1988, 2005) articulated the collapsing of time as the traumas of one generation become expressed in the next. Davoine and Gaudilliere's *History Beyond Trauma* (2004), focused on psychotic expressions of World War II trauma in Europe as seen in their treatment of the post-war generation. In 1946, perhaps a decade after his move to the U.S. and less than a year following the end of World War II, Erik Erikson advised that the "analysis of the ego should include that of the individual's ego identity in relation to the historical changes which dominated his childhood milieu" (Erikson, 1946, p. 395). It would have seemed irrational, given what he saw and lived through, to try to understand a person's psychological development in isolation from the dramatic and disruptive events a child in Europe in the late 1930s and early 1940s would have experienced. And American analysts and psychologists have written about the traumatic residues of slavery on the African American psyche, as will be discussed in more detail below and particularly in the next chapter.

Related developments have enabled psychoanalysis to think about individual subjectivity not only transgenerationally, but also in the context of the effects of contemporary realities beyond the consulting room or family home. Psychoanalysts who have pushed to open up the clinical field in order to look at social and environmental implications for understanding the individual and psychoanalytic process include Altman (1995) dealing with race and class in a public clinic, and looking at history in therapy (2005); Dimen (2011) on a variety of cultural complications in the lives and practices of fellow clinicians; Boulanger on the psychic impact of immigration as discovered in her analytic work (2004, 2015), and in her work with psychotherapists in the aftermath of Hurricane Katrina (2013); Grand (2010) on analysis of a Vietnam veteran;

and, as will be described further in later chapters, Leary (1997a, 1997b, 2000), Hamer (2002, 2006), Vaughans (2014a, 2014b), Suchet (2004), Gump (2010), Holmes (1999, 2006), and others describing some of the complexities regarding race and racism in psychoanalytic treatment. "Culture," as Muriel Dimen (2011) wrote, "saturates subjective experience" (p. 4).

These writers are all talking about working with patients in a way that situates the patient in his or her real world. When historical context is sidelined, as Layton (2006) warns, a patient can mistakenly identify understandable feelings of pain over a distressing situation as an illegitimate reaction to a personal failing. Or an action by another that is felt to be an injustice can be discounted, misidentified, and perceived by its victim to be a universally accepted norm. The inability of the therapist to consider historical context can thus lead the therapist and client into sharing a distorted understanding of the meanings of events in the client's life. However, when the therapist does think historically, clinical material may require the therapist to introduce into a session an observation or recollection of historical, sociological, or political material. Such an intervention, although atypical, may be the most clinically appropriate response. When a woman berates herself for becoming angry following an incident in which she was racially profiled, as did my patient Tracy, crying, "I used to be able to handle that stuff," it is sometimes important to let her know that her reaction of anger to a real insult is not a sign of pathology as much as it is an understandable reaction to hostility, particularly as it was one of a life-long and intergenerational series of such insults. We will learn more about Tracy in later chapters.

Not only are patient and therapist both subjects and objects of history, but each therapy treatment also takes place in a unique historical moment, in which patient and therapist are both players and witnesses. A particularly clear examination of the inseparability of internal experience and the events of the "real world" is Boulanger's *Wounded by Reality: Understanding and Treating Adult Onset Trauma* (2007), in which she elaborates on the issues that emerged while working in her Manhattan office with fellow New Yorkers suffering from the effects of trauma in the aftermath of the attacks on the World Trade Center. But therapists must also think about the impact on themselves and their patients of current events and social forces that are experienced only indirectly, through the media. These printed and televised realities of daily life in America certainly figure into the discussions of case material throughout the book, as events such as the rise of Barack Obama or the death of a teenage African American boy walking home with a bag of Skittles weave their way into the minds of both patients and therapists. From time to time, a news event may actually be the catalyst for the decision to seek therapy or to move an existing therapy in a new and unexpected direction. In 1991, a middle-aged woman came to see me at the clinic where I worked, saying she wanted to finally talk about her childhood experience of being touched inappropriately by her uncle, an event that had filled her with shame and confusion, and which she had never revealed. It was only after a few sessions that she mentioned that watching Anita Hill testify at the confirmation hearings for Clarence Thomas that year, in which Hill spoke openly about having been sexually harassed by Thomas, made the client begin to entertain the possibility that she could talk about her experience and somehow integrate it into her history.

It is not feasible to honor history without encountering the problem of injustice. On some level, all psychotherapy revolves around the experience of injustice in the context of important relationships: the sibling who takes the other's toys, the spouse who does not pull his or her weight around the house, the tyrannical boss, and, of course, parents who, in their own emotional dysfunction, withhold the unconditional and nurturing love each child needs and deserves. The frustration, pain, rage, and loss of self-esteem that the common human experience of injustice can evoke are thus familiar to all psychotherapists. The patients I will be discussing grapple with all of these forms of injustice, but they do so within a society that forces an additional load of injustice on them, because it seems forever to be structured in ways that undermine and threaten their abilities to feel safe and comfortable in the world. These are people for whom, in varying degrees, contemporary America is not benign, and this is a reality which psychotherapists, especially white therapists, must understand when trying to comprehend the emotional lives of their African American clients.

Who We Are

The collaborative effort of individual psychodynamic psychotherapy, then, is a relationship comprised of history embodied in the psyches of two people, meeting together in a particular time and place. In the remainder of this chapter I will try to provide some basic orientation to the participants in the therapy relationships from which the vignettes of this book are drawn. You will be meeting several African American patients, and to protect their confidentiality I have given them new names and have disguised many specifics of their stories. In some cases, individuals described are composites. At the same time, I have tried to preserve their actual words as much as possible so as to provide a reliable understanding of the clinical interactions reported, and also because their often lively eloquence is very much part of who these clients are. I have tried to accurately report my own words, which has not always been a comfortable process. Writing from my session notes at times left me wishing I'd questioned a client's comment further, responded to something on a more empathic rather than interpretive level, been more articulate, or simply kept my mouth shut. I see my clinical work as presented here as a work in progress, as, I suppose, all psychotherapeutic work must be. I have tried to include these reflections when I am aware of my omissions and mistakes.

These patients are each, of course, very individual personalities with very specific histories. Still, because my practice is located in Berkeley, California, and I opened my practice at a certain moment in time, these women and men constitute a particular historic and geographic demographic among black

Americans. Most—though not all—are children of the Great Migration, specifically the offspring of parents who left the South for northern California in the 1940s and 1950s, seeking safety and/or greater opportunity for economic stability, a phenomenon that will be discussed later in this chapter. Thus, most of the people I will be discussing were born in the San Francisco Bay Area; those born elsewhere are from the South and came to California as children or young adults. These clients have been nearly all women, a gender ratio that is somewhat more skewed than that of my non-African American patients. This is a discrepancy that might be understood by factors that will be described in Chapter 6. Most, though not all, initially sought treatment because they had suffered from workplace injuries, either harassment or severe physical injuries that resulted in a level of emotional distress that rendered them no longer able to function in their work and daily lives, or a combination of both. They were referred to me through an agency with which I was affiliated that provided mental health services to workers through collaboration with their unions, and their treatments were paid for by workers' compensation insurance. They had been typically diagnosed with either major depressive disorder or posttraumatic stress disorder and were thus compelled to do something none had ever imagined doing: to see a psychotherapist. Only because they were experiencing such dramatic senses of collapse of their psychological well-being, and because workers' compensation insurance would cover their psychotherapy, did they turn to a treatment form that was suddenly available to them. Others came through word of mouth and have paid for their psychotherapy using other insurance, Medicare, or by taking advantage of my sliding scale.

The age range of these patients is relatively narrow, with birth dates ranging from approximately 1940 to 1960, dates that situate their formative years, and the lives of their parents, at particular points in our history. They are mostly from working-class families; a few from the middle class; and a few from real poverty. Approximately half come from single-parent families. Most have held or still hold blue-collar jobs, although a few have held or continue to hold white-collar jobs. Some are no longer working due to unemployment or disability. Some are now very poor. For the most part I will be presenting vignettes from the treatments of six women and one man, with brief references to the cases of a few other men and women. Because their stories will be scattered throughout the book, and it may therefore be challenging at times to keep straight who is who, I have provided a brief, descriptive list, a *dramatis personae*, which can be found at the end of this chapter.

As the psychotherapist in these relationships, I am also a subject and object of history. For one thing, the specificity of my identity or that of any psychotherapist creates a very particular transference and countertransference dynamic for each treatment relationship. I am clearly white. I was born right in the middle of the two decades represented in the group of patients that are the subjects of this book, but my family and I came to this country only in the late 1950s, when I was a child. Thus, while I lived in this country during much of the same historical period as my clients, I do not have a shared experience of American life before my immigration. Many of the historical and cultural forces surrounding the Civil Rights Movement and its aftermath, events that had such tangible significance for the patients represented here and their families, were known to me only via contemporary television and newspapers, and did not affect me directly.

I am Jewish, which will figure somewhat in the case material. I spent ten years of my childhood in Southern California, rarely encountering African Americans except as service workers. Like my clients, however, I have spent my entire adulthood in Berkeley and Oakland, California. I have never lived anywhere else in the United States and have very little extended family in this country. Not surprisingly, as an immigrant and also as a Jew born in England in the aftermath of World War II, I grew up with a sense of being an only partly legitimate American. I suspect that both my own sense of marginalization, and my parents' liberal to left leanings, have affected my politics and particularly my urge to understand anyone else who feels marginalized in white, Christian, America. Because I was born not long after the devastation of Nazism, the concept of trying to survive a frightening, racist, national environment, while not something I ever experienced directly, was also not just hypothetical; so when I learned about the history of slavery, lynchings, and the Jim Crow laws, and then as a child saw for myself on the evening news stories about the bombing of a black church in Birmingham that killed four young girls, the murders of civil rights workers in the South, and other atrocities, I was, like many of my generation, deeply affected. Furthermore, as my clients are children of men and women who seized any opportunity available to escape from both the economic repression and the physical dangers of African American existence in the Jim Crow South, so am I one of many of my generation's European Jews whose parents grasped any chance to flee Nazi danger. My own parents entered England in the late 1930s as "illegal immigrants."

Woven into my professional self are feelings of rootlessness, inauthenticity, and ambivalence about my identity: I am an American, but not 100 percent American. I am very attached to the geography and ambiance of Northern California, while at the same time am often highly critical of much about this, my, country. I am Jewish, but my attachment to my Jewish identity is also complicated, as I squirm at narratives that portray Jews as perpetual victims, rage at Israeli policies towards Palestinians, yet also value my cultural ties to Jewish life. Because of these particular ambivalent tugs, there are times that I imagine that my own confusions are parallels to those experienced by African Americans as they think about their national identities, who, on the one hand, are closely identified with much of what constitutes our culture, but who also are rightfully angry at how they are viewed and have been treated by their country, reduced at times to caricatures of themselves as helpless victims, or criminals, intruders into white middle-class sanctity, and providers of the pleasures of sports, music, and pungent slang to that same white world. Like me, my African American clients both value and are critical of many aspects of their national identity.

How might the relationship be different for the same patients were they working with a Latino or Asian American, a South Asian or Middle Eastern, or Italian émigré with an obvious accent? The subject of bi-cultural psychotherapeutic relationships other than white/other is one that I hope will be increasingly taken up as our field continues to become more diverse. There have been some excellent articles (e.g. Holmes, 2006) that include discussions of cases in which African American psychotherapists treat African American clients, but this is obviously also an area that can use more exploration.

Psychoanalytic thinking in recent decades has placed considerable emphasis on countertransference and the therapist's unconscious role in the therapeutic relationship. Although I have worried about the danger of letting my "politics" foreclose my perceptions of the individual in my office, I believe that as I have come to appreciate something of the complexity of human relations and the meanings of race in the U.S., I have begun to feel some confidence that I can integrate political and historical understanding into our psychological narrative without having it obscure my client's uniqueness. I would even now say that my anger at the injustice of racism, while rarely visible, subtly enhances the development of therapeutic alliances with my patients, and that access to righteous indignation is actually necessary for our work. Another way of putting it is that when we integrate our understanding of historical context into psychodynamic thinking, by necessity we also integrate our politics into our work, understanding that politics is essentially grounded in our interpretation of history and of events taking place in the world around us; and our ideas about history and the functioning of our society inevitably circle us back to questions of justice. By politics I do not, of course, mean any particular partisan or political cause, bumper stickers on cars, or campaign buttons on jackets. Instead, I am talking about a point of view that recognizes the role of the socio-economic world in people's lives, one that does not, as rigidly libertarian or right-wing positions maintain, imagine individual effort and responsibility as the sole drivers of people's lives. In this way, I see that curiosity about the workings of our society and their differing impacts on members of our society is a political position, and one that is relevant to the practice of psychotherapy. In order to work effectively with the patient and to be able to hear clearly a patient's account of his or her experience, the therapist needs to understand enough about the nature of the patient's world, and to have a fundamental curiosity about it. As will be discussed more thoroughly in Chapter 6, a failure to take on that challenge can severely limit the therapist's ability to help the client and, more importantly, shut down an avenue for relief and growth for the client.

Where Are We

The chronological markers of clients', their ancestors', and their therapists' lives influence the therapeutic process, but all history takes place in specific geographical spaces, so I have decided to present here a very brief description of Oakland, California, and its African American history. While my office is in Berkeley, it actually sits on the border with Oakland, and, more significantly, almost all the clients whose stories I tell live, have lived, and/or worked in Oakland. The city is itself, in some ways, a character in this story, as its demographics, its history and its African American history, its reputation, and its politics all play a role to some degree or another in the lives of my patients.

African American presence in Oakland seems to have really begun in the 1850s. Elizabeth Flood opened the city's first school for African American children in 1857, and by the 1890s there were already black newspapers in the Bay Area, such as the *Mirror of the Times, San Francisco Elevator, The Oakland Sunshine*, and *Oakland Illustrated Guide*. In 1890, African Americans made up just 3 percent of Oakland's population. But that population was growing, and it was doing so in an interesting way. In the late 1800s, George Pullman, determining that his new, luxury railway passenger cars should deliver flawless service, "ordered that each Pullman car should have a black porter to keep the car meticulously clean, to change the bed linens daily, and to be constantly on call to provide personal services to passengers" (Bagwell, 1982, p. 83). The requirement for a black porter may seem odd, yet it was consistent with the history of domestic service that Americans had come to associate with African Americans. With Oakland as the western railroad terminus, many of these porters chose to settle there.

Pullman's hiring decision was fateful in ways he could not have imagined. Being a Pullman porter was a highly valued job among African Americans. For one thing, the travel inherent in the job afforded these men opportunities to be exposed to passengers of many backgrounds and to see different parts of the country, giving them an education and broad viewpoint that few if any other kinds of work available to them did. Another development that Pullman could not have predicted took place in 1925, when Oakland's Pullman porters organized the all-black Brotherhood of Sleeping Car Porters, the country's first major labor union open to African Americans (Bagwell, 1982, p. 83). According to historian Robert Self (2003), Oakland's Pullman porters and employees of the Southern Pacific Railroad sparked the creation of other African American institutions in West Oakland, where they settled, including "the city's two oldest African American churches, the Alameda County NAACP, fraternal and civic associations, women's clubs and auxiliaries," a recreation center, and "substantial black commercial and professional districts" (p. 50). Crucially, the porters would bring home with them black newspapers from cities and towns on their routes. Out of this combination of African American concentration in West Oakland (since they were barred from housing elsewhere in the city) and the benefits of nationwide networking, there emerged in black Oakland a "cosmopolitan laborite culture that blended politics, trade unionism, and human rights," aimed at ending economic and social segregation. It was a culture that was heterogeneous in its political makeup, ranging from "the communist left to the liberal center" (p. 50).

World War II saw the next influx of African Americans into Oakland, as the newly mobilized military and the shipyards in the East Bay required so many new workers that they were forced to turn to people who were normally excluded from employment, most notably women and African Americans. The black population of Oakland went from approximately 8,000 in 1940 to 21,770 just four years later (Self, 2003, p. 47), one incidental consequence of which was that Oakland in the 1940s became an important incubator of black music—as it continues to be in the present. The war had also "elevated racial liberalism from the margins of political discourse to the center of the nation's wartime antifascism" (p. 52).

African American history and the war effort also collided in ways that produced tragic consequences. The Naval Ammunition Depot in the small port town of Port Chicago, located about 30 miles northeast of Oakland, was the site of the war's "worst disaster on home soil" (USMM.org, 2002). On July 17, 1944, as the mostly African American naval enlisted men were loading ammunition onto the Liberty ship S.S. *E.A. Bryan*, an accidental explosion blew up the ship, setting off shock waves felt hundreds of miles away, and killing 320 sailors, 202 of whom were African American. Workers had been quietly complaining in vain to their superiors that the loading procedures that were imposed on them were unsafe, so grief and fear were infused with outrage. After the disaster, 258 African American navy replacement workers refused to return to loading munitions without improved safety protocols. Two hundred and eight of the men were tried in courts martial for bad conduct and forced to forfeit three months' pay for disobeying orders. Fifty, however, were charged with mutiny, a charge that is punishable by death. None was so sentenced; instead they were given eight to fifteen years of hard labor. However, in January 1946, all were released from prison but forced to remain in the Navy, sent to the South Pacific, and gradually released. Loading safety procedures were eventually introduced, and the case drew attention to the injustices of segregation within the military, revelations that contributed to President Harry Truman's Executive Order 9066, integrating the armed forces in 1948 (www.blackpast.org/aaw/port-chicago-mutiny-0, www.usmm.org/portchicago.html).

In 1994, the Navy rejected requests by four California lawmakers to overturn the "mutineers" courts-martial rulings, and most of the Port Chicago 50 refused to ask for pardons, asserting that they had done nothing wrong for which they should be pardoned. Many are no longer alive, but efforts to exonerate them continue (https://en.wikipedia.org/wiki/port_Chicago_disaster).

The call for justice in the case of the Port Chicago 50 became part of a national African American wartime movement, the Double-V campaign, which "called for victory over racism in Europe and victory over racism at home" (Self, 2003, p. 53). Despite the more racially liberal national context, the NAACP and the Urban League continued to make little progress locally in their fight against discrimination in employment. The various military sites in Oakland and nearby Alameda did provide some jobs and a path to the middle class for African Americans, especially men, and many of these jobs continued after the war. The government thus created a "community bulwark against the more pervasive bias in the private sector and the large-scale post-war layoffs in shipbuilding" (p. 57). Some of the clients you will read about are the children of men who left the South for these jobs, or in some cases, of the girlfriends who followed them, or the relatives who heard of the migrant's improved situation.

However, these jobs were certainly not enough to outweigh the losses in employment opportunities that befell Oakland in the post-war years. In a story familiar throughout the urban centers of the U.S., new housing and businesses moved to the newly created suburbs, taking with them industry and tens of thousands of white residents. It is probable that between 1950 and 1970 Oakland lost nearly 10,000 jobs and 23,000 residents (https://oakland planninghistory.weebly.com/early-history.html). Those left behind tended to be African American, "who could not afford to leave or whose race prevented them from moving into more desirable neighborhoods even if they had the money," due to ongoing, legalized housing discrimination (Bagwell, 1982, p. 251). The shift was stunning in Oakland where, by 1970, a full 59.1 percent of the population was African American, and 34.5 percent was white. "White flight," as this trend was called, "had the effect of lowering the commercial and economic base of the city while at the same time creating greater demands for human services for the troubled classes left behind" (p. 251). Housing discrimination within Oakland continued to restrict the areas in which African Americans could live to West Oakland and parts of North Oakland.

Although the drive to ban discrimination in employment throughout the 1940s and 1950s, led by African American organizers Byron Rumford and C.L. Dellums (uncle of future long-time congressman and eventual mayor of Oakland, Ron Dellums), eventually resulted in California's 1959 Fair Employment Practices Law, discrimination in hiring and at the workplace by no means ceased. Rumford's and Dellums' efforts, along with work by other black activists, to end housing discrimination culminated in the 1963 Rumford Fair Housing Act, but, as will be discussed in Chapter 5, it was repealed a year later in a general election with the passage of Proposition 14. Proposition 14 won approval from 65 percent of California voters and 55 percent of Oakland voters, this in an election in which more than 60 percent of California voters supported Democratic presidential candidate Lyndon Johnson. In Oakland, the greatest support (70 percent) for the repeal came from the most homogeneously white hillside areas of the city, where residents had the least contact with African American Oakland residents (Self, 2003, pp. 167–168). For patients who spent their childhoods in segregated Oakland, a silver lining was the sense of a safe community of neighbors, fellow African Americans, who effectively shielded the children from early encounters with direct racism. The relative safety of those neighborhoods was to become history, however, during their adult years, as we shall see a bit later.

And then came the 1960s and the Black Panthers, probably Oakland's most famous contribution to African American political history. If liberalism, in the forms of the legal victories of the Civil Rights Movement and Johnson's ambitious War on Poverty programs were sources for optimism for black Americans, their failures to make significant, community-wide, positive changes led to equally painful disappointment. Out of this disappointment came "a rich and contentious period of debate and conflict over the direction of the African American community in Oakland and its relation to the larger city" (Self, 2003, p. 222). Self sees the Black Power movement of the 1960s and 1970s as "a poignant effort to advance a political strategy beyond desegregation" (p. 218), and that "black power and self-determination politics," far from being a homogeneous movement, "always contained contradictions of class, struggles over leadership, and broad ideological conflicts that divided African Americans as much as the symbolic notion of community united them" (p. 220). Huey Newton, whom we will meet briefly later in this book, and Bobby Seale, fellow students at Oakland's Merritt College in the mid-1960s, joined the Afro-American Association, founded in 1962 as "the West Coast's first indigenous black nationalist organization," which served as an intellectual and activist base that "fused black capitalism, Afro-centrism, and Garveyite self help," stressing "education and skill acquisition as the way to create African American economic power" (p. 222).

But in 1966, Newton and Seale parted with the Afro-American Association, Seale calling its members the "cultural nationalist 'college boys,'" and the two men created the Black Panther Party. The party's 10-point platform included demands for "full employment, decent housing and black history in the schools," and a commitment "to defending our black community from racist police oppression and brutality" (Self, 2003, p. 226). This last point was to become at times the most visible and controversial representation of the Panthers, who recruited both "sincere young black intellectuals and political figures as well as street toughs" (p. 228). Violence as a Panther practice was real, in the form of threats, or worse, of retaliation to local merchants who refused to donate to their social programs, and the party was accused of "involvement in illegal markets in weapons and drugs" (p. 228). As if to prove the Panthers' accusations of police brutality, "white-led police" and F.B.I. Counter Intelligence Program (COINTELPRO) also crossed boundaries of violence and illegal activities, as the Oakland Police Department responded to the Panthers "with nothing short of guerrilla warfare—no less than three black men were killed by Oakland police in the spring of 1968 alone" (p. 229).

But just as Panther violence was real, so, too, were their humanitarian accomplishments, including a free breakfast program for schoolchildren (1968), a free ambulance program (1974), founding of Liberation Schools (1969) in which students learned "about class struggle in terms of black history", free clothing (1970), establishment of the Sickle Cell Anemia Research Foundation, providing free sickle cell testing (1970), and a free food service (1972). Although much of their program was a continuation of the work of prior activists, the Panthers added anti-capitalist discourse, and held that desegregation efforts "could not ultimately deliver liberation" (Self, 2003, p. 227). In a later chapter, we will meet Francis, who came to Oakland from the South as a young woman, and received her political education as a volunteer in the Panthers' school lunch program, an education that continued to affect her ways of encountering the white world more than 40 years later.

In the 1970s, party membership declined as its leaders engaged in increasingly vicious, even violent, internal battles and purges, as they dealt with accusations of shootings and beatings, and some, such as Eldridge Cleaver and for a while Huey Newton, went into exile. The Panthers, nevertheless, had left their mark on the city.

Subsequent decades have presented Oakland's black community with many challenges, the most tragic of which was the crack cocaine epidemic of the 1980s. My anecdotal experience as a psychologist at a mental health clinic of an HMO (health maintenance organization) in Oakland at that time, and reports I have heard from clients in the many years since, have driven home the heartbreaking reality of how destructive that period was for the black community. At the time of the crack cocaine explosion, our clinic was suddenly encountering addicted middle-class and working-class African American members of our health plan embarking on their descents into poverty and despair. Drug treatment was expensive and hard to come by, even for those who were willing to enter rehab. But we also saw the other victims, the wives whose hardworking spouses who had gone from decent jobs to addiction and unemployment, draining the hard-won family resources, and who, worst of all, had changed into erratic, emotionally unavailable husbands and fathers. Women, too, fell into addiction. Families that had succeeded in making it into the middle class were falling apart. We saw middle-aged couples who were suddenly raising grandchildren when their sons and daughters turned to drugs and were on the streets, often tumbling into the mass incarceration that characterized the war on drugs. Neighborhoods that had once seemed relatively safe became dangerous, homes were neglected, some turning into crack houses, and parents or grandparents became reluctant to allow their children to walk to school or play outside. The addicted person's impact reverberated throughout the family. Their now-adult children must contend with the effects of childhoods of abandonment and chaos. Years of connection and presence that were lost cannot be restored. Years of education, undermined by childhood anxiety and depression, cannot be replicated. In a later chapter, we will look at the resulting fractured family and community support systems of the 2000s in which some of my patients live.

As happened throughout the country, Oakland and surrounding areas faced continued draining of blue-collar, union jobs from the 1970s onward, and finally, in the 2000s, a housing bubble that priced many out of the city, forcing a struggling black population into the exurbs or even to other states with cheaper housing. Three of my clients have already made the move to exurbia, and some speak of friends and relatives who have left the state in search of affordable housing. In an irony that can make a person's head spin, several have chosen to move to the very places in the South from which their parents fled.

As a result, Oakland's African American population, while still double the national average, is shrinking. From nearly 60 percent in 1970, it dropped to 43.9 percent in 1990, and as of the 2010 census was 28 percent—still well above the national average of 13.2 percent, but a steep drop from its previous heights. The white population has remained relatively constant at about 34 percent, with Latinos and other immigrants replacing the black emigrants (www.census.gov/quickfacts). In economic terms, while some of Oakland's black citizens are successful, middle-class residents, the majority are struggling, with approximately 71 percent of their children eligible for the schools' free lunch program, and unemployment in the poor black enclaves of East Oakland possibly "as high as 28 percent, five times the national rate" (Nazaryan, 2015). As of this writing, one cannot walk down a commercial street without encountering a homeless person or drive far in this city without passing an encampment of indigents, often under a freeway ramp, a high proportion of whom will be African American men and women.

Probably not unrelated, Oakland's crime rate is well above both California's and the national averages. One undated account calculated 570 crimes per square mile in Oakland, compared with 83 per square mile state-wide, and the national rate at 32.8 (www.neighborhoodscout.com/ca/oakland/crime). On the other hand, the riches of Silicon Valley have spilled over into Oakland, keeping Oakland property values high and bringing some new, unfamiliar, chic to the city. But predictably, as Nazaryan points out

> . . . there isn't a united Oakland that shares both the newfound wealth and the long-standing burdens of poverty. There is, instead, a white Oakland, a black Oakland, and a brown Oakland, and on those rare occasions when those Oaklands speak to each other, the conversation is often impolite.
> (Nazaryan, 2015)

As an Oakland resident myself, my own observation of relations between African Americans and whites, at least, is not quite as gloomy as Nazaryan depicts, but camaraderie is probably mostly visible within class affiliation, in the few neighborhoods that have remained integrated, and among professional colleagues. It seems that Oakland is emblematic of a typical mid-sized American city in which some middle- and working-class neighborhoods are integrated, but a large part of the city still suffers from *de facto* segregation.

To make matters worse, the public schools are chronically among the lowest performing in the state, in large part because of the extraordinary number of immigrant children for whom English is not their native language, but also thanks to the flight of many middle-class families, who historically are white. This flight of the white middle class makes a difference, because even in a public school in a financially starved school district, a P.T.A. with middle-class families can fundraise for services the school lacks—the weekly arts teacher, a music program, and so on. In 2010, for instance, out of 3,442 graduating seniors in the Oakland public schools that year, 92 of the students were white, as parents with the means pulled three out of four white children out of the public system and transferred them to the suburbs or private schools by the end of high school. The children left behind are challenged with learning in underfunded schools with underpaid teachers, while their parents or guardians grapple with a community that is in economic distress, plagued with crime, and trying to recover from the fallout and the losses from the drug wars.

The news has not been all bad. There remains in a good deal of Oakland's politics and life a spirit of optimism and a pride in being a place that works toward the possibility of a healthy multicultural community. Oakland has had three white and three African American mayors since 1977, and since 1971 has been represented by the same two Democrats in Congress, both black: Ron Dellums and Barbara Lee. Despite declining membership as the African American population drifts out of the city, black churches abound, providing free food, other support programs, and even school scholarships to the community. And there are a number of initiatives and organizations of African American citizens that foster the arts, provide mentorship for young people, and preserve local and non-local black history, such as the excellent African American Museum and Library at Oakland.

Oakland's Office of African American Male Achievement is

> ... the country's first department within a public school district that specifically addresses the needs of its most vulnerable children: black boys, who have stubbornly remained at the bottom of nearly every academic indicator, including high school graduation rates in most states, according to the Schott Foundation for Public Education.
>
> (Brown, 2016, p. 18)

Out of this office has come an intriguing program based in the city's middle and high schools, and includes Afrocentric core courses that meet University of California prerequisite standards, peer mentoring, conferences, and a student leadership council. It is early days yet to assess the impact, but there have been improvements in absenteeism and suspensions, and senior boys are heading for college with the aid from a local nonprofit fund (Brown, 2016, p. 19). Such programs and institutions described above can be found in most towns with even a small black population. In other words, life for black Americans in Oakland is and has been a mixed bag, and it has been within this context that the psychotherapy patients whom I will be discussing have been born or have, at least, spent their adult lives.

References

Altman, N. (1995). *The analyst in the inner city: Race, class and culture through a psychoanalytic lens*. Hillsdale, NJ & London: The Analytic Press.

Altman, N. (2005). Historical context in clinical work. *Psychoanalytic Dialogues*, 15: 909–916.

Bagwell, B. (1982). *Oakland: The story of a city*. Novato, CA: Presidio Press.
Boulanger, G. (2004). Lot's wife, Cary Grant, and the American dream: Psychoanalysis with immigrants. *Contemporary Psychoanalysis, 40* (3): 353–372.
Boulanger, G. (2007). *Wounded by reality: Understanding and treating adult onset trauma*. Mahwah, NJ & London: The Analytic Press.
Boulanger, G. (2013). Fearful symmetry: Shared trauma in New Orleans after Hurricane Katrina. *Psychoanalytic Dialogues, 23*: 33–44.
Boulanger, G. (2015). Seeing double, being double: Longing, belonging, recognition, and evasion in psychodynamic work with immigrants. *The American Journal of Psychoanalysis, 75*: 287–303.
Brown, P.L. (February 7, 2016). #Blackmindsmatter: Rewriting the script of racial inequality and underachievement for the country's most vulnerable students, African-American males. *New York Times*, Education Life: 18–20.
Davoine, F. & Gaudilliere, J. (2004). *History beyond trauma: Whereof one cannot speak, thereof one cannot stay silent*. New York: Other Press.
Dimen, M. (2011). Introduction. In Dimen, M. (Ed.), *With culture in mind*. New York & London: Routledge.
Erikson, E.H. (1946). Ego development and historical change—clinical notes. *Psychoanalytic Study of the Child, 2*: 359–396.
Faimberg, H. (1988). The telescoping of generations: Genealogy of certain identifications. *Contemporary Psychoanalysis, 24*: 99–117.
Faimberg, H. (2005). *The telescoping of generations: Listening to the narcissistic links between generations*. London & New York: Routledge.
Grand, S. (2010). *The hero in the mirror: From fear to fortitude*. New York & Hove, UK: Routledge.
Gump, J.P. (2010). Reality matters: The shadow of trauma on African-American subjectivity. *Psychoanalytic Psychology, 27* (1): 42–54.
Hamer, F.M. (2002). Guards at the gate: Race, resistance and psychic reality. *Journal of the American Psychoanalytic Association, 50*: 1219–1237.
Hamer, F.M. (2006). Racism as a transference state: Episodes of racial hostility in the psychoanalytic context. *Psychoanalytic Quarterly, 75*: 197–214.
Holmes, D. (1999). Race and countertransference: Two "blind spots" in psychoanalytic perception. *Journal of Applied Psychoanalytic Studies, 1* (4): 319–332.
Holmes, D.E. (2006). The wrecking effects of race and social class on self and success. *Psychoanalytic Quarterly, 75*: 215–235.
Krystal, H. (Ed.) (1968). *Massive psychic trauma*. New York: International Universities Press, Inc.
Layton, L. (2006). Attacks on linking: The unconscious pull to dissociate individuals from their social context. In Layton, L., Hollander, N.C., & Gutwill, S. (Eds.), *Psychoanalysis, class and politics: Encounters in the clinical setting*. London & New York: Routledge.
Leary, K. (1997a). Race in psychoanalytic space. *Gender and Psychoanalysis, 2*: 157–172.
Leary, K. (1997b). Race, self-disclosure, and "forbidden talk": Race and ethnicity in contemporary clinical practice. *Psychoanalytic Quarterly, 66*: 163–189.
Leary, K. (2000). Racial enactments in dynamic treatment. *Psychoanalytic Dialogues, 10*: 639–653.
Lifton, R.J. (1968/1991). *Death in Life: Survivors of Hiroshima*. New York: Random House.

Nazaryan, A. (March 25, 2015). Fighting to reclaim the future of Oakland's young black men. *Newsweek*, www.newsweek.com/2015/04/03/oak-town-mans-316548.html (accessed November 1, 2017).

Self, R.O. (2003). *American Babylon: Race and the struggle for post-war Oakland*. Princeton, NJ & Oxford: Princeton University Press.

Suchet, M. (2004). A relational encounter with race. *Psychoanalytic Dialogues, 14*: 423–438.

USMM.org (2002). Port Chicago disaster—July 17, 1944. www.usmm.org/portchicago.html (accessed November 1, 2017).

Vaughans, K. (2014a). Disavowed fragments of the intergenerational transmission of trauma from slavery among African Americans. Paper presented at Division 39 meetings, New York City.

Vaughans, K.C. (2014b). Disavowed fragments of the intergenerational transmission of trauma from slavery among African Americans. In Vaughans, K.C. & Spielberg, W. (Eds.), *The psychology of black boys and adolescents*, Vol. 2 (pp. 563–575). Santa Barbara, CA: Praeger.

Dramatis Personae

The individuals described below and throughout the book represent clients with whom I have worked. Their identities have been disguised, and some are composites of more than one patient. In instances in which I felt there was a danger of recognition, I have obtained consent from each person to use her material for this book.

Althea: With one brother and one sister, she was very conscious of being the darkest member of her family in which white and fairer skin were highly valued. She began therapy in her 40s while suffering from a major depression following several years of harassment at her white-collar job. She was born in the South but moved with her family to Oakland in middle school. Her lively verbal style gives her a unique voice. She has a college education and is a single mother, following a divorce many years prior to beginning treatment.

Barbara: Barbara and her younger sister came to Oakland from the urban South as children. She began therapy with an older white male therapist, whom she greatly respected, and had lost her job a year before beginning therapy. Upon her first therapist's sudden death, she was referred to me. Her Christianity is very important to her. She suffers from health problems that highlight her difficulties with medical professionals, and struggles with a troubled relationship with her mother.

Cheryl: On the younger end of the age continuum of the group, she was born and raised in Oakland. She sought treatment for major depression following sexual harassment at her blue-collar job. As she recovered and was able to make use of vocational rehabilitation. She moved out of Oakland to a nearby suburb and has settled there, working at clerical jobs. She is light-skinned, feels envied and rejected by her mother in part on that basis, and is reluctant to admit to noticing racism. She is a single mother of one daughter.

Dwayne: We worked together briefly when Dwayne was in his 60s, referred by a co-worker at their blue-collar job. He was suffering the effects of posttraumatic stress disorder after having witnessed the work-related death of another co-worker. He has been self-medicating with alcohol.

Francis: Divorced and the sole support of her daughter, Francis works at a white-collar job. She grew up in poverty in the rural South, and after high school, followed family members to the Bay Area, where she attended college and joined the Black Panther Party. She retains a high sensitivity to evidence of racism in her life.

Glenda: Born and raised in Oakland, she is the youngest in her family. Her parents left the South for the Bay Area during the jobs boom of World War II. She is a feisty union organizer, and has had struggles at her job because of her outspokenness. She says she did not become aware of her race or racism until she visited her grandparents in the South with her mother. She is divorced and the mother of two children.

Loretta: An only child, she was born in Kentucky, and came with her parents to Oakland when her father was in search of a good job. He briefly joined the Black Panthers before returning to Kentucky, while her mother remained. Hers was a respected, professional, African American family in her hometown, but, in fact, she was abused physically and sexually by her father, an alcoholic, and was unprotected and rejected by her mother, who became addicted to crack cocaine once the family arrived in Oakland.

Tracy: She was born and raised in San Francisco, but moved to Oakland as an adult. Her parents left lives of danger in the deep South and worked hard to provide a middle-class life for their children. Tracy felt proud of her life of hard work, altruistic participation in her community, and her goals of a career—all of which came to an end when she was severely injured in an industrial accident that has left her virtually disabled and in chronic pain. She battles with symptoms of posttraumatic stress disorder related to her post-injury battles for health care.

2 Chains

Brutal Centuries

It is February again. Barbara, a 40-year-old African American patient, takes me aback in the middle of our session as she exclaims, "I hate February, Black History Month!" I look at her clearly puzzled. "Because there's all that stuff on TV about slavery. Lets everyone know we were slaves," she explains. "It's embarrassing!" This remark took place in 2013. It had been almost 400 years since the first slaves arrived on the shores of Virginia, and 148 years since the Confederate Army surrendered and the ratification of the 13th Amendment, which effectively brought slavery to an end in the U.S. Barbara is still embarrassed.[1]

After all these years and despite the Civil Rights Movement, revisions in the teaching of U.S. history, and a wealth of novels, poetry, television documentaries, and histories by brilliant African American writers tackling the subject—not to mention an African American family in the White House—the history of being descended from enslaved Africans and often from their white masters continues to have the power to humiliate. Obviously this history affects each person differently, but there can be no doubt that it endures in the psyches of today's African Americans, permeating their identity formation. That slavery was traumatic is obvious, "whether grief from the loss of everything and everyone familiar, the despair of captivity, the helplessness and rage of physical abuse, or the rage and shame of rape" (Gump, 2010, p. 46). Ashram Rushdy described slavery as "the family secret of America" (Vaughans, 2014, p. 573), for the legacy of slavery and its psychological damage lives in all Americans, black or white. In his classic historical work on African American folk traditions, Lawrence Levine (1977/2007)[2] tells of one former slave who regrets he did not "die fighting rather than be a slave again"; Lena Horne said that her grandmother, "the direct issue of a slave owner," never spoke to Horne about slavery: "She dismissed it, by force of will, I think, from her consciousness" (p. 386).

To return to Barbara, I went on to ask her how the history of slavery is embarrassing to *her*. She replied, "I know it makes no sense, because everyone knows we were slaves, but when all those other ethnicities keep hearing how we were slaves, it's just embarrassing." I noted to her that it was interesting that it was the slave owners whose behavior was barbaric, yet it was *she* who felt embarrassed. Barbara looked surprised, and seconds later gave a gentle smile. "I guess that's true. You know, I never honestly thought that way—that they're the ones who should be embarrassed. I can't wait to tell my sister. She goes on and on about other ethnicities hearing that we were slaves." Barbara and her younger sister were born in the South, and spent their early childhoods there before the family moved to California. Could the white Southern attachment to its antebellum past be so embedded in their consciousness, despite decades in the Bay Area, because of those formative years spent in the South? The angry reaction of many white Southerners to plans to remove monuments to heroes of the Confederacy and of post-Civil War white supremacists lets us know that Southern culture has not repudiated its antebellum and Jim Crow ethos. I wonder with Barbara, "Your sister may have internalized the slave owners' claims that the slaves were not valuable as people. That must be confusing for her." Barbara replies, "Yes, she is very confused. There are lots of stories about how we have to love those above us." "Above?" I ask. "Yes," says Barbara. "Nothing wrong with a maid who loves her mistress." Now I am the one who is feeling a confusion of emotions. All I can muster to say at the moment is, "Well, we are all very complex, and I suspect these complicated feelings contribute to your sister's low self-esteem" (a topic she has discussed before).

Barbara's sister is not unique in her reactions. One former slave explained to a teacher at a black college several years after Emancipation that he preferred not to talk about his years of slavery: "I feel as if folks mightn't believe me, and then, if I think too much about them myself, I can't *keep feeling right*, as I want to, toward my old masters. I'd do anything for them I could, and I want to forget what they have done to me" (Litwack, 1980, p. 204). That confusion with which Barbara and her sister struggle is obviously not new, its roots reaching deep into slavery's muddy soil.

Despite its marginalized defenders, most contemporary Americans of all races do not condone slavery. Even Thomas Jefferson's brilliance and humanism fade in the face of his refusal to free his slaves. To be a slave owner was to profit from a system that was cruel, immoral, and exploitive. To have been a slave was to have been a victim of such a system. But whatever one *thinks* about the justice or injustice of one's oppression, to actually live in the position of powerless victim can be felt as a humiliating denigration of one's selfhood and worth, and particularly so when the whole society in which you live is structured to defend the system that maintains your oppression and to confirm your devaluing, and does so over a period of more than 200 years. Barbara can still feel the shame attached to her ancestors' powerlessness and humiliation. She did seem to experience a moment of relief, on her own and her sister's behalf, when reminded of how that history looks to her therapist, a white woman who has had the liberty to contextualize the moral scales of slavery at a distance from both slaves and slave owners. I say "a moment of relief" as opposed to a major transformation, because obviously the journey towards a comfortable sense of self is a long process made up of many interactions and experiences.

Barbara has a lot on her plate as a single mother, with an ex-husband who does not support his children. She had lost her job more than a year earlier, and a fair amount of self-confidence seemed to have gone with it. Yet this one small piece of reframing can provide a building block towards a more realistic understanding of Barbara's place in the world.

Other psychotherapists have reported therapeutic evidence similar to the vignette described above. Gump (2010) asserts that the echoes of "the historical fact of slavery" can be heard "infusing and determining both intrafamilial and societal traumatic acts" (p. 48). Suchet (2004), a Caucasian therapist, bumps up against the emotional legacy of slavery as she describes the flight of her African American patient from a successful and close treatment relationship at the moment that the woman began "to bare her deepest feelings of self-disgust and despair regarding her family . . . The profound shame she was examining," she explains, "carried with it the states of slavery" (p. 435). In this chapter I am going to look at how and why the traumas of American slavery of Africans and the more than four million African Americans who were living in bondage at the beginning of the Civil War continue to occupy important, if unacknowledged, spaces in the minds of the African Americans with whom I have worked. We are all inheritors of our particular family histories and of the traumas, ruptures, and economic and historical catastrophes from which even the most privileged among us have not been entirely free, and are part and parcel of living as historical beings. But for African Americans, aspects of their historical inheritance have remained especially embedded psychologically by reason of the visible color of their skins, and by an ongoing experience of consistent discrimination in their country. In fact, understanding the effects of racism against African Americans is impossible without coming to grips with the experiences of slavery.

But the issues are complex. It took many years after the 1945 liberation of the Nazi concentration camps for the traumatized survivors to begin to tell their stories and for others to emerge who could listen to them. The capacity to tell and to listen required a cultural shift. Krystal (1968) and his colleagues, looking at the long-term effects on individual survivors of Nazi concentration camps, confirmed the reality of posttraumatic stress, and in doing so debunked the wishful adage that "time heals all wounds." As more has been revealed and continues to be revealed since 1945, we have learned more about what occurred in the camps and the complexities of the inmates' experiences. The process of being able to speak and to listen has been key in developing the capacity to imagine the variety of psychic trauma, the humiliation, the moral dilemmas, and the coping strategies of the camp survivors.

We know now that descendants of traumatized parents in many ways take in the residual emotional states, generally unprocessed and unconscious, of their parents' traumatic experiences (Davoine & Gaudilliere, 2004; Faimberg, 2005). Through hints and whispers, the emotional states of parents, and even their silences and the holes these leave in family history, children become the inheritors of the traumas experienced by parents and grandparents.

Contemporary psychologists have written, and continue to write, about the effects of centuries of racism, and the echoes of slavery in particular, on African American psyches. Understanding slavery's complexity is complicated; after all, it took place over a wide geographical area with no centralized authority, and, unlike the Shoah, it took place continuously for nearly 250 years.

Thus, it is well beyond the scope of this chapter to give a full description of the 250 years of our country's enslavement of Africans and their descendants. There is a long and full historiographical tradition of study of the institution of American slavery, with its own evolution, conflict, and controversy. Nevertheless, for our purposes, I am going to look at a few of the themes that have seemed strikingly consistent in descriptions of the slaves' experience and which continue to carry emotional weight in the psyches of their descendants. The story is ugly, making all the more remarkable the vast evidence of the slaves' resilience embodied in their creative responses to their circumstances; while trauma is clearly transmitted from generation to generation, so too are the psychological tools for survival.

Living as Property

One day Althea, an African American woman I see in weekly therapy, was describing her neighbor's ne'er-do-well relative, a man whose work ethic as an itinerant handyman is less than stellar. "Well," she declares, "I wouldn't own a cousin like that." I'm struck by an application of the word "own." She is playing with the trope of a family member as property, a thing to be owned. This same patient had also once told me about coming to my office that day by driving on surface roads rather than risk "taking that rust bucket of mine on anybody's freeway." This time she has translated the notion of a publicly owned freeway, which by rights is hers, into the property of somebody, "anybody." Here are two uses of the concept of property remodeled and applied to things that are not normally viewed as possessions of individuals. In truth, there is a delightful, almost whimsical feel about this linguistic mixing and play in Althea's words. But as is often the case with humor, a harsher truth is embedded in the play that is hard to ignore, suggesting a more sinister, inappropriate concept of property.

A frequently reported story tells of a slave who was caught eating his master's pig. The slave, so the story goes, defended his action by pointing out that since both he and the animal were the master's possessions, nothing was lost: "Yes, suh, Massa, you got less pig now but you sho' got more nigger" (Levine, 1977/2007, p. 309). Thus, again with the healthy recourse to humor, the story-tellers have let be known their judgment of a system that equates them with farm animals, essentially laboring flesh and economic possessions. For Althea, the dreadful knowledge that for many generations her ancestors were, in fact, legally held to be someone's property to be bought, sold, worked, named, fed, starved, insured, bred, imprisoned, humiliated, whipped, hunted, and barred from literacy plays in the back of her mind. What are the psychological implications of this history?

One of the most traumatic characteristics of the slave system's process of transforming people into property was the master's freedom to sell a slave at will, thereby wrenching the man, woman, or child from family, connections, and surroundings. Just how deeply wounding this practice was is demonstrated by this fact: "Except for punishment, no other factor had accounted for as many runaway slaves . . . [as the] attempt to reunite with loved ones." Similarly, slaves reported that those same ties were, for many who contemplated running away, a primary reason to refrain from doing so (Litwack, 1980, p. 230). Harriet Jacobs (using the pseudonym of Linda Brent), in her memoir, *Incidents in the Life of a Slave Girl. Written by Herself* (1861/2000), describes in particular the pain of New Year's Day in the South, as experienced during her years as a slave in North Carolina from the 1820s to 1840s. It was on that day each year that slaves were bought and sold. Thus, "to the slave mother New Year's day comes laden with peculiar sorrows . . ." (p. 761). In fact, much of her memoir recounts her own story as a mother and her dangerous and often heartbreaking attempts to keep her children from being sold away from her or to get them out of bondage. In describing life in the South immediately following Emancipation, Litwack tells movingly of the sweeping movement of the former slaves to re-establish separated families or establish new marriages, with "mass wedding ceremonies a common sight in the postwar South" (1980, p. 240). Southern whites chose to view these marriages as nothing more than "a desire to imitate their superiors" (Litwack, 1980, p. 241).

Women who were enslaved faced the additional terror and degradation of being considered sexual property. Whether they occurred through brutal rape or less violent means of coercion and seduction, master/slave sexual relationships were never voluntary for the female slave and thus denied girls and women autonomy over their bodies and their sexuality. The effects of this widespread practice were deeply felt. Jacobs, a victim of sexual abuse by her master from the age of 12 onward, writes effectively of the realities of such a relationship, for which

> . . . there is no shadow of law to protect her from insult, from violence, or even from death; all these are inflicted by fiends who bear the shape of men. The mistress . . . has no other feelings towards her but those of jealousy and rage.
>
> (Jacobs, 1861/2000, p. 773)

Against this background, says Jacobs, "Even the little child" will become "prematurely knowing in evil things." And "If God has bestowed beauty upon her, it will prove her greatest curse" (p. 774).

Thus under slavery, commitments of fidelity and protectiveness between husbands and wives, no matter how deeply and sincerely felt, were often untenable. Not only could an owner claim a man's wife for his own sexual pleasure, but he could also separate married couples through sales of either of them to another plantation, and, for purposes of "breeding," even force marriages on slaves who had spouses from whom they had been forcibly separated. Occasionally, masters would allow visits between separated spouses if the two plantations were near to each other. One former slave, whose parents had thus lived five miles apart, reported that this type of relationship produced "confusion, mix-up, and heartaches" (Litwack, 1980, p. 235).

Familial ties, then, under slavery were painful and confusing, their viability and sustenance in constant peril, at the complete mercy of the legal bondage of individual slaves to their owners. While some slave owners encouraged family relationships among their slaves as a means of ensuring stability of their workforce, most worked to undermine the possibility of those relationships, either out of fear of competing alliances or out of a need to deny the humanity of their slaves by deeming them to be incapable of the kind of affections for spouses, children, or other kin which they believed were possible only for white people. A set of marriage vows created by one master for his slaves' weddings both trivializes the meaning of marriage among slaves and demonstrates the master's ultimate domination over the couple:

Dat yo' wife
Dat yo' husban'
Ise yo' Marser
She yo' Missus
You're married.
           (Litwack, 1980, p. 240)

Not surprisingly, the structure of slavery also warped parent/child relationships. Child slaves learned early that they belonged to the slave owner, not to their biological parents. Children were often given to masters' children as playmates and were trained to tell their masters and mistresses of infractions they observed by other slaves. According to Vaughans, one effect of this demand was that adult slaves "never spoke of important matters in front of their children, and if they did, it was very much disguised." The parents, according to ex-slaves, "usually spoke in metaphors." Meanwhile slaves were to raise their offspring to be suitably submissive and obedient to their "owners," while still maintaining loyalty to their own families (Vaughans, 2014, p. 568). This balancing act of parenting must have been extremely challenging to achieve successfully.

The devaluing of slaves' family life was not unintended. One slave recalled being whipped for saying to a mistress, "'My mother sent me.' We were not allowed to call our mammies 'mother.' It made it come too near the way of the white folks" (Litwack, 1980, p. 238). Yet for all the energy that slave owners exerted to oppose the maintenance of the family unit, the slaves managed to forge strong familial bonds. Historical records show that the lives of the slaves appear to have been organized around traditional two-parent family units (p. 238; Gutman, 1976, pp. 3–44). Pittman (2014) points out that there was a good deal of variation among plantations as to the preponderance of two-parent families, depending typically on the size of the plantation. Small plantations were more typical in the Mountain South, where 20 percent of slave families were headed by two parents, in contrast with the Lower South, where there were more large plantations and where 50 percent of slave families were headed by two parents (p. 234). There were also variations among plantations and slave owners regarding degrees of antipathy to their slaves' familial integrity, but, as noted above, masters who did not interfere with their slaves' desires to form and maintain families were rare.

For the most part, generations of slaves faced masters and mistresses who manipulated, ruptured, and diminished the significance of their attachments to partners and family. We know from records that these experiences of assaults on their marital and familial relationships were experienced with great pain. One former slave, after describing a tragic separation from her husband and the suffering it caused, said, "White folk's got a heap to answer for the way they've done the colored folks! So much they won't never *pray* it away" (Litwack, 1980, pp. 246–247). Even after Emancipation, "nothing could erase the still vivid memories of the fear and experience of forced separation from loved ones and the innumerable tragedies and complications which such separations . . . had inflicted on their families" (p. 246). Not only were the separations difficult to endure, but, according to the reports of former slaves, many of the post-war reunions of these separated families were troubled, even traumatic. In some cases, infants who had been snatched from their mothers now had attached to other figures and could not reconnect with the women who had so grieved at their loss.

Living for generations in this environment, in which the white population claimed to be models of the stable and virtuous nuclear family, African or African American slaves were told in word and deed that they were neither capable of nor permitted to enjoy secure familial relationships. These persistent negative messages from those in power concerning the rights of slave husbands and wives to love and protect each other, or of parents to assume the nurturing role and protective authority of mother or father, and command the love and respect that went with that parental role, confronted the slaves with a demoralizing challenge.

In her book, *Post Traumatic Slave Syndrome*, De Gruy (2005) encourages African Americans to understand themselves in the context of this very history. She speculates that black men may have resented black women "for not fighting against the master's sexual advances," even though it was clear that a female slave had no power in the situation and wonders if black women felt contempt for black men for failing to protect them, despite knowing that "any interference on his part could cost him his life?" (p. 153) Harriet Jacobs seems to share De Gruy's view:

> Some poor creatures have been so brutalized by the lash that they will sneak out of the way to give their masters free access to their wives and daughters . . . What would *you* be if you had been born and brought up a

slave, with generations of slaves for ancestors? I admit that the black man *is* inferior. But what makes him so? It is the ignorance in which white men compel him to live; it is the torturing whip that lashes manhood out of him; it is the fierce bloodhounds of the South, and the scarcely less cruel human bloodhounds of the north, who enforce the Fugitive Slave Law. *They* do the work.

(Jacobs, 1861/2000, p. 790)

Despite her compassionate analysis, this assertion "that the black man *is* inferior," is a jolting admission of what we would today call internalized racism. To what degree was the idea of their inferiority internalized by male slaves, and unconsciously absorbed by black women, such as Jacobs, and subsequently reinforced by post-slavery generations of white racism?

During a session in which she recounted yet another example of her mother's lack of affection and tendency to exploit her, Althea said the following: "I imagine my mom's mother was just as screwed up as she was. I don't watch much daytime TV, but I saw a judge show where a woman had to sue her own mother. But the mother went on and on repeating, 'That's *my* child.' But she took no responsibility for what she'd done. It's like your child becomes your property. That's a view that is so prevalent in my community." I was interested in her linking of the idea of one's child as one's "property" with "my community," so I asked her to explain. Surprised by my curiosity, she admitted she didn't know whether that attitude also was true among whites, so I asked if she was referring, in a roundabout way, to slavery and the idea of people owning people. Althea did not answer directly, but instead told the story of a young man in her neighborhood who had been gunned down some months ago. "I've seen his mother," she said disapprovingly, "and she was not grieved."

We hear again the troubling confusion between the idea of attachments based on love or familial commitment, and attachments based on ownership. Althea is struggling to articulate that uncomfortable sense that something is amiss in some of the relationships around her. Her immediate association is to the tragic and sadly not uncommon story of the mother who loses a son to gun violence. There are at least two ways one can understand the meaning of Althea's observations, whether or not they are, in fact, accurate. Against the backdrop of slavery, she may have absorbed in a corner of her mind the white slave owners' refusal to acknowledge real familial relationships amongst their slaves by the insistence that a black woman might be a "mammie," a woman who could serve as a generic maternal caretaker to any child, but never a mother, with the respect and profound emotional bond that latter title implies. Perhaps, consciously or unconsciously, Althea may have been referring to the need of mothers for some form of emotional protection against the ruptures that dogged their lives, whether resulting from the system of slavery or the violent world of her neighborhood.

In the twenty-first-century urban United States, for African Americans the chances of sudden, tragic separation especially from the young men in their lives—sons, nephews, brothers, uncles, and fathers—can lead to a similar desire for some kind of coping strategy for those loved ones left behind. According to a 2012 report, African American men are six times more likely to be murdered and seven times more likely to murder than their white counterparts (Hennekens et al., 2013). That statistic alone means that a black family is many times more likely to lose a son, father, brother, or uncle to death by murder or capital punishment, or to life imprisonment, than is a white family. Many years ago, I was working in a clinic where I treated briefly a middle-aged African American woman with three adult sons. She was depressed over a work-related problem, but she told me, with little affect, that she lived in constant fear of receiving a phone call informing her of the arrest or, worse, death of one of her children. No, they were not particularly involved in dangerous activities, but they were young black men, and they did go out at night with friends, and were subjected to traffic stops, like everyone else, and probably bought and smoked marijuana as well. We need only think of the more publicized cases of Trayvon Martin, Michael Brown, and Oscar Grant, not to mention the victims of drug trade wars and gang rivalries, to realize how understandable her fears were.

According to Litwack, "Few memories of bondage elicited greater pain in black parents than the humiliation they had suffered in watching their children whipped or abused by a member of the white family" (1980, p. 238). Vaughans (2014) suggests that in his experience, contemporary black parents emphasize their authority over their children, as if to defy the structure of slavery that deprived parents of that parental function, putting all power in the hands of the slave owners. The following vignette may, in some way, illustrate Vaughans' point.

Unlike Althea, Glenda was born and raised in northern California, the youngest child of parents who migrated from the South during the 1940s. This exchange followed a visit to her son and his family. She tells me about her grandson. "You tell him to pick up his jacket, and he'll say 'No!' I think of you, because there's no way you cannot pop 'em." I ask, "Do your son and daughter-in-law hit the kids as well?" "Yep, they've got to," she replies. "It's the only way they listen." The earlier exchange to which she was alluding when she said, "I think of you . . ." dealt with the topic of disciplining children. Glenda had then insisted on the need to "whoop" children from time to time to produce well-behaved youngsters. I had suggested to her that corporal punishment ends up backfiring, and that it sends the message that if a person feels justified, it is all right to hit someone, that it humiliates and angers the child, and whatever else I had learned in child development classes in graduate school. This time I say, "Well, there are other ways." Forcefully, she tells me that time-outs don't work. She rebuts the idea that the child who is spanked might then turn around and hit others: "You know, blacks been gettin' beat forever. We know the difference. No whites complained when they beat the slaves, but now it's 'violent' and 'undisciplined' to do it." I said that she seemed to feel my position was a "white thing," and encouraged her to tell me more of her thoughts. As she had in our earlier discussion of this topic, she reported that her parents had beaten her and her siblings "when we deserved it," implying that doing so had done her no harm. This time, however, the memory of those experiences changed and expanded.

As she described her father's disciplining of her, she eventually admitted, "Later on, when I thought back on it, I thought our whoopings was child abuse. My dad beat me all over my body, and I still have marks. My older brother had big welts on his back from being hit with an extension cord." I asked if she thought her parents accomplished what they hoped to do with their disciplining. She replied, "We're not criminals." There was a brief pause. "Well, my brothers did some robberies and went to prison, but not recently, and none of the girls went to jail." She also added that although she did swat her children at times, she had decided never to beat them as her father had done his children.

Glenda's association to white masters whipping slaves is intriguing, suggesting that, through some complicated process of identification, her father has asserted the right to discipline his own children, using the methods that had been used by the antebellum masters. Perhaps, more to the point, her father has continued the imperative of the slave parent to impose a fearful obedience and submissive stance vis-à-vis his or her white authority. Failure to do so would both reflect badly on the parent and, more significantly, endanger the child. Glenda has absorbed and modified this legacy. Of course, people of all ethnicities have been using corporal punishment on children world-wide, including pervasively in this country, yet Glenda's association to speaking to her white therapist about her hitting children takes us back 150 years to slavery. In the U.S. the post-World War II shifts in child-rearing practices, most famously seen in the writings of Dr. Benjamin Spock, have evolved to greatly discredit physical punishment and to criminalize the kind of abuse she describes her father having used. But for some African Americans, there continues to exist a mistrust of white people once again usurping their parenting authority, now with their "expert advice." As Glenda noted, she didn't hear about whites complaining about other whites beating slaves.

Under a Bushel

In the mid-1990s, Althea, whom we met above, came to see me after initial treatment elsewhere for a major depressive collapse. She had been taken off work when she had become too depressed to function at the white-collar job she'd held for many years. She described having endured two years of increasing harassment and humiliation. By the time she initially sought treatment, she had no longer been able to concentrate on her work tasks, suffered from crying spells, and had become so depressed that she stayed in her apartment, barely able to get out of bed in the morning. By the time she came to see me, she was doing better, and had benefited from both psychotherapy and antidepressant medication. As our work progressed and we began to look at her relationship to the job over the years she had worked at the company, some interesting material emerged.

An African American woman with a college education, born in the early 1950s, and working in a primarily white and Asian American setting, she let me in on some aspects of her experience that had not been initially apparent. We began to talk about the self-deprecating way in which she spoke to me at times, which corresponded to her descriptions of her ultimately futile attempts to rescue her position at work. Her body language, her walk, and her posture in her chair seemed to reflect a sheepishness that was at odds with her often astute observations. She reported that on one level she had realized that something was very wrong at work, but that she tried to deny to herself that she was being singled out for humiliating extra scrutiny by her white supervisor. Instead, she bent over backwards to ingratiate herself to him, hoping that if she could make him like her, her job might be safe. One way she had assumed she would be able to make herself agreeable was to downplay her education in his presence, while privately using all her skills as best she could to do her job well. In our work together, she began to realize she had slipped into a strategy of making herself as unthreatening as was possible, having decided on some level that the supervisor was angry at thinking of her as competent and well-educated, possibly even more so than he. I say "slipped" into this strategy because she was barely conscious of the shift, and it is this very lack of awareness or conscious decision making that is telling. Rather than using her considerable intelligence to figure out what was going on politically in her office, she relied on adopting a role that had roots in African American history, a role that involved concealing one's abilities to think independently or critically.

Martin Jackson, a former slave, described first-hand a precedent for this patient's experience as he tells of the need slaves felt to suppress the strength of their perceptions and intelligence. He also alludes to the lingering effects of this habit:

> Lots of old slaves closes the door before they tell the truth about their days of slavery. When the door is open, they tell how kind their masters was and how rosy it all was. You can't blame them for this, because they had plenty of early discipline, making them cautious about saying anything uncomplimentary about their masters.
>
> (Litwack, 1980, p. 104)

Much of the narrative of Harriet Jacobs' life as a slave and her journey out of the South describes her quiet vigilance and constant use of deception, which she describes as "the only weapon of the weak and oppressed against the strength of their tyrants" (1861/2000, pp. 846–847). Clearly for the slaves it was unsafe to be heard voicing honest and rational responses to their situation, but what is significant is Jackson's observation that the sense of peril in openly sharing one's thoughts persisted in the freed slaves even after Emancipation. Despite the fact that the house slave was in many ways deemed to be more fortunate than the field slave, he or she was especially compelled to assume the defensive strategy employed by my patient. Unlike the field slave, the house slave was always at the beck and call of the master and mistress and had to

> ... submit to indignities without protest, to submerge his feelings, to repress his emotions, to play "dumb" when the occasion demanded it, to respond with the proper gestures and words to every command, to learn the uses of flattery and humility, to *never appear overly intelligent.*
> (Litwack, 1980, p. 158; emphasis added)

Many African American folk tales, beginning in the time of slavery, warn against "undue pride and self assertiveness," and in his analysis of early African American folk tales, Levine explains that it was "dangerous for black men and women to forget who or where they were, and this danger constituted a motif running through Negro tales" (1977/2007, pp. 96–97).

Within the business operations of slavery, some African Americans achieved a certain amount of responsibility. Another figure of complicated status on the plantation was the black foreman or slave driver, often carrying "at best a mixed reputation" among fellow slaves (Litwack, 1980, p. 159). A small series of recorded letters of both house slaves and black slave drivers to and from their masters and mistresses is revealing. The letters primarily were intended as reports on the day-to-day operations, both commercial and domestic, of the plantations when the owners were away and wanted to be kept up to date. Letters from the driver included reports not only of the status of crops, but also of the health of the animals and the slaves, as all were considered equally as business investments and property. In the owners' replies, we see some small expression of affection for both of the latter. At the same time, the black foreman or driver offers details of incidents of disciplinary whippings he has meted out to the field slaves, reported in the same tone as was used in recounting the crop prices or seeds planted. The slaves' letters voice admiration and respect for the masters and their families, and those from the house slave in particular are saturated with flattering and adulatory comments to the mistress, along with the requisite details of the domestic affairs of the house (Starobin, 1988/1994).

These "privileged" slaves must have developed complex psychological coping strategies in order to manage what forbidden resentment they may have felt, being forced into adopting obsequious positions, while at the same time having the daily experiences of their master's or mistress's imperfections. In a letter dated July 12, 1856, plantation owner William Pettigrew writes to his driver, Moses. As a slave, Moses was barred from literacy, so a white neighbor had to serve as intermediary. Moses, left in charge while Pettigrew vacationed with friends and family, had been sending regular reports on the daily operations of the plantation. In response, Pettigrew tells of sharing Moses' letters with his friend. "You see from this, Moses," he writes

> ... how much interest Mr. Johnston takes in you and your people, and that should things take an unfavorable turn, in consequence of my long absence, not only would I be distressed, but he would also; and you & all your people would not only be disgraced in my estimation but also in his.
>
> (Starobin, 1988/1994, p. 3)

How would Moses have processed emotionally receiving such a letter with its veiled threat in response to having been given significant responsibility, seeming to be executing that responsibility without problems, all the while remaining unpaid chattel as the master gives himself a holiday? The contradiction between the obvious value accorded to Moses and the degrading way in which Pettigrew treats him creates a confusion that could well have affected Moses' self-image and sense of reality. And yet, as we know, Moses, if he is to survive his servitude, must cope privately and in silence, likely by splitting off his observations and any rebellious feelings they engender.

Similarly, more than a century and a half later, Althea felt it unsafe to let on that she had the insight to know she was being treated unfairly. She further believed, as she later revealed, that to disclose anything that might challenge her supervisor's presumed belief in his racial superiority to her would be dangerous and was to be carefully avoided. She felt dependent on her job to support herself and her children. Sadly, her panic and resulting refusal to admit even to herself what was happening prevented her from taking proactive measures, such as looking for another job. As our further therapeutic work together has also made clear, Althea has paid an additional price for her reliance on the skill described by Martin Johnson that was adaptive for Moses and the slaves, but can prove self-defeating in today's context. As it turned out, years before the problems at her job, she had faced hostile responses by her white fellow students and professors when she took advantage of a then new affirmative action program to attend a good university. She was not going to subject herself to that painful experience again. In the case of this patient, we discovered that not only was her attempt to forestall hostile responses unsuccessful, but in trying to be non-threatening by creating a facade that papered over her strengths, she was reinforcing an internal image of herself as inferior—an image that had reflected her mother's own projections of inadequacy and racial inferiority on to the patient, an issue I discuss later in this book.

Probably no line of W.E.B. Du Bois has been quoted more often than the following words from his seminal work *The Souls of Black Folk*. "It is a peculiar sensation, this double-consciousness, this sense of always looking at one's self through the eyes of others ... One ever feels his twoness—an American, a Negro ..." (1903/1986, p. 8). Living out Du Bois' description, Althea is ever conscious of how she will appear to the white world, while she also tries to fulfill her very human desire to discover who she is as a person in her own community. Maintaining that dual consciousness is hard work, and not always successfully achieved, as she knows only too well.

Crabs in a Bucket

It was Glenda who introduced me to what she told me was an old African American term, "crabs in a bucket." We were exploring her recollection of feelings of loneliness and abandonment by friends and family during her period of difficulties at work. She said, "It would take forever to explain, but we blacks are so screwed up. Have you heard the expression, 'crabs in a bucket?'" I asked her to tell me about it. "As one crab climbs up the side to get out, the others pull it down," Glenda explained. De Gruy describes "crabs in a bucket" as "an uncanny tendency amongst many blacks to orchestrate and plot the demise of other blacks, sometimes even friends and relatives." Her interpretation of this term offers a sensitive and more sympathetic understanding of the destructive impulse inherent in the crabs' behavior than Glenda could initially muster, suggesting that "layered between the resentment and envy are issues of fear or panic, coupled with feelings of abandonment and shame . . . a fear of being left behind by the very people who we have embraced as equals" (2005, p. 161). De Gruy sees the seeds of "crabs in a bucket" in slavery's structure and the slave owners' manipulation of their chattel so as to promote distrust amongst the slaves "as a way of preventing slave uprisings," by rendering them "less prone to unite against their common enemy, namely the slave owners" (p. 203).

Whether or not De Gruy is correct in her speculation, it is clear that through disrupting family and kinship connections with unpredictable forced separations, disempowering individual slaves in as many ways as possible, and creating a caste system among the slaves, the institution of slavery seemed to strive to prevent slaves from forming and maintaining stable and mutually supportive connections among themselves. Glenda is not the only one to complain about feeling undermined in this way. Althea also has often given vent to her perception of having been dragged down by fellow "crabs," including coworkers, strangers, friends, and siblings. Just as she hid her education from her white supervisor at work, she believed her college degree put her at a disadvantage among her African American coworkers. "My education worked against me," she told me one day. "I can't tell you how many black people resented seeing white graduates rise above them, but they couldn't take it out on them. Instead they showed their anger to me." I commented, "So you were getting it from both sides, white and black." Nodding, she added, "They thought that I'd think I'm better than them, so I'd try to be 'down' with them, and be careful with them in my conversations." "You mean you had to play dumb?" I asked. "Yes, but I had to do well in my actual work at the same time. I just didn't know where I stood with people."

In a different session in which she was revisiting the history of her challenges at her job, she talked about another supervisor to whom she was later assigned, as the pressures of the harassment began to affect her work performance: "She was a tall, loud-mouth black woman. She seemed to delight in seeing that I couldn't keep up. She hadn't gone to college, and this is where the insanity comes in. If a young, white woman came in with a college degree, that was okay, but she had a real problem with a black person who'd been to college."

In considering the dynamics of workplace rivalries and insecurities, we all have an intuitive, if not experiential, understanding of the perils and intricacies of hierarchical relationships, such as Althea is describing. These could be female boss/male underling; or a 24-year-old charged with supervising a 50-year-old employee; not to mention any variety of inter-ethnic combinations. Yet as we look further into relationships involving African American men and women at work or in the public sphere in general, whether race is a determining factor or not, for many like Althea it is never forgotten.

These speculations about the effects on African American families of "the peculiar institution," as antebellum Southerners so euphemistically labeled slavery, cannot fully describe the complexities and varieties of lives and relationships of the descendants of the four million men, women, and children who were enslaved at the time of Emancipation. To forget that reality inevitably takes one into dangerous territory, as became evident in 1965 with the eruption of anger surrounding a U.S. Department of Labor report by then Assistant Secretary Daniel Moynihan.

The report (Moynihan, 1965), originally drafted as an internal document intended to influence federal jobs policy, was entitled "The Negro Family: The Case for National Action." Moynihan took the position that despite having finally achieved civil rights, "Negro Americans" would be unable to bridge the existing social and economic gaps between them and white Americans for two reasons: 1. "the racist virus in the American blood stream still afflicts us," so that blacks will have to continue to deal with white racism. 2. "three centuries of sometimes unimaginable mistreatment have taken their toll on the Negro people . . . The fundamental problem (resulting from that mistreatment) . . . is that of family structure." (p. 1) Citing a 1964 book, *A Profile of the Negro American* (Pettigrew, 1964, pp. 13–14), Moynihan wrote that because of many of the abuses of slavery, "the slave household often developed a fatherless matrifocal (mother-centered) pattern." He added that post-Emancipation white hostility was focused on keeping black men "in their places," while deeming that "the female was not a threat to anyone." This pattern, he believed, perpetuated this "matrifocal" family structure (1965, Chapter III). Much of Moynihan's report, which was used, as he intended, to promote the implementation of jobs and training programs, with the expected benefit of increasing African American male employment, was spent outlining the forces working against African American equality in this country, including poor housing and education, crime, and, of course, discrimination. Yet he concludes with the following: "Nonetheless, at the center of the tangle of pathology is the weakness of the family structure" (Chapter IV). It was this final claim, and his emphasis on the "tangle of pathology" throughout the report, that led to the eruptions that followed.

Coming at the moment of the Black Power movement's emergence as well as of feminist critiques of patriarchy and assumptions about the nuclear family structure, Moynihan's unflattering descriptions of disempowered African American men, and inadequate "matrifocal" African American families, sparked intense reactions. An immediate response in *The Nation* magazine was a pivotal article by psychologist William Ryan, who challenged Moynihan's research as "weak" and "insufficient," which encouraged

> ... (no doubt unintentionally) a new form of racism ... and seduces the reader into believing that it is not racism and discrimination but the weaknesses and defects of the Negro himself that account for the present states of inequality between Negro and white.
>
> (Ryan, 1965, p. 380)

In Ryan's view, Moynihan's attribution of the poor conditions of African Americans to "the Negro's history of being enslaved and oppressed—*generations ago*" (original emphasis) represents "an ingenious way" of ducking responsibility for contemporary oppression by blaming history for having created the troubled state of African American life in 1965 (p. 383). Interestingly, Ryan's prescription to end the inequality essentially echoes Moynihan's: "re-education, by training, by any means that become necessary," to raise African American employment. His concluding proposed solution is "to bring a real end to real discrimination and segregation" (p. 384), no small task. Ryan went on to elaborate these themes in a 1971 book in which he coined the expression "blaming the victim." His analysis of Moynihan's text illuminates the danger of what Anne Anlin Cheng (2001) describes as "naturalizing injury" (p. 5). As she cautions, "it can be damaging to say how damaging racism has been" (p. 14).

Historian Herbert Gutman, in the introduction to his 664-page work on the black family, states that he wrote the book in response to "the bitter public and academic controversy surrounding" the Moynihan report, which he characterizes as reproducing "conventional academic wisdom" in viewing the black family as primarily pathologically dysfunctional, and tracing this dysfunction back to the evils of slavery. He describes Moynihan's attribution of the origins of these problems: "It was by destroying the Negro family that white Americans broke the will of the Negro people" (Gutman, 1976, p. xvii). Gutman counters Moynihan's report with his exhaustive study of census schedules, records of Freedmen's bureaus, and many other writings, to document the outlines of familial behaviors and structures that undermine this conventional articulation by Moynihan, that slavery destroyed the black family, and that black families have failed to function successfully ever since. To be sure, slavery and its legacy have taken a heavy toll on the black family, as we have seen, but by labeling the single-parent black family as a form of "pathology," Moynihan seemed to shift the blame for the difficulties faced by African Americans to the family itself. This attribution may well have been unconscious, as Moynihan also demonstrates obvious sympathy for the obstacles, both current and historical, facing African Americans. Nevertheless, he appeared unable to imagine that African American families, like those in all societies, adapt to the realities of their given circumstances, and that these adaptations could be seen to represent creative solutions to challenging environments.

Resistance, Survival, and Creativity

When Barbara spoke of the shame she feels when reminded that she is a descendant of slaves, she was reflecting both the transmitted traumatic experiences of abduction and enslavement, and the denigrating projections of the white slave owners onto their slaves. The humiliation that accompanies complete subjection, reinforced by the abuse and dehumanization required to render people powerless, affects everyone touched by these relationships. Yet toxic as those memories are, many, like Barbara, tend to seem unaware of the omnipresent resistance to their situation mounted by the slaves. With the persistence of white racism over the centuries, it is not surprising that this history of resistance is less known to twenty-first-century Americans of all ethnicities, or is taken for granted even by African Americans who participate in the culture that emerged in that resistance. The affirming elements of black life, then, are rarely raised in psychotherapy sessions. Yet it is important not to forget the foundations of the culture that has sustained the slaves and their descendants and that is so essential to our national identity.

While antebellum life for blacks was one of hardship, fear, and often desperation, it would be a serious mistake to think of the slaves exclusively as terrorized victims, rendered passive, brainwashed, and beaten down by their situation. Ex-slaves and their immediate descendants reported that the image they had of themselves was not as

> ... a cowed and timorous black mass but of a people who, however circumscribed by misfortune and oppression, were never without their means of resistance and never lacked the inner resources to oppose the master class, however extreme the price they had to pay.
>
> (Levine, 1977/2007, p. 389)

Many families proudly held onto and passed down stories of rebellious slave ancestors who stood up to white owners.

Not only did some slaves openly resist their oppressors, but, perhaps more significantly in the long term, the slaves evolved for themselves communities comprising a cultural world that they developed and maintained mostly beneath the radar of their white masters, and that could provide them with means of psychological self-determination. And even if those descendants do not consciously register that legacy, it has been in many ways sound enough to continue to serve African Americans throughout the dangers and hardships they have faced since Emancipation. The enslaved Africans and their descendants managed to subvert slavery's constrictions on their lives by forging and adapting cultural tools for psychological survival and creativity that served and continue to serve their descendants. These cultural tools enabled them to hold on to aspects of their identities as Africans while mobilizing to respond to their current realities, creating "the necessary space between the slaves and their owners and were the means of preventing legal slavery from becoming spiritual slavery" (Levine, 1977/2007, p. 80).

The establishment and maintenance of a stable sense of identity is a fundamental human need. While it begins its formation within the dyadic relationship between mother and infant, one's sense of self becomes increasingly and vitally affected by the larger family and community. It is hard to imagine that the effects of the many traumas involved in abduction, the "Middle Passage," the relocation in a strange landscape and language, and final entrapment by the brutality of slavery would not have had an impact on the nature of the slaves' senses of self, self-esteem, and peer relationships. Even voluntary immigration inevitably challenges the immigrant's sense of self and identity. But for the man or woman who had gone from being a member of a community with familial and cultural roots, and the means of earning respect within that society, to becoming a deracinated human being, whose role and worth is now to be assessed in terms comparable to those of livestock, literally as chattel, this challenge is unfathomable. As Gump (2010) notes, "the self receives affirmation by dint of the other's recognition . . . mutuality of recognition must be sustained if both subjectivities are to exist," a mutuality that is impossible between master and slave (pp. 49–50). Yet in the midst of coping with this crisis of identity, as well as the psychological effects of terror and powerlessness, being able to integrate aspects of one's "old" life—religion, customs, styles, family ethos, and language— with the "new" life can mitigate the blow to the self-esteem caused by the uprooting (Grinberg & Grinberg, 1989). Thus, despite unpromising odds, the slaves' preservation of their cultural roots reflected their will to survive psychologically as they coped with, adapted to, and made something of their harsh circumstances and ultimately succeeded in defining much of what we consider vital and original in American culture today.

Folklorists from the nineteenth and twentieth centuries discovered that despite the fact that the slaves were drawn from different African tribes, with a variety of languages and religious customs, there were nevertheless common attitudes and a similar ethos among them. By the time scholars were collecting their data, the presence of purely African etiology had been significantly reduced by both active attempts by slave masters to destroy their slaves' cultural heritage and the inevitable results of contact with and appropriation of Euro-American forms.[3] Folklorists and anthropologists have argued for decades over the degree of persistence of African influence in black American consciousness, but it would be foolish to deny that during slavery African structures of belief and expression played a significant role in the lives of the exiles and their descendants, if only because the slaves were denied access to much of the culture of their owners. This continuity with their African roots proved critical to their cultural development (Belgrave & Allison, 2010, p. 44).

Long after the end of slavery, that "cultural refuge" of African heritage has continued to serve as a means of self-affirmation that does not rely upon acceptance by the European/white environment. The Black Power movement of the 1960s, for instance, distinguished itself from the broader Civil Rights Movement by emphasizing both resistance to and independence from white society. Its organizers included in their mobilization efforts renewed attention to the African cultural roots of their people and campaigned for Black Studies departments at universities across the country. For an energized sector of young African Americans at the time, connection with African roots struck a responsive chord. Possessing a sense of connection with a land and peoples before enslavement provided a source of pride, a sense of history, and an affirmation of opposition to white domination. The use of African-based names exploded, and a small but significant percentage of African American families began and continue to celebrate Kwanzaa after its introduction in 1966.

A reminder of the ongoing importance of a sense of recognition of one's roots occurred in my practice during the treatment of an African American man whose severe industrial injury had forced him off work. After many years of pride and pleasure in his profession and a sense of camaraderie with coworkers, he was angry and hurt, bereft at the loss of what had been a powerful source of identity for much of his adult life. Although he claims he had never been much of a student in high school, he now found himself fascinated by the pyramids of Egypt, and began to read everything he could in Egyptology. In one session in which he had expressed his deepening awareness that he would never return to his job and his anger at how he was treated once he was injured, we began to discuss the delicate subject of what he might do, once he was well enough, in lieu of his usual work. "I would like to go to school to study the Egyptians," he said. "I'm fascinated with what they did, and I get frustrated when people say they were not smart enough to last, and with the arguments over the skin color of the Egyptians." I said that it sounded as though he felt people now did not appreciate the accomplishments of these people. He added, "You know, these people moved around. The Nubians conquered Egypt; there are really more pyramids in Sudan than in Egypt." I speculated that maybe he felt a special identification with these peoples whose accomplishments he feels are not fully appreciated, given how he had been treated by his employer. He did not respond to what I said, so I am not sure my comment was on the mark, but for a man in his 40s who says he never had any interest in history when he was in school to be captivated by the grandeur of ancient Egypt it is hard not to think about the meaning of such a development.

The Sacred Under Slavery

Few ethnic groups in this country live as close to their religious beliefs as African Americans. The power of spirituality was from the start vital to the slaves' ability to cope with the forced exile from their homelands and their enslavement. Religion during the centuries of slavery was a fluid and evolving combination of African beliefs and practices, and, after eventual conversion to European-American Christianity, something else that was neither and both. White slaveholders were at best ambivalent about whether or not to introduce their slaves to Christianity. In fact, there was a good deal of fear that exposure to Christianity and ideas about equality before God could give the slaves dangerous ideas. Furthermore, there were more mundane, practical considerations, such as the Bible's prohibition of work on the Sabbath, and time needed to attend church services—both of which would cost the slave owners financially by taking away from time their slaves could be working. And, of course, there was the difficulty in accepting the idea that the Africans, whom the masters took such pains to devalue, could be worthy co-religionists with white Christians (Levine, 1977/2007, p. 60). The slave owners' withholding of Christian teaching from their slaves did not prevent the latter from creating and inhabiting their own sacred universe, where they could hold to a form of meaning and order in the chaotic and brutal environment in which they lived (pp. 54, 62).

Many slaves defied their masters and, at some peril to themselves, formed groups to hold clandestine night-time prayer meetings. Even when they were allowed to attend church with the masters' families on Sunday mornings, in the evenings they would often hold their own secret services, generally outdoors and away from their quarters, where their masters would not see them (Litwack, 1980, pp. 464–465). These gatherings must have been powerful experiences for the slaves. It was there that they were able to create a Christianity that made sense to them. There they were able to establish and celebrate the idea of a distinction "between the eternal power and justice of the 'Master' (God) as opposed to the short-term temporal power of the 'Massa'" (Levine, 1977/2007, p. 98). The "massa" may control their lives on earth, but there was an omnipotent and omniscient God who was ruler of master and slave alike, who saw the cruelties inflicted on His people, and who maintained the power to eventually right wrongs. Simply by the very act of worshipping secretly, they were acting out that resistance to their earthly masters, sabotaging those masters' beliefs that they could control their slaves' very souls. As we shall see in other ways, these moments of covert defiance and evasion of the masters' crude attempts to repress any suspected instance of self-determination or autonomy figured prominently in the cultural lives of the slaves.

These secret prayer meetings must have provided the slaves with a sense of comfort by worshipping, learning, and singing among their peers. Living in a dangerous world as they did, where they were "faced on all sides by doubt and the threat of personal disintegration, by the thwarting of instincts and the annihilation of values," the slaves turned to a God whom they adapted to suit their needs (Levine, 1977/2007, p. 33). This God was no abstraction; He was "as intimate, personal, and immediate as the gods of Africa had been" (p. 35). As one ex-slave put it, "We must see, feel and hear something, for our God talks to his children" (p. 36).

I have been periodically struck by the ways in which my patients' God remains an "intimate, personal, and immediate" being. Barbara described her Christianity to me one day: "I talk to God all the time and ask him to show me the right way." Among my patients, she is not alone in this practice. God is not an abstraction or a remote figure. By their accounts, He continues to intervene directly in their lives: in one instance allowing misfortune to fall on the person as a painful means of teaching a lesson; at another perfect moment producing a sympathetic bureaucrat who dealt courteously with her insurance claim; and on another occasion by bringing a loved one back to health from a serious illness. Barbara remarked to me one day, "I don't know if you are religious or believe in God, even. I sure hope you do." When I inquired as to what made that important to her, she replied, "Because it's such a comfort." In Chapter 5 Tracy recounts how her appeal to God and His intervention prevented her from taking action that would have had devastating consequences.

Additionally, in the whites' Bible, the slaves found themes and stories that they readily translated to serve them in their own circumstances, providing vital compensatory narratives to combat the denigration and powerlessness they experienced on a daily basis. The belief in being "the chosen people," for instance, figures prominently in slave songs (Levine, 1977/2007, pp. 33–34), providing a spiritual counterforce to their masters' disrespect for them, and turning on its head the message conveyed by their white captors, of having been a people "chosen" by the slavers to be exploited and dehumanized. Now, by adapting the Scripture to their needs, they could create together a positive group identity, that of a people who had been marked by their suffering, but seen as special in the eyes of God.

Another instance of the working of a biblical tale to provide a potential tool for resilience can be seen in the story of Cain and Abel. Anglo-American mythology explained blackness as God's punishment of Noah's son Ham, and many added the curse of Cain as an explanation for blackness and justification for slavery, but an African American slave preacher taught his fellow slaves that it was *whites* who were derived from Cain after God turned him *white* as a punishment for his murder of Abel. This latter version of the Scriptures continued to be told in the South into the twentieth century (Levine, 1977/2007, pp. 84–85), as well as through the teachings of Black Muslim Elijah Muhammed.

Similarly, biblical heroes who confronted and conquered powerful enemies, despite the seemingly unlimited power of their opponents, also played important roles in the slaves' spiritual mythology, and are frequent subjects of their spirituals. David's fight with Goliath, Moses matching wits with the Pharaoh, Samson and the Philistines, and Jesus' confrontation with the authorities of his time—all were tales that were eagerly adopted by the slaves. Not surprisingly, it is Moses, who led the enslaved Israelites out of Egypt to freedom, who figured most prominently in the slaves' biblical pantheon. As one Northern army chaplain who spent time with the slaves during the Civil War noted, by comparison, Christ was seen "not so much in the light of a *spiritual* Deliverer, as that of a second Moses" (Levine, 1977/2007, p. 50; original emphasis). How gratifying it must have been—and continues to be—to hold in mind, to sing of, and to tell these exciting stories of people like themselves who eventually triumph over and are liberated from the swaggering bullies who brought misery to them and their people. One patient told me that when she feels overwhelmed with rage at being treated unjustly, "I try to get over the anger with my religion. At first the Pharaoh wouldn't let the people go, but eventually Moses took them to freedom. Why should it be any different for me?"

Inherent in these stories that fill the sacred world the slaves created is the promise that justice will eventually punish the oppressors. What could be better suited to this desire for justice and the triumph of good over evil than the concepts of heaven and hell? There is much evidence to confirm that slaves believed, or at least hoped, that slave owners, or even all whites, not only would be denied access to heaven, but would instead end up in hell. A fugitive slave named Charles Ball said: "Heaven will be no heaven to him (the slave), if he is not to be avenged of his enemies (whites)" (Levine, 1977/2007, p. 34). This theme was so widespread that it was a regular feature of slave humor. In one example, a master is dying when he says to his slave: "Good-by Jack; I have a long journey to go; farewell." Jack replies, "Farewell, Massa! Pleasant journey; you soon be dere, Massa—*all the way down hill*" (p. 25; original emphasis). A song dating back to slavery, but still heard in rural Louisiana as late as the 1930s, went as follows:

> My ole mistress promised me
> Before she died she would set me free . . .
> Now she's dead and gone to hell,
> I hope the devil will burn her well
>
> (p. 193)

The Arts of Survival

While the slaves retained faith in the promise of the ultimate justice their religious beliefs offered, they also were realists. Every day they confronted hardship and danger, and the art they created reflected and responded to those challenges. Blending their African traditions with expressive forms they encountered in North America, they created a new cultural tapestry of folk tales, magic, music, and humor to satisfy their aesthetic, emotional, and social desires. What evolved provided them with three important elements: 1. the opportunity to represent the cruelty and chaos of their lives in aesthetically rewarding ways, 2. the creation of a community of shared culture, knowledge, and experience, and 3. the ability to express themselves safely, within the repressive world of the plantation, by using artistic forms that veiled their messages so as to avoid antagonizing their owners.

One art form they brought from their countries of origin that was well adapted to their situation was story-telling. Devoid of sentimentality and romanticism, African American folk tales depict characters endlessly engaged in acts of cruelty and violence, mirroring with psychological accuracy the slaves' lived experiences (Levine, 1977/2007, p. 117). Most popular were the trickster tales in which the protagonist typically is a weak animal, often a rabbit, who thwarts more powerful animals by relying solely on his wits. The unthreatening rabbit represents a truth about the lived experience of the slave. It is physically vulnerable to its predators, yet it can think of ways to survive and even to triumph. Still no matter what victory it achieves in a particular story, at the end of the day, it is still just a puny rabbit. Because the characters in the trickster tales are animals, the story-tellers were safely able to comment on their situations without arousing the slave-masters' anger. To the white master, these animal stories may have been amusing trifles. The slaves, however, were not fooled: "The trickster's exploits, which overturned the neat hierarchy of the world in which he was forced to live, became their exploits; the justice he achieved, their justice; the strategies he employed, their strategies" (p. 114).

In a way, these often violent tales also can be seen as attempts by the slaves to come to terms with the traumas of their lives by representing their experiences symbolically, thereby externalizing traumatic memories of their experiences of oppression into artistic form, hopefully to achieve a momentary distance from the painful and disorienting feelings stirred up by the awareness of their situation. (I wonder if some examples of the violence described in rap music also represent attempts to master the terror of a different, but still dangerous, world.)

Probably no African American art form has had a deeper impact on American culture than the music created by the slaves and their descendants. Jazz virtuoso Sidney Bechet gives us a clue as to the centrality of music in a world where people are denied autonomy: "The onliest thing I've ever been sure of how it was going is the music; that's something a man can make himself if he has the feeling" (Levine, 1977/2007, p. 297). The black slaves constantly and consistently produced songs of great artistry, in particular the spirituals, thematically based on their newly acquired Christianity, rich in poetry and filled with an emotional intensity that keeps them alive today. W.E.B. Du Bois described the spiritual as "the singular spiritual heritage of the nation and the greatest gift of the Negro people." (1903/1986, p. 537) These songs managed to express both sadness but also hope and confidence. After all, "Did not old Pharaoh get lost . . . in the Red Sea?" (Levine, 1977/2007, p. 40)

One of the cultural artifacts brought from Africa and also frequently noted by white observers were work songs, whether sung in the fields or on boats. These songs were an important source of communal comfort for the slaves (Levine, 1977/2007, p. 33; Epstein, 1977, p. 79), characterized by pathos, but also by humor satirizing the figures in their lives who were oppressing them. One of the most important tools for maintaining sanity under adversity is humor, and the slaves made good use of it. John Bernard, a British actor and comedian who lived in the U.S. in the early nineteenth century, claimed that the slaves were "the great humorists of the Union" (Levine, 1977/2007, p. 30). The cakewalk was a perfect example of this kind of wit that becomes art. Born out of slavery, the cakewalk was to become enormously popular worldwide in the 1890s. Papanikolas (2015) cites the words of a woman who had been a young slave in the 1840s as she described the genesis of the dance:

> Us slaves watched the white folks' parties where the guests danced a minuet and then paraded in a grand march, with the ladies and gentlemen going different ways and then meeting again, arm in arm, and marching down the center together. Then we'd do it, too, *but we used to mock 'em*, even step. Sometimes the white folks noticed it, but they seemed to like it; I guess they thought we couldn't dance any better.
> (p. 52, and in Stearns & Stearns, 1994, p. 22; original emphasis)

As Papanikolas describes, "the rigid backs and the military strut of the cotillion . . . become exquisitely exploitable by black caricature," with each feature of the white performance exaggerated into its own new form (p. 53).

Political humor, for that is what this kind of satire represents, can be inspirational in the face of feelings of impotence against one's leaders and the damage they inflict. Those moments of shared laughter, experienced in community with other likeminded souls, provide the group with a pleasant sense of having publicly stripped the emperor of his myth of righteous authority, and upturning the power relationship under which those subjected to him live. I wonder if the function of story-telling has shifted to professional comedians, and while my patients do not tell B'rer Rabbit stories, they often speak with the same humor, irony, and satire found in the old tales, employed to make sense of an often hostile and perplexing world.

Addressing his son in *Between the World and Me*, Ta-Nehesi Coates (2015) writes, "Never forget that we have been enslaved in this country longer than we have been free. Never forget that for 250 years black people were born into chains—whole generations followed by more generations who knew nothing but chains" (p. 70). Yes, we see that the traumas of slavery reverberate in the emotional lives of my patients, but so do the means of resistance as well. We also know that Emancipation did not end the racial divide or the oppression under which African Americans lived and continue to live. The next chapter will explore the psychological ramifications of Jim Crow, the Great Migration, the Civil Rights Movement, and other events in African American history, as we work to make sense of the African American experience.

Notes

1 On August 20, 1619, the first Africans were unloaded onto the shores of Virginia, and by 1865, 597,000 Africans had been brought to this country (Tadman, 2000). By the time of the Civil War there were more than 4,000,000 African Americans living in the U.S., and they comprised close to 40 percent of the population of the South (Litwack, 1980, p. 3).
2 The writings of Herbert Gutman, Lawrence Levine, Leon Litwack, and Eugene D. Genovese are classic historical works that deal with U.S. slavery. The New Deal's WPA project, *Born in Slavery: Slave Narratives from the Federal Writers' Project, 1936–1938*, with its 2,000 interviews of former slaves, has been invaluable for historians, and there have been many more recent studies on aspects of slavery.
3 An exception was the Gullah, a community of slaves who had been settled on the islands off the Georgia and South Carolina coasts, where the isolation from the mainland served to preserve elements from African language and lore (Dorson, 1956, p. 17).

References

Belgrave, F.Z. & Allison, K.W. (2010). *African American psychology: From Africa to America*. Thousand Oaks, CA: Sage.

Cheng, A.A. (2001). *The melancholy of race: Psychoanalysis, assimilation, and hidden grief*. Oxford: Oxford University Press.

Coates, T. (2015). *Between the world and me*. New York: Spiegel and Grau.

Davoine, F. & Gaudilliere, J. (2004). *History beyond trauma: Whereof one cannot speak, thereof one cannot stay silent.* New York: Other Press.
De Gruy, J. (2005). *Post traumatic slave syndrome: America's legacy of enduring injury and healing.* Portland, OR: Joy de Gruy Publications, Inc.
Dorson, R.M. (1956). *American Negro folktales.* New York: Fawcett.
Du Bois, W.E.B. (1903/1986). *The souls of black folk.* In *Writings.* New York: The Library of America College Editions.
Epstein, D.J. (1977). *Sinful tunes and spirituals: Black folk music to the Civil War.* Urbana, IL & London: University of Illinois Press.
Faimberg, H. (2005). *The telescoping of generations: Listening to the narcissistic links between generations.* London & New York: Routledge.
Grinberg, L. & Grinberg, R. (1989). *Psychoanalytic perspectives on migration and exile.* New Haven, CT & London: Yale University Press.
Gump, J.P. (2010). Reality matters: The shadow of trauma on African-American subjectivity. *Psychoanalytic Psychology, 27* (1): 42–54.
Gutman, H.G. (1976). *The black family in slavery and freedom: 1750–1925.* New York: Vintage Books.
Hennekens, C.H., Drowos, J., & Levine, R.S. (2013). Mortality from homicide among young black men: A new American tragedy. *American Journal of Medicine, 126* (4): 282–283.
Jacobs, H.A. (1861/2000). Incidents in the life of a slave girl. Written by herself. In Child, L.M. (Ed.), *Slave narratives.* New York: Library Classics of the U.S., Inc.
Krystal, H. (Ed.) (1968). *Massive psychic trauma.* New York: International Universities Press, Inc.
Levine, L.W. (1977/2007). *Black culture and black consciousness: Afro-American folk thought from slavery to freedom.* Oxford & New York: Oxford University Press.
Litwack, L.F. (1980). *Been in the storm so long: The aftermath of slavery.* New York: Vintage Books.
Moynihan, D. (1965). The Negro family: The case for national action. U.S. Department of Labor, www.dol.gov/dol/aboutdol/history/webid-moynihan.htm (accessed November 1, 2017).
Papanikolas, Z. (2015). *An American cakewalk: Ten syncopators of the modern world.* Stanford, CA: Stanford University Press.
Pettigrew, T.F. (1964). *A profile of the Negro American.* New York: Van Nostrand.
Pittman, L. (2014). African American families: Still a band of slaves? In Akhtar, S. (Ed.), *The African American experience* (pp. 229–269). Lanham, MD: Rowman and Littlefield.
Ryan, W. (1965). Savage discovery: The Moynihan report. *Nation, 201* (17): 380–384.
Starobin, R.S. (1988/1994). *Blacks in bondage: Letters of American slaves.* Princeton, NJ: Markus Wiener Publishers. http://nationalhumanitiescenter.org/pds/maai/enslavement/text4/mosesandhenry.pdf (accessed October 24, 2017).
Stearns, M. & Stearns, J. (1994). *Jazz dance: The story of American vernacular dance.* New York & Cambridge, MA: De Capo Press.
Suchet, M. (2004). A relational encounter with race. *Psychoanalytic Dialogues, 14*: 423–438.
Tadman, M. (2000). The demographic cost of sugar: Debates on slave societies and natural increase in the Americas. *The American Historical Review, 105*: 5.
Vaughans, K. (2014). Disavowed fragments of the intergenerational transmission of trauma from slavery among African Americans. Paper presented at Division 39 meetings, New York City.

3 From Lash to Backlash: Invisible Chains

By now it must be clear that traumatic history does not disappear with the passage of time. The psyches of people whose forebears have been subjected to persecution and oppression are infused with that history, as it is passed from generation to generation. As we will see in this chapter, the traumatic residue of early African American history is particularly persistent because many of the same destructive aspects of that history have persisted to reinforce rather than disconfirm the mental residue of earlier traumas. Under slavery, African Americans lived with an omnipresent threat of physical harm, a threat intended to maintain them in states of perpetual fear and powerlessness. Furthermore, in their need to justify the slave system, those who supported and were supported by it created a mythology of the inherent inferiority of the African slaves and their descendants—a mythology that was constantly expressed, elaborated, and defined by social and economic constrictions and enforced through violence. This chapter looks at how, despite the defeat of the Confederate Army and the end of legal slavery, these conditions of oppression, threats of violence, and psychological abuse may have adapted to changed circumstances but in reality continued unabated. They, too, have left and continue to leave their marks. In order to understand the psychological effects of these conditions, historical context, again, is critical.

But to begin that survey, I want to look at a phenomenon of relatively recent history that illustrates the psychological persistence of the events following the end of slavery. It happens to be one of the most atypical events in American history: the 2008 election of Barack Obama to the presidency. In spring of 2007, as the competition for the Democratic nomination was gearing up, Althea first voiced her thoughts to me about Obama. "I love him for saying that we're 'a mean society.'" Laughing, she added, "I know he's not going anywhere." In her next breath, she complained about right-wing television personality Rush Limbaugh, telling me, "He'd called Venus and Serena [Williams] 'animals.' Well, they're not shrinking violets, that's for sure. But that stuff is so prevalent. It's all over the Internet." I asked how the ugliness of these kinds of insults felt to her. "Oh, it didn't affect me," she replied. "We should all be outraged at the mean-spiritedness, but it's the whole system. It's much too hard to do anything about it. It's like knowing that I'll never get my mother's approval. That's been easier to cope with now that I understand it."[1]

These thoughts voiced by a middle-aged African American woman express some of the complexity of the relationship between her sense of herself in the larger society, her feelings about a younger, African American politician, and her experience of being her mother's child. Her initial gratification in hearing a black candidate confirm aloud the "mean" quality of a society by which she felt so often injured was coupled with her light-hearted assumption that such a candidate could never become the Democratic nominee. I wish now that I'd asked her the meaning of her laugh; what did she really feel about her conviction that he could never be elected? In a sense, however, she does reveal how she feels just seconds later when she brings up the crude racism of Limbaugh and others on the Internet, opining that while we should "all be outraged," racism is so entrenched that the idea of an African American president is as hopeless as her ever gaining her mother's approval. Her feelings include outrage at the racism, outrage at the lack of general outrage ("we should all be outraged"), and hopelessness. Was she also offering a critique of my question about how *she* felt about the insult, as if perhaps I was distancing myself from feeling the outrage "we should all" feel?

But she also links two impossibilities that seem on the surface unrelated, eliminating racism in this country and feeling loved by her mother. In fact, the simile is not random. Her mother, like Limbaugh, places low value on dark skin, and Althea, as the child with the darkest skin of her siblings, was always made to feel less valued by her mother. (The issue of color and shading will be discussed in more depth in a later chapter.) Althea is, in fact, a statuesque, dark-skinned woman, who dresses with becoming and tasteful flare; but, of course, that reality provides no immunity to her mother's painful messages. Over the years, however, she has come to understand that her mother's inability to love her was a manifestation of her mother's traumatic familial and ethnic history as a poor black girl and woman raised in the deep South during the 1930s and 1940s, a history that had left her unable to truly nurture any of her children. She may have made Althea feel badly about her color, but her mother's profound level of depression and troubled psychological functioning, as described by her observant daughter, wreaked psychological havoc on the whole family. In other words, some of the inadequacy Althea had felt about herself all her life was generated from within her mother's tortured psyche and did not represent anything intrinsically inferior in Althea, or, in the case of Limbaugh's own twisted inner world, Serena or Venus. What makes Althea's maternal deprivation additionally toxic, then, is the fact that her mother's projected self-hatred was confirmed for Althea by the larger society, as she stepped outside the family, particularly but not exclusively in the southern state where Althea and her mother were raised. Very little in the outside world was available for the young girl to disconfirm her belief that her darker complexion made her a less valuable person. She achieved some relief as a young adult through changes in circumstances for African Americans, in particular by affirmative action, but it has been only through a careful and persistent exploration of both sources of denigration of her black identity and our discovering the links between the two that Althea has begun to take some distance from these injurious projections and to see her mother, herself, and the environment in a more realistic way.

In any event, by the time Obama actually did win the nomination, Althea's attitude shifted. "They'll kill him," she pronounced one day. Glenda also voiced the same worry, but she was able at the same time to enthusiastically campaign for Obama, and scrimped and saved to fly from the West Coast to Washington for his inauguration. It turns out that Glenda's concern and Althea's more emphatic ambivalence about an Obama candidacy based on fear of assassination were far from unique. Princeton political science professor Melissa Harris-Lacewell is quoted as saying, "For many black supporters, there is a lot of anxiety that he will be killed. It's on people's minds" (Gardner, 2008). Cheryl Boyd, a cleaner in Memphis, told a reporter:

> People say that if he makes it, someone will have him killed . . . I'm trying not to let it worry me. I pray that if he is elected then he serves his time and goes on with his life. But he's black and if he wins the presidency over a Caucasian, then it would be trouble.
>
> (Harnden, 2008)

Jelani Cobb (2014) reported in *The New Yorker* that in the lead-up to the 2008 South Carolina primary, "black voters told me that they considered voting for [Hillary] Clinton as a favor to Michelle Obama," referring to the fearful expectation that her black husband would not survive such a victory.

So what do we make of this pervasive fear? There is certainly the likelihood that Althea, for instance, has projected onto Barack Obama her own fears of succeeding in a white world, incurring retribution from whites, as well as envy from fellow African Americans. Ethnicity aside, the psychological phenomenon of internal conflict between the drive to do well and the fear of outdoing a loved object, who could retaliate by withdrawing love or worse, is a basic precept in psychoanalytic thinking. Yet for African Americans, this Oedipal anxiety can often become enacted beyond the nuclear family in ways that it does not do so readily for non-African Americans. We discussed in the last chapter how Althea had worked hard to play down her education at her job so as not to threaten her white supervisor. If we look at American history since the Emancipation, we see that challenging the white belief in superiority and control can be dangerous in very real ways. Congressman John Lewis explained the phenomenon of African American panic at an Obama nomination this way: "Those of us who lived through Martin Luther King Jr.'s assassination have never gotten over it" (Cobb, 2014). One message expressed in the fears of these black citizens is that white Americans would not be able to tolerate the presence of an African American man with more power and authority than they have, and certainly would not allow the survival of an African American holding perhaps the most powerful position in the world. The danger here is not withdrawal of love, but death.

In her session two days after election night and Obama's victory, Barbara was jubilant: "What a night!" she sighed. "My neighbor on the porch screaming, and I started singing 'Amen.' It was something to see. It does give you hope." However, she immediately added, "The skinheads are plotting to kill him, I heard. I said that America is just not ready for a black president. I have aunties and uncles who never discussed politics, but this election had them fired up. Obama handled himself so well. My auntie says it's the white in him." The only way, it seems, that her auntie can understand Obama's ability to win the election and "handle himself so well" is by remembering that he is only half black. As the Obama presidency proceeded, Barbara became quite critical of some of his political decisions and periodically referred to him as "our half-black president." Perhaps she was also hoping that the white half of him would keep him safe.

Even when Barack Obama was well into his second term, echoes of the fears expressed in 2008 continued to reverberate, as evidenced by response within the African American community to news of serious lapses in performance by the Secret Service, the corps tasked with protecting the president and his family. The mishaps were widely reported and even led to the resignation of one Service chief. The news evoked a particular reaction within the African American community. Peter Baker reported in the *New York Times* (2014) that many African Americans believed that the Secret Service had been deliberately lax in order to expose Obama to assassination. Donald Tucker, a retired Secret Service agent and one of the first African Americans to protect a president, told the reporter, "I would say that more than 75 percent of the African American community are suspicious," believing the security failures to be deliberate. While he acknowledged the mistrust, he related that he believed the Secret Service "is doing its best" (Baker, 2014).

Thus many African Americans continued to fear that white anger over the rise to power of an African American man would destroy their leader. In fact, the Southern Poverty Law Center (S.P.L.C.) reported in 2013 that since Obama's first election, "we've tracked a huge increase in the numbers of racist and hate groups and so-called Patriot groups . . ." (Beirich & Schlatter, 2013). Perhaps most telling is Michelle Obama's 2007 casual shrugging off of any fear of assassination of her husband when asked about it on *60 Minutes:* "I don't lose sleep about it, because the realities are, as a black man, you know, Barack can get shot going to the gas station." (Cobb, 2014) Obama's presidential career merely highlighted a widespread fear and expectation of the danger of challenging white superiority and power, a danger that has a deep history.

Backlash

What the S.P.L.C.'s statistics reveal and what the African American men and women cited above were afraid of is called "white backlash," a phrase that emerged in the 1970s to refer to resentful white reaction to the civil rights advances of the 1960s and 1970s. Affirmative action, the policy that opened previously denied educational and job opportunities to minorities and women, became a target at which whites could express their resistance to African American progress. Though generally somewhat coded, the backlash against affirmative action was powerful. One African American patient, Loretta, who had moved from Kentucky as a teenager in the 1970s, described how coming to California meant leaving "the old slave mentality back there." However, she was quick to add, "But at least back there it was open. 'We don't like niggahs around here,'" she mimicked. "Here, they say they're not prejudiced, but when they talked in school about affirmative action, their true colors came out— teachers talking about the pros and cons. I didn't get in on no affirmative action, but it affected how white people looked at you." I asked what the effect of those remarks was on her. Loretta: "Made me very insecure, on top of the bad dynamics that were going on at home."

A sense of how divisive the issue was at that time is shown in this brief moment during a session. Althea talked about her friendship with a white former co-worker, Kathy, and the sadness she felt at their estrangement. Althea says she had become fairly close to Kathy until "I began to feel she was hiding something from me. Then we were sitting around in the coffee room with a bunch of other people. I was the only black person there, and they were all complaining about affirmative action—in front of me! This was during the time of Bakke.[2] To think that this man is somewhere now practicing medicine. I sure wouldn't want to be treated by him." The betrayal she felt by Kathy's participation in the complaints opened a rift between them that she was never willing to attempt to heal.

Another contentious outgrowth of the Civil Rights Movement and the demand to desegregate public schools was school busing, through which children were bused to schools outside their neighborhoods in order to achieve racial balance, and with the goal of offering black children education opportunities equal to those afforded white children.[3] Opposition was loud and sometimes violent in certain cities in the 1970s, most famously Boston. By the 1980s, the backlash was in full swing, flourishing during Ronald Reagan's presidency, when he coined the derogatory term, "welfare queen," a "not-so-subtle code for [a] 'lazy, greedy, black ghetto mother'" (Alexander, 2011, p. 49).

Thus, while Obama's election was celebrated as a sign that America had moved forward in electing a black man to the presidency and giving a sense of empowerment to the African American voter, the event also generated its own negative white reaction—a backlash that was fearfully and not unreasonably anticipated by a population that was accustomed to angry, even violent, white response to any advance by its black fellow citizens. The 2016 election of Donald Trump and the subsequent surge in reported hate crimes may well be seen as part of that backlash. Although the phrase "white backlash" may have surfaced in the 1970s and continued to apply in the years following Obama's rise, the phenomenon has a long history. The late nineteenth and early twentieth centuries saw an increased self-confidence among African Americans, as a generation that had never experienced slavery came of age. But along with that rise in self-confidence came an upsurge in white racism (Levine, 1977/2007, p. 152; Wilkerson, 2010, p. 43). In the 1830s, when a militant abolitionist movement emerged, it was followed by a "reactive proslavery counterattack" (McPherson, 2015, p. 69). Harriet Jacobs (1861/2000) describes the aftermath of the 1831 slave rebellion led by Nat Turner in southeast Virginia, characterized by paranoia and increased repression on the part of slaveholders near her in South Carolina that provided "a grand opportunity for the low whites, who had no negroes of their own to scourge," and proceeded to destroy the "little church built by the colored people" (pp. 813–814). Jacobs noted, with a good deal of psychological insight, that these "low whites" failed to recognize "that the power which trampled on the colored people also kept themselves in poverty, ignorance, and moral degradation" (p. 810). Thus, by the time the slaves were actually freed, it is not surprising that white reaction was angry and destructive.

Emancipation

Although the Emancipation Proclamation was signed on New Year's Day of 1863, it was not until the fall of Richmond and the final defeat of the Confederacy in April 1865 that the end of American slavery became truly possible. Juneteenth, a holiday still celebrated by many African Americans, commemorates June 19, 1865, the day when Union troops arrived in Galveston, Texas, to declare and enforce the emancipation of all slaves in Texas—two years after the actual Emancipation Proclamation was instituted, making Texas the last state to free its slaves. In reality, the promise of a slave's freedom was essentially as good as the presence of Yankee soldiers to make sure it happened. That presence was varied and, for the most part, short lived, especially in rural regions, where responses by the plantation owners also varied according to how willing they were to adapt to the changed status of their former slaves and the overturning of their economic and social world that came with that change. Slavery's end was thus implemented in fits and starts, yet ultimately it did happen and seemed to the slaves to be an answer to their prayers. With Emancipation came concrete improvements in their lives. Litwack (1980) believed that the most important of the changes to the slaves included "securing of families," "sanctification of marital ties," "the taking of a new surname or the revelation of an old one," "the opportunity to achieve literacy," and "the freedom to hold religious services in their own churches, payment for labor, and reuniting with family members separated by slavery" (p. 229). These outcomes were all extremely significant for the freedmen and -women of the South, despite the tremendous limitations that continued to be imposed on them.

Shortly before the Civil War ended, the Freedmen's Bureau had been created to ease the freed slaves' transition to lives of freedom, for which they had been deliberately ill-prepared, and limited, as the freedom proved to be. The Bureau provided food, established schools, and gave other assistance to the newly freed slaves. Literacy was now possible and highly sought after (Levine, 1997/2007, p. 472). About 5,000 northern teachers, mostly from New England, descended on the South to educate the former slaves. In addition to teaching literacy, their goal was to "civilize" their students, to root out the emotionalism of their religious practice, and to train them to embrace white models of behavior (pp. 140–144). The end of the war and the introduction of Reconstruction made possible an explosion of African American opportunity from 1865 until the end of Reconstruction in 1877. In addition to the work of the Freedmen's Bureau, the Reconstruction era saw the establishment of a public education system for blacks and whites, the 13th Amendment abolishing slavery, full citizenship given to African Americans, and passage of the 14th Amendment, providing for equal protection under the law. Literacy expanded, and blacks held political office for the first time.

Yet while the end of slavery is understandably viewed as a milestone in this country's progress, Reconstruction was sabotaged and curtailed from the start by strong southern white ambivalence to the idea of providing equal opportunity to black Americans. In the decade following the end of the war, radical Republican influence in the South diminished as the Ku Klux Klan kicked into action (1866) and the attention of sympathetic northerners shifted to a faltering economy and the Indian wars. The final blow came with the disputed presidential election of 1876 between Republican Rutherford B. Hayes and Democrat Samuel J. Tilden. When a final compromise was reached in 1877, Hayes was given the presidency in exchange for, among other things, a promise to withdraw all federal troops from the South, thus enabling the collapse of the last remaining Republican Reconstruction governments.

Reconstruction was reportedly rife with corruption, and perhaps more importantly in the long run, it failed to address the question of reparations for the freed slaves' years of unpaid labor, thus condemning them to economic dependence on capitalized whites. The ramifications of that failure will be explored in more depth in Chapter 8. Land grants were denied to ex-slaves and many whites refused to sell or rent land to African Americans (Litwack, 1980, p. 407), a hint of what was to continue, in both the North and the South, for generations to come. Vaughans (2014a) writes that the colossal failure of the short-lived Reconstruction project and the concomitant crushing of the hopes of the freed slaves "embedded forever the core boil of a transgenerational trauma within American Black Culture" (p. 569).

The departures of emancipated slaves from the plantations created logistical hardship for the slaveholders at a time of economic devastation. No longer legally able to force African Americans to work for them, many planters or their agents used violence, and even murder as a warning model to others, to make former slaves return to work (Litwack, 1980, p. 303). Predictably, there were many instances of employers cheating their workers, even though some former slaves organized to deal with their grievances collectively (pp. 414–437). The occupying Union Army and federal officials, who were supposed to enforce the terms of Emancipation, tended to comply with the planters' wishes to force the freedmen to work and to keep them generally under control. As one freedman put it, "Whenever a new Provost Marshal comes he gives us justice for a fortnight or so; then he becomes acquainted with planters, takes dinners with them, receives presents; then we no longer have any rights, or very little" (p. 375). Local Freedmen's Bureaus often sided with the plantation owners and pressured blacks to be patient with the exploitation and abuse in their workplaces. Litwack maintains that the Bureau "ultimately facilitated the restoration of black labor to the control of those who had previously owned them" (pp. 379–386).

Although the period following Emancipation was far from idyllic for the former slaves, the dramatic upending of the slave system and the changes implemented with Reconstruction were enough to produce a situation ripe for white backlash. Alexander (2011) describes the white response as a "temporary anarchy and state of mind bordering on hysteria, particularly among the planter elite. But even among poor whites," she adds, echoing Harriet Jacobs' observation, "the collapse of slavery was a bitter pill," since during slavery, "the lowliest white person at least possessed his or her white skin—a badge of superiority over even the most skilled slave or prosperous free African American" (p. 27). The reality of four million newly freed slaves generated panic among southern whites of all classes, and the response was a scramble to develop new systems of control over their black compatriots, whom they increasingly viewed as potential threats. Litwack points out that freedmen "quickly discovered in the aftermath of emancipation how much more vulnerable and expendable their lives had become" (1980, p. 275).

Another theme underlying much of the white panic at that time was the fear of sexual mingling of the former slaves with whites. Of course, such "mingling" had been taking place for the duration of the "peculiar institution," but those sexual relationships, as described in Chapter 2, were primarily manifestations of white domination over black women and their families. But Emancipation generated a fear that non-authoritarian propinquity could lead to "miscegenation," a word that seems to have been coined by an American journalist in an 1864 pamphlet. Interestingly enough, decades earlier, Thomas Jefferson gave voice to that worry about possible intermarriage once the slaves were freed. After a lengthy explication of the intellectual and aesthetic inferiority of blacks—except, in his view, in the areas of music, integrity, and memory—he concludes that if the slaves were to be freed, they could not, as the Roman slaves had been, be allowed to remain in society with their former masters, or they might "mix" with white people. Since the Roman slave was seen as white, he "might mix without staining the blood of his master." For the black slave, in contrast, "When freed, he is to be removed beyond the reach of mixture" (Jefferson, 1787/1984, p. 270). I assume Jefferson was not alone in his confused feelings about his black slaves, as his denigrating remarks and insistence that they be deported upon their freedom cannot be completely divorced from his long-term liaison with Sally Hemings, a slave with whom he fathered six children.

African Americans were not unaware of this white preoccupation. One black newspaper in Augusta, Georgia, seems to have accurately interpreted the "obsession" with inter-racial sex:

> By his loud out-cry against the *dreadful* thing, he [the white man] seems to be afraid that some of his daughters may do what a good many of his sons and himself has done time and again, and therefore he wants laws made to prevent *them* from doing so.
>
> (Litwack, 1980, p. 267)

With this fearful white sexual anxiety as part of their underpinning, the Black Codes were created to govern and constrain African American social and economic behavior.

Emancipation and Reconstruction were a complex set of events that played out in a variety of ways that created situations for the freedmen that were promising, liberating, but also far from idyllic. Given the opposition with which white society responded to the changed circumstances, and the difficulties they made for the former slaves, it is no surprise that the years following the Civil War were emotionally confusing for the African Americans. Initially, thousands expressed their satisfaction that slavery had been abolished, by leaving the plantations on which they had been slaves and moving, mostly to other plantations or to towns in their area. Doing so enabled them to separate from their pasts as slaves, while also retaining important ties to family and friends. These moves were felt as a means of enacting their newly granted freedom, and as one woman put it to her former mistress, "If I stay here I'll never know I'm free" (Litwack, 1980, p. 297). For others who initially remained on the plantations as workers, "the tension between the urge toward personal autonomy and the compulsions of the old dependency grew increasingly intolerable," at which point many would leave (pp. 360–363). This struggle between autonomy and independence is understandable, as they faced the end of a condition that, despite burdening them with insecurity and powerlessness in just about every meaningful aspect of their lives, and despite its brutal repression, had provided some guarantee of being fed and housed, albeit extremely poorly.

An indication of the complexity of the emotional struggles confronting African Americans during Reconstruction can be seen in DuBois' description of the daunting challenge faced by the Freedmen's Bureau, the federal agency that really represented the face of Reconstruction: "Thus did the United States government definitely assume charge of the emancipated Negro as the ward of the nation . . . a tremendous undertaking." These wards, he writes, were

> . . . black men emasculated by a peculiarly complete form of slavery . . . and now, suddenly, violently, they come into a new birthright, at a time of

war and passion, in the midst of the stricken and embittered population of their former masters.

(Du Bois, 1903/1986, p. 378)

I would add to DuBois' description of the challenges confronting the "emancipated Negro" the reality that emerging from slavery and the Civil War were millions of men, women, and children who had been traumatized by their experiences as slaves. Many had been brutalized and had seen others brutalized, had lost family to slave auctions, and suffered rapes by white overlords. In some of the reports of their reactions to their newfound freedom, compromised as that freedom obviously was, we can recognize attempts at managing the painful and confused feelings stirred up by the traumatic memories of their lives as slaves. Litwack describes a commonly noted attitude that eschewed "feelings of remorse or hatred for their former masters," but instead "would have been perfectly content never to see them again" (1980, p. 206). Booker T. Washington described slavery "as something to be forgotten and left behind like a dead skin" (Vaughans, 2014a, p. 596). About ten years after the end of the war, an older student at Hampton Institute, a black college, explained his reluctance to talk about his life under slavery:

> I feel as if folks mightn't believe me, and then, if I think too much about them myself, I can't keep feeling right, as I want to, towards my old masters. I'd do any thing [sic] for them I could, and I want to forget what they have done to me.
>
> (Litwack, 1980, p. 204)

These comments speak not only to the desire to avoid painful memories, and confused feelings towards his masters, but also to the belief that "folks mightn't believe me." In cases of both child abuse and torture, the overwhelming power of the abuser and torturer leaves the victim feeling so impotent as to be unable to imagine being believed or understood by the world outside the torture chamber or the site of the abuse. The plantation as a site of brutalization was an enclosed world that sheltered its cruelty and secrets. No wonder the man at Hampton Institute doubted that his perceptions of reality would be accepted beyond the plantation borders.

The loss of connection to a benign outside world is one of the great tragedies of traumatized people, because without the validation by a witness to their reports of their experiences in that outside world, the survivor is left alone to question his or her realities and perceptions. This same expectation of not being believed was widely reported among survivors of Nazi concentration camps in the period following World War II. Boulanger (2007) tells of Primo Levi's account of the S.S. officer at Auschwitz, "who jeered at him that if he survived the concentration camp, no one would believe the story he had to tell." More painful to Levi than the taunt was the fact that years later, he found himself unable to feel sure of the reality of his memories (p. 68). Krystal (1968) and his colleagues treating camp survivors years after the war repeatedly observed that many of the patients who did attempt to speak of their experiences met with defensive denial on the part of well-meaning, but obviously overwhelmed, interviewers or caregivers. The fear of not being believed is often sadly confirmed by a world that cannot tolerate the survivor's story, condemning him or her to an internal isolation filled with shame and self-doubt.

Vaughans, in reflecting on the findings of his and Warren Spielberg's study of black male youth, sees continuity with the reluctance to speak of painful memories in the observation that, while the children's parents were able to tell each other and researchers about painful experiences of racism, only one parent of the group had actually shared his experience with his children (2014a, p. 570). The others had maintained a silence about these pieces of their histories and daily lives. This "Not Knowing," Vaughans believes, exemplifies the pressure to not acknowledge the pain of slavery and its aftermath, and "is parallel to a collective cultural and racial amnesia throughout the African American community and throughout America that has come full force since the revisionist history of the Reconstruction Period" (p. 572). Vaughans postulates that this contemporary

> . . . wall of conscious silence between parent and child is also driven by unconscious needs to protect the parents from being viewed by the child as vulnerable, ineffectual, and impotent, as well as a need to distance themselves from their own horrendous fears involving loss, shame and humiliation.
>
> (Vaughans, 2014a, p. 570)

This formulation makes a good deal of sense, particularly resting on the collective memory of capture and enslavement and the feelings of impotence and humiliation attached to those experiences. The silence, says Vaughans, "risks promoting a sense that the unspoken issues are too powerful and shameful to bear," and "seems to inhibit the development of an empathic bond between parent and child, especially, I suspect, between father and son" (2014a, pp. 570–571).

The backlash that resulted from the legal end to slavery and its interwoven system of white domination became the model for the relationship between whites and blacks in this country. As with the backlashes that came later, this one rested on a variety of mythological justifications, in addition to the fear of widespread racial mixing. Litwack, for instance, writes:

> Whether he had ever owned slaves or not, almost every white man remained convinced that only rigid controls and compulsion would curtail the natural propensity of blacks towards idleness and vagrancy, induce them to labor for others, and correct their mistaken notions about freedom and working for themselves.
>
> (Litwack, 1980, p. 365)

With the loss of their compulsory work force, it does not take much imagination to see where the seductive quality of a myth of black idleness would serve white farmers. And whites had the power to turn this mythology into law. Anyone found "without legal employment" could be jailed as a vagrant. As they moved from the plantations into the nearby towns, the former slaves faced "restrictions, harassment, and violence," with accusations of "idleness if not insolence if they declined to work for a planter" (Litwack, 1980, p. 321). In fact, "Any freedman who refused to work at the prevailing wage in a particular area could be defined as a vagrant. . . .." Furthermore, freedmen were defined exclusively as agricultural workers or domestic servants, and some towns had curfews for African Americans who lacked requisite permits from their employers (p. 368). The vagrancy laws that emerged as a method of continued domination of African Americans in the white backlash following Emancipation remained in force well into the twentieth century and continued to be used not only against African Americans, but against poor people in general.

Tracy: "We're all workaholics"

It took Tracy a while to discover that she might be something of a workaholic. She worked hard, and when she wasn't working she was raising children, volunteering in the community, working on her home, biking, skiing, or working out. All of these activities ground to a halt when she was severely injured at her job, and after trying to continue to work in pain, she was finally forced to leave her employment. She was pushed into psychotherapy by family members who informed her that because she seemed to pass all her time in her darkened bedroom, was brusque and irritable when they tried to speak with her, and had essentially cut herself off from everyone, she was probably depressed. When she began therapy, she told me that she supposed her relatives were right, but awareness of her mental suffering was difficult for her to grasp. Workers' compensation accepted her psychological incapacity as a major depression related to her disabling, job-related injury and chronic pain, and we began treatment. In fact, as the work progressed, it became clear that Tracy's diagnosis was complicated, with more beneath the surface than could be explained by her injury alone. A traumatic event occurring in the context of the injury will be discussed in Chapter 5. But the piece of Tracy's presenting problem that is relevant here is that, from the outset of her psychotherapy, her grief was focused on her loss of ability to work—not just to continue her occupation, but to do any kind of meaningful physical labor at all, including most of the activities described above, all of which had been important parts of her life prior to her injury.

When she began to see me, Tracy was in her mid-30s and unmarried, and had raised a number of children in the family whose parents were, for one reason or another, unable to do so. There were also godchildren who had lived with her for extended periods, whom she also had helped to set on track. She was the backbone of her family, owned her own home, provided ministry to those in need, and had, since her teens, steadfastly rejected the lure of the drugs, alcohol, and violence that she saw destroying many around her. It was clear to me fairly quickly that her inability to perform physical and constructive work was causing her a level of distress that could not be explained solely by the very real and typical losses that being unable to work entailed, such as the removal from the social world of the workplace and, of course, loss of income. Furthermore, as we began to realize, her attempts to keep physically busy, which seemed to have a calming effect, led her to exacerbate her injury and increase her dosages of pain medications in order to do the chores she attempted. Slowly, she began to become conscious of these behaviors, of which she often had not even been aware, and their problematic effects. She began to monitor herself and over the course of several years has learned to try to pace herself. As the months and years of our work passed, I learned that this compulsion to work is familial. "We're all workaholics," she told me. Her father had died in middle age after continuing to work hard, even after being warned by his doctor not to. Over the course of our work, I have also learned that her uncles also had continued to work hard well beyond retirement age and when they could well afford to retire. In recent years, she has been often frustrated with her now elderly mother, who ignores both her own and Tracy's physical limitations to insist on both of them performing physically demanding home maintenance tasks, despite the pain and damage doing so causes them, and despite the fact that her mother could easily afford to hire people to do these tasks. Tracy is very aware of the irrationality of her mother's behavior, and sees in it a mirror of her own struggle against being willing to rest.

Tracy's parents came to California as adults from the rural South after World War II. By working hard and living frugally, they were able to provide their children with a middle-class life, and ultimately became quite comfortably off. But despite their success in the West, the South lived inside them. Tracy's mother was raised in an atmosphere of terror. She had to obey white people and to work so hard that she could never be accused of being lazy, whatever the consequences to her own well-being. Although the dangers of her youth were behind her in San Francisco, her emotional structure migrated with her. What began as need to live as a workaholic in order to survive became a moral and characterological compulsion that helps to define a person's self-worth. Uncoupling this link between constant physical labor, self-esteem, and safety from criticism or worse from whites has been a challenging project of Tracy's psychotherapy. The powerful forces that embedded the workaholism in her family's culture are reflected in the resilience of the symptom within Tracy herself.

Tracy's family culture is not unique. In one session, Althea revisited with me the hurt and frustration she had experienced at her job, and how painfully demeaning her boss had been towards her. "He told me he saw signs of laziness in my performance," she said, tears in her eyes. "My poor old grandfather, he worked so hard. He had a good job for a black man, walking behind the asphalt truck laying roads. Then Saturday he worked in a meat plant, and early Sunday morning he was singing in the church choir. We're a family of hard workers.

So to have someone call me lazy, that really hurt." C.L. Thompson (2012) describes the case of an African American patient, "Juanita," whose family held that partaking in pleasurable activities "was unacceptable because it meant they could be perceived as 'lazy, childlike Negroes'" (p. 342).

Of course, the economic environment for African Americans of Tracy's parents' generation, subject to the deprivation of opportunity in education, property rights, and job equality that continued long after Reconstruction, often made hard and non-stop physical labor a necessity. The vagrancy laws that were instated so soon after the end of slavery were part of her parents' environment, so that when Tracy recently sighed and said, "We just have to keep going," when recounting her latest battle with her mother over the latter's compulsion to push herself beyond her physical limits, the historical foundations of her meaning were clear. The confluence of the history of the use of vagrancy laws against African Americans, and the tendency of workers' compensation insurance claims examiners to approach with skepticism workers' claims of on-the-job injuries and disability, adds additional levels of fear and pain to people like Tracy, who are raised to feel they must always prove their willingness to work, and to work hard.

One day Tracy began talking to me about how her brain "freezes over" and she can't think when she begins to consider the severity of her injuries and her level of disability. I said, "It's as if you are afraid of what you will learn if you think at those moments." Tracy rejects my idea: "No, I don't see fear." I am not surprised at her reply, as I had been noticing for some time that while Tracy had no difficulty acknowledging other emotions, such as anger and sadness, the one that seemed unavailable to her was fear. I was curious, so this time I pointed out her easy rejection of the idea of fear and asked her how fear was talked about in her family. She replied, "We didn't talk about fear. We were taught to be prepared," and reminded me that her parents had sent her and her siblings to self-defense classes from early childhood.

RF: It occurs to me that for your parents in the South in the 1930s and 1940s fear must have played a huge role. Maybe they felt that once they got to California they didn't want to go there—to a place of fear—again.

TRACY: That's for sure! They just told us always how to be prepared for everything.

RF: So what does fear mean to you?

TRACY: When we'd go back South, and my grandmother would say, "Don't look at the white people," or "Don't go where the white people are." She was freaking out. She'd say, "Shh. Be quiet." It was puzzling to me. I didn't feel fear, myself, but I saw it. The only time I saw fear at home was once, when I decided to go to church in a bad neighborhood, and my dad didn't want me to go. The only time I saw him with fear. Fear is something they just can't handle.

A few years after this session, the subject of fear re-emerged, and Tracy voiced with surprise that she was, in fact, becoming aware that underneath the anger that had so predominated her traumatic memories, she felt fear. "I know you always talked about fear," she said, "but now I think I can say I feel it." I asked if she remembered feeling fear as a child. "Never!" she claimed. Interestingly, she again associated to the family vacations to relatives in the South, but this time she introduced new material. She recounted the journeys every summer from San Francisco along Route 66, in which her father would drive them all in their big car, crammed with their suitcases and plenty of food. Her parents would prepare meticulously for the long rides, preparations that enabled the family to travel in safety. By coincidence that morning's newspaper had carried an article about *The Negro Motorist Green Book,* published from 1936 to 1966, which had listed eating places, motels, gas stations, and rest stops along Route 66 that were safe for African American travelers to patronize. I had shoved the article into my bag before leaving for work. Tracy described the sense of security she and her siblings felt in the car with her parents. Her mother and father would alternate driving so that they could keep moving until they reached a place to rest that would accept black visitors. Gasoline was carefully monitored, and sometimes her father would pull up somewhere, warn them to stay in the car, walk to the back of a building, and return with food for them.

"Sometimes," she said, "we could get out at a rest area and run around." She remembered one favorite place they stopped. "All I remember is it had Indian murals all over, and souvenirs, and I got an Indian doll that I loved." As it happened, the morning's article had singled out a Hopi motel and coffee shop in Albuquerque as an example of a safe place listed in the *Green Book.* The text of the article described the murals as she had, so I showed Tracy the newspaper photo of the exterior. She beamed and believed she recognized it, but mainly reveled in the happy memory of being on these adventures with her family, of feeling happy and protected by her parents' careful precautions. I noted to her how happy the memories seemed to make her. She confirmed she felt "delight" at the photo, the fact of the article, and the fond associations it provided. She had never, by the way, heard of the *Green Book,* although it was in wide circulation from 1936 through 1966.

There is something both revealing and, to me, quite moving about Tracy's linking of the awareness of fear and the feeling of safety in the movable shelter and of her parents' attention to the dangers of their environment. She obviously felt secure and protected as a child in her family, but she also absorbed an awareness that that security came from her parents' constant efforts to protect their children, not only from danger, but also from feeling endangered. I imagine that Tracy's parents sheltered their children from knowledge, even, of the *Green Book,* as well as the full story of what they were protecting them from, instead focusing on the need to be prepared. There is, to me, something touching about the heroism of parents' attempts to provide their children with something they could not have experienced in their own childhoods in the Jim Crow South. Until trauma knocked Tracy down, her parents had seemed to have achieved that hope.

Violence

The visits to her grandparents as a child had shown Tracy the fear of white violence with which her relatives and other African Americans in her parents' home town lived. A recent visit to the town confronted her with the realization that while much had changed, the condition of white domination enforced by threat of violence had not. Her cousins told her of an African American boy, a high school student in the next town, who had been invited to a party hosted by a white girl. He was shot and killed as he walked up to the door. Another incident happened to her at a hardware store during the visit. She was about to pay for her purchase when the cashier turned away to serve a white man who had come in, and proceeded to serve all the white customers now behind her in the line before serving her. No one said a word. It is the combination of these two stories that explains much of African American life since the end of slavery: second-class citizenship enforced by threat of violent retaliation.

It was the willingness of whites to use violence that gave force to the Black Codes, so that their psychic legacy endures to this day. (Recall the fear of the Obama assassination.) "How many black men and women were beaten, flogged, mutilated, and murdered in the first years of emancipation will never be known," writes Litwack. He reports assaults of "barbaric savagery and depravity" against blacks, with black teachers and clergy frequent targets of white violence, and schools and churches often set afire (1980, pp. 276–279). When whipping was banned by the federal government in some areas, outraged white employers devised other forms of "discipline," including tying the laborers up by their thumbs, or feeding them only bread and water. The belief was that only fear of physical harm yielded good work performance (pp. 371–372). And when it came time for the freedmen to exercise their rights to vote, whites used every sort of intimidation to stop them. Notably, African Americans did not give in to those intimidations and "voted in overwhelming numbers in their first exercise of political power" (p. 555).

Lynching and its Legacy

From the late nineteenth through the first half of the twentieth centuries, nearly 4,000 African Americans were lynched in this country. The Equal Justice Initiative (E.J.I., 2015) describes lynchings as a form of "racial terror," staged as "violent and public acts of torture that traumatized black people throughout the country," acts that were "largely tolerated by state and federal officials" (p. 3). Any minor social transgression by which an African American failed to show total deference to whites or failed to demonstrate inferiority or fear of them could result in a lynching. In a reflection of Jefferson's fears of "mixing," close to 25 percent of lynchings were associated with an alleged "sexual assault," a charge that required neither a claim of force nor even an identified victim. In a typical example, Keith Bowen was lynched in 1889 in Mississippi for "allegedly trying to enter a room where three white women were sitting" (p. 10). The Louisiana Creole musician Amede Ardoin's music laid the foundation for zydeco with his brilliant blending of blues and European music traditions. According to a "widely accepted account," he was performing at a white dance hall and asked a white farmer whom he knew for a rag to wipe off his perspiration. In response, the farmer's daughter handed him a handkerchief. After leaving his show, he was beaten savagely by a group of white men, and by some accounts also was run over with a car, in punishment for that momentary and insignificant interaction with a young white woman. While he barely survived the beating, he was destroyed psychologically. He died at the age of 44 in 1942 in a state mental hospital (Robertson, 2015). Lynchings were particularly widespread in Florida. Wilkerson (2010) reports that in 1950 the government's special investigator noted that there had been so many acts of mob violence against African Americans in one Florida county that it "never had a negro live long enough to go to trial" (p. 62). Lynchings and other kinds of assaults, such as occurred to Ardoin, were frequent enough that for many they amounted to a powerful reason to escape from the South and to join the Great Migration to the North and the West (E.J.I., 2015, p. 5; Wilkerson, 2010, p. 533).

It was under this constant danger that African Americans, particularly in the South, tried to live their lives. What made lynchings and mob attacks so frightening was that simply doing something that is part of being a normal human being could be dangerous *if the person was black*. The same actions that were taken for granted for a white person—accidentally touching someone while walking past on the street, entering a room where there are white women, proudly wearing one's army uniform in public when home on leave—triggered unexpected violent, even deadly, response when the actor was African American. This kind of environment demanded psychological adaptations that took an emotional toll on each person who had to contend with it. Tracy's report of her grandparents' and mother's fearful admonitions to the children to stifle themselves around whites demonstrate that parents, for instance, operated in a state of hypervigilance regarding their children's behavior in public, always anxiously coaching the child to keep a low profile so as not trigger a violent response from an irrational, powerful, and hostile white person.

The anxiety behind the admonitions was conveyed to Tracy with an urgency that, even as a child, she recognized as revealing her parents' and grandmother's fear. An important need for all of us is to believe we are recognized, acknowledged, and, at a deeper level, understood. Yet for African Americans in the South feeling safe and believing that what you say and even your nonverbal expressions will be viewed benignly and more or less accurately by those around you must have felt risky, even foolhardy—and, as Tracy learned on her visit, remains the case in some areas today. And being viewed as the bearer of untrustworthy motives, lascivious impulses, or envious hostility cannot help but set up an extra set of obstacles in the path to development of a healthy self-image or sense of oneself in one's community. A black child could thus readily develop an idea that safety would lie in being invisible. How much of this confusion of developmental needs has lived on? For that matter, how much has actually changed in the environment of blacks in the United States? There are ordinary activities of daily living, of just going about one's business, that have their own perils for African Americans: driving while black, shopping while black, being ill while black, acting like a teenager while black, and reaching for a cell phone while black, can be dangerous or even deadly.

To return to Tracy's therapy, the subject of fear came up again about a year after the session cited above. Tracy is very preoccupied with her tendency to move into rage before she is even aware of feeling angry, in reaction to a group of triggers that evoke a trauma associated with her accident. (Again, this case will be examined in more detail in a later chapter.) I had occasionally and tentatively suggested that the traumatic experience must have frightened her, and that perhaps her responses to the triggering incidents were reflective of fear as well as anger. I said, "I think you suppress the fear you feel and zoom right away to rage." This time her response seemed a little less insistent, and her tone reflected curiosity rather than certainty.

TRACY: But it doesn't *feel* like fear.
RF: You were taught not to be afraid. I remember when you began seeing me you'd tell me that you'd do what you could to walk from your car to my office without your cane so that no one could tell that you were injured. And when I'd asked why that mattered, you'd said that you expected to be robbed or attacked if a person suspected you couldn't defend yourself.
TRACY: True. When we'd go south to see my grandma, we learned, "Don't show fear." My grandma would say, "Don't look at them! Just look normal. Don't let them think you're afraid!" We had to be careful not to drink at the wrong fountain or sit in the wrong place. And I've learned that in fear I can't think, so maybe that's why I switch to anger.
RF: At least in anger you have a primitive strategy—fight or flight—to deal with the situation.
TRACY: Yeah, like a shark. Yes, I can see skipping fear to anger.

Tracy's resorting to anger emerged only in the context of the posttraumatic stress disorder that has plagued her since her initial accident-related trauma. A traumatic rupture exposed her psyche to the unmediated impact of generations of fear and rage that her parents were compelled to repress and which they taught their children to repress as well. It is significant that, although the injury and the additional trauma that followed were not overtly racial in character, many of her triggering events have involved her encounters with twenty-first-century, northern Californian racism. When she laments the loss of her beautifully controlled self, she says with frustration, "But those things used to not bother me! I'd just let them roll off my back." At what cost did she and do other African Americans let racist affronts "not bother" them or "roll off their backs?"

Each of the four million African Americans emancipated in 1865, and all of their descendants, have had to grapple with living in an environment in which threat from members of the white majority has been all too real. We cannot have read the non-stop reports of police killings of unarmed black men and women without seeing that the waning of lynching did not bring the threat of being killed by angry white people to a close. Gang- and non-gang-related shootings, of which African Americans are so often victims, also make life for blacks dangerous. Recall Michelle Obama's statement that she's no more afraid of her husband being assassinated than of him being shot pumping gas, a worry that had obviously flickered across her mind. Althea arrived for her session one morning in an agitated state: "I am so angry at my niece." The young woman phoned her the night before, upset because she had just been pulled over by a police officer. Her car had a broken tail light. She was calling her aunt for comfort, as the officer wrote the citation. Althea exploded at her: "Are you crazy? You pulled out a cell phone in front of a cop?! You could have been killed!" She was clearly still shaken by the incident.

Althea's fury was mirrored in a YouTube clip that went viral in the aftermath of the demonstrations in Baltimore following the death of Freddie Gray, a 25-year-old African American, from spinal injuries at the hands of the police in April 2015. The video pictured an African American woman chasing her young adult son, slapping him, and berating him for participating in the demonstration. She was quoted later: "I didn't want to see him become another Freddie Gray." One writer commented, "Dating back to slavery, black moms have had to hold a strong grip on their children's behavior. Only a foolish mother would risk boosting her child's self-esteem to the point where he might be perceived as uppity by whites" (Caviness, 2015, p. 3). In *Between the World and Me* (2015), Ta-Nehisi Coates describes with passion the profound sense of fear that he believes permeates the consciousness of African American parents. "My father was so very afraid," he writes. "I felt it in the sting of his black leather belt, which he applied with more anxiety than anger, my father who beat me as if someone might steal me away, because that is what was happening all around us" (pp. 15–16). Coates' book is driven by a constant awareness of physical danger in which white racism and its destructive effects on black communities places African American bodies. "When I was your age," he writes to his teenage son, "the only people I knew were black, and all of them were powerfully, adamantly, dangerously afraid. I had seen this fear all my young life, though I had not always recognized it as such" (p. 14).

In a talk given in 2014, Vaughans (2014b) said that it is the "sequestering of the collective memory, the abject failure of Reconstruction, as well as its humiliating and terrorizing aftermath that set the tone for the unresolved trauma" buried in today's African American population. How can that not be true? Each African American develops a particular relationship to that fear and traumatic memory: Althea, who copes by striving to keep a low profile, minimizing any possibility of psychologically challenging a white person; Tracy, who combines a preoccupation with safety and preparedness with a denial of the experience of feeling personally fearful; the gang member, who seeks security in making allies while counter-phobicly courting danger and being dangerous himself.

One sharecropper fled Louisiana with his wife and toddler son in 1943, after he "had barely escaped a lynching . . . for talking back to his white overseers." He settled in Oakland, California, and his son, Huey Newton, founded the Black Panther Party, reveling "in discomfiting the white establishment with his black beret, rifle, and black power rhetoric" (Wilkerson, 2010, p. 186). To what degree did that history of fear and trauma play into the son's assertion of armed resistance? One patient said her grandparents in rural Mississippi kept shotguns in every room of their house as they quietly listened every night for unfamiliar noises outside. It is hard to live with fear in one's body every day. To work, love, and participate in society, people need to maintain some minimal trust their social environment. Lacking that assurance, most African Americans have become expert survivors who "just have to keep going."

The memory of lynching continues to cast an ominous power over African Americans. A 2015 article in the *San Francisco Chronicle* reported on a lawsuit filed by a local construction superintendent at a large real estate development company, who "was working at his desk . . . when he felt something hit the hard hat he was wearing. He looked up and saw a noose with a hangman's knot hanging over his cubicle wall." He heard his supervisor laughing with a co-worker about the noose, which he continued to dangle. Upset, the African American superintendent left work early, but found the noose still hanging in his office when he returned to work the next day. He later "found a wanted poster of an African American man hung in the noose with his name on it," according to the man's attorney. After reporting the incidents to the company owner, the noose was removed but his supervisor was heard threatening to bring his rifle to work. Within a few days, the superintendent "was hospitalized for high blood pressure because he was at risk for having a stroke." His attorney claims that he has since been "diagnosed with post traumatic stress disorder, suffers from nightmares and flashbacks and avoids construction sites, effectively ending his career." The supervisor was fired only after an E.E.O.C. (Equal Employment Opportunity Commission) suit was filed (Williams, 2015).

Post-lynching and After the Dream

In some ways, the nation's criminal justice system has taken over some of the enforcement role that lynching and mob violence once played. Research suggests as much, reporting that incidents of lynching declined in the South with the increased use of capital punishment, typically imposed "following an often accelerated trial" (E.J.I., 2015, p. 6). With the waning of lynching and legal segregation, and the increase in legal protections for African Americans from acts of overt racist discrimination, white resistance to the loss of privilege took new forms. For one thing, legal bars against discrimination based on race led to a greater care to avoid the use of language that was openly racist. Most white Americans cleaned up their acts, and many became genuinely more conscious of wanting not to tolerate racism, or later, sexism and homophobia.

But for those who continued to consciously oppose racial equality, these changes meant that racist sentiments could not be openly expressed.

One avenue available for the continuation of black subordination was through the criminal justice system. As Michelle Alexander demonstrates in her 2011 classic, *The New Jim Crow*, the focus of American policing on black communities is not accidental, but in fact represents a stealth backlash against the civil rights gains of the 1960s and 1970s. She documents how a confluence of high unemployment and the emergence of crack cocaine in America's inner cities were manipulated to create the "War on Drugs" (p. 51) and the eventual mass incarceration of African American citizens. She reports that the result was an increase in the U.S. prison population from about 300,000 to more than 2,000,000 in less than 30 years, with a disproportionate percentage of them African American (p. 6).

Paul Butler, law professor at Georgetown University, said, "Mass incarceration is ahistorical, criminogenic, inefficient, and racist" (Toobin, 2015, p. 27). But why should a battle against drug use result in the mass incarceration of African Americans? After all, research has shown that whites and non-whites "use and sell drugs at remarkably similar rates," and, if anything, "white youth are somewhat more likely to engage in drug crime than people of color." Nevertheless, African American males in some states go to prison 20 to 50 times more than do white males (Alexander, 2011, p. 7). A study by the Vera Institute of Justice, a New York-based research and policy group, focused not on police arrests but on decisions by Milwaukee prosecutors to charge, or not to charge, people arrested for various crimes. The researchers discovered that the prosecutors "declined to prosecute forty-one per cent of whites arrested for possession of drug paraphernalia, compared with only twenty-seven per cent of blacks." In other words, the prosecutors were 14 percent more likely to proceed with prosecution if the arrested person was black than if a person arrested for the same crime was white. Similarly, black women defendants were more likely to be charged for prostitution than their white counterparts, and charges of resisting or obstructing an officer were carried out against 80 percent of blacks compared with 66 percent of whites arrested (Toobin, 2015, p. 24). With good reason Alexander asserts that this mass incarceration of African Americans is akin to a "new Jim Crow," and is the most damaging manifestation of the backlash against the Civil Rights movement" (2011, p. 11).

According to Alexander, support for the War on Drugs and "tough on crime" positions by whites correlated highly with resentment of the appearance of progress for blacks through the enforcement of civil rights laws, and the introduction of affirmative action programs—a correlation that was far greater than actual crime rates or experience of being victimized by crime. Despite the irrationality of these policies in terms of cost and, more importantly, of their failure to address causes of crime or drug use, their one visible feature was to offer "whites opposed to racial reform a unique opportunity to express their hostility towards blacks and black progress, *without being exposed to the charge of racism*" (2011, p. 54; emphasis added). Both Presidents George Bush, Republican, and Bill Clinton, "New Democrat," solidified the gains of the backlash movement, the former by opposing affirmative action, continuing the drug war, and inhibiting civil rights law enforcement; the latter with his immediate embrace of anti-crime rhetoric, dramatized by his decision to interrupt his 1992 presidential campaign to fly back to Arkansas to oversee the execution of a mentally disabled black man. Clinton continued to play into backlash sympathies by both punishing and demonizing the poor through his project of "ending welfare as we know it." Penalties for drug-related convictions, under Clinton's legislation, extended to losing the right to federally subsidized housing and lifetime ineligibility for food stamps or other welfare benefits (pp. 54–57).

Edward Ball, the great-great-grandson of a South Carolina slaveholder, likens contemporary police behavior towards black men to that of antebellum slave patrols: white men who would stop African Americans and demand to see whether they had the proper papers allowing them to travel outside the plantations on which they were enslaved and who "routinely punished young black men, and faced no punishment for doing so" (Ball, 2015). "Deadly force was often used against slaves who resisted being taken into custody," he writes. Ball suggests that this history "provides police action with an unconscious foundation," and African Americans with feelings that combine familiarity and heightened anxiety in such encounters. After Emancipation, as we saw, vagrancy laws performed a similar function.

The sense of continuity and inevitability Ball is suggesting has been somewhat disrupted recently. The Black Lives Matter movement, aided by the proliferation of cell phones that can function as cameras, has been drawing attention to disturbing instances of lethal encounters between police and unarmed black citizens, raising the question of whether members of the police force are brutal racists, just looking for opportunities to pull their guns on black men and women, responding as Ball would suggest to the "unconscious foundation" of antebellum history. I believe something else might be at play and that police officers are as racist as the general U.S. population, but that they are focused on people doing bad things, and they are heavily armed and trained to respond with those lethal weapons whenever they feel threatened. When African American patients report to me their common experiences of being followed by store employees as they browse the aisles, it seems clear that the store clerk's implicit assumption that an African American woman must be planning to shoplift could easily be translated to a police officer's assumption that, in a country awash with guns, the same African American woman who opens her purse at a traffic stop, or the young man who runs away from a police officer, must be armed, dangerous, and generally up to no good. The consequences of the shopping experience are humiliation and anger. The consequences of the latter could be deadly.

Thus African Americans have, since the 1970s and 1980s, been living in a nation in which they often continue to experience the effects of white racism and backlash against any sign of progress in racial justice, but in which that racism is mystified, coded, and covert. Yes, many African Americans truly have been able to benefit from the opening up of opportunities enabled by the Civil Rights Movement. In many ways, Americans are proud of the successes of Oprah Winfrey, Barack Obama, Colin Powell; of the many black professionals they see around them; of city mayors, congressional representatives; of artists and athletes, Supreme Court justices, physicians, bankers, and so on. However, for average African Americans who continue to experience racist affronts and who are unable to attain or maintain decent standards of living, these successes also challenge them with the question, "If they can succeed, why can't you?" This is a question put to them by white society, by fellow African Americans, and most painful of all, by themselves. The juxtaposition between the assertion that the playing field has been leveled (which no one can honestly believe), with their lived experience can be painfully confusing, leaving people partially persuaded that they are living in a "post-racial" America, but in which they know that they continue to be subjected to racial discrimination, albeit often masked as something else. Without some kind of reality check, many will internalize the contradiction so as to blame themselves. There are times when people can easily see the racism through the veil, but even then, the fear and hostility embedded in racism can have an insidious psychological effect when their perceptions tell them they have been victimized because of their race but the social environment refuses to validate those perceptions. One consequence of this mystification is that "because our society continues to deny racism as an everyday experience, some African Americans do not experience it as traumatic" (Jackson, 2000, p. 7).

This ambiguity plays out in the therapy office, in particular with a white therapist. Among my African American patients, it took quite a while for each of them to talk about experiences of racism, although after many years of developing our therapeutic relationships, each did. My sense is that the fear of having one's perception of racism dismissed may have made patients cautious, partly to avoid the pain of that invalidation, but also to avoid a risk of discovering that I do not understand the realities of African American life, or worse, that I am a racist. If the client wanted to preserve what was otherwise a useful relationship, she or he might want to minimize the chances of being disillusioned about me. One woman, however, was much quicker to bring up racism.

Francis was struggling with conflicts with her employer, feeling that she was being passed over consistently for promotion in favor of white colleagues. She had also observed and commented on the short tenures of African American managers in the company, while white managers seemed to stay in their jobs. A short, stocky woman with close cropped hair, Francis had come to California from an impoverished family in the South as a young woman, and through determination and hard work, managed to go to college. Despite a life-threatening illness in her 20s, she had been able to be the primary support of her daughter once she and her husband divorced. Francis seemed to have no problem in recounting to me patterns of what she saw as racism. It was only late in her work with me she mentioned having been a member of the Black Panther Party as a young college student. At an important developmental stage she had begun a process of political education, one that was geared to actively name and resist white racism. She thus remained alert to any pressure to submit to the forces of white backlash. But this vigilance came with a price.

One day she arrived at my office fuming because, she said, a driver had cut her off as she was trying to park. She was certain that the woman did so solely because she, Francis, was black, and that she would not have done so had Francis been white. I was dubious. Imagining the speed with which these parking incidents take place, I thought it was unlikely that the patient's color had played a role, but instead, that the other woman was just a bad driver. Francis and I had, by that time, been working together long enough that I felt I could question her certainty, without her experiencing me as someone who was denying the existence of racism. After probing the details of the interaction, she, too, began to have her doubts that race had played a part in the incident, and actually seemed slightly relieved at the idea that she had not been targeted. Our discussion led to consideration of how confusing it can sometimes be for her to sort out whether she is being treated a certain way because she is African American or not, and what a mess American history has created for relationships between black and white Americans.

Althea, whose education proved to be a source of difficulty for her with both white and African American colleagues (see Chapter 2), was also vulnerable to the deliberately misleading language of white backlash. She reported that when her career fell apart, her family and childhood friends regarded her with disdain, occasionally verbalizing their opinions that she had little to show for her "fancy schooling." The implication was that education was useless, a position that was often backed up with tales of friends who had achieved financial success without college, and that something must be wrong with her if she had not parlayed her degree into greater success, assuming as true the myth that the "playing field" was now level. They would bring up examples of other educated African American women in their community who had achieved prominent careers, suggesting that Althea had squandered what opportunities she had been given. Part of this punitive attitude expressed by Althea's family towards the striving represented by her decision to go to college may constitute what Holmes (2006) sees as a taboo against African American success that is conveyed by the larger Euro-American society and that is internalized very early in an African American child's development. She speculates that this taboo "may also be internalized in one's superego, leading one to punish oneself for any pursuit of success, as well as to anticipate punishment from real oppressing forces" (p. 219).

Thus primed, Althea believed both messages, but especially the second, which landed comfortably onto her depressed psyche. When I would hear these reports I felt protective of her, but also sad and angry that the people in her life had so readily bought into the primacy of financial success and the assumption that Althea's troubles were solely of her own making. Over a period of time, I worked with her on two fronts around this issue. She had mainly loved her college experience, which she felt opened up new cultural worlds to her, but there had been a dark undercurrent to the experience as well. She described thinly veiled hostility from some white students and professors who were bristling at the introduction of affirmative action into their program. Her education was not an indulgence by a benevolent university, but she began to believe that she was undeserving, as she unconsciously assimilated the attitudes of those who resented her presence.

We also talked about how to assess the value of her education. She sometimes complained about the overvaluing of nice cars, and "bling," and would blame fellow African Americans for having bad values. I reminded her that these were not values exclusive to her community, so when she viewed education solely as a visa into the land of money, she seemed to be accepting those same "bad values." Althea had a great interest in politics and was a careful analyst of what she read and heard. I reminded her that she seemed to be a lot more well-read and careful in her thinking than the friends and relatives who were minimizing the value of her degree. Her education, I told her, was something that no one could take away from her—the books she read, the papers she wrote, the discussions in which she participated. She had made very good use of her education, after all.

There are times when the veil that normally hangs over racist enactments is lifted in a public way, and those moments can have therapeutic value. Tracy had once again recounted an incident of being followed while browsing at a hardware store. As it happened, during the following week an article had appeared in the *New York Times* (Feuer, 2015) reporting on a class-action lawsuit filed by black and Latino former store detectives employed by CVS in New York, charging that their supervisors had ordered them to target African American and Latino shoppers. The article also mentioned that almost a year earlier, New York's attorney general had negotiated a $650,000 fine against Macy's over complaints that "minority shoppers faced heightened surveillance and, in some cases, wrongful detention at its flagship store in Midtown," and a similar deal for $525,000 with Barneys New York over the same issue. Both stores also had to address and rectify their policies. I had brought the article to the office for my session with Tracy, and despite the fact that she did not bring up the subject of being profiled in that session, I did something fairly unusual for me and for a psychodynamic treatment in general: I read relevant excerpts from the article to her. She was excited and pleased, both that her experience was actually being acknowledged in a newspaper, but also that these brave men and women were taking action.

In this chapter, I have tried to look at the psychological effects on my African American clients of the seemingly perpetual dynamic of progress and backlash that represents America's dysfunctional, contradictory, and often mystified relationship between its citizens of African descent and those of European descent. As of this writing, younger African Americans, through the Black Lives Matter movement and student activism, are opening up and protesting, often with great eloquence, the kinds of marginalization that Althea has experienced in painful isolation. They are speaking some truth about the country in which they live, demystifying some of the national pathology around race, and, in doing so, hopefully achieving a nascent sense of validation and internal clarity about the challenges of grappling with racism.

Notes

1 Limbaugh was not the only figure to strike out at the Williams sisters. Claudia Rankine's prose poem, *Citizen: An American Lyric* (2014), includes a powerful and eloquent account of the racism that has pursued Serena Williams relentlessly throughout her successful tennis career.
2 Allan Bakke was a white man who sued the University of California when he failed to get into medical school at its Davis campus, claiming that he was denied a slot based on the school's affirmative action program's use of quotas. In 1978, in a complex decision reflecting divisions among the justices, the Supreme Court ruled that affirmative action programs were constitutional, but that they could not use quotas to achieve their goals.
3 About a hundred years later, the same belief in the power of education motivated black parents to launch the ground-breaking case of Brown versus the Board of Education of Topeka, resulting in a unanimous ruling that segregated schools deprived non-white children of equal education, an opportunity to which all children are entitled.

References

Alexander, M. (2011). *The new Jim Crow: Mass incarceration in the age of colorblindness*. New York: The New Press.
Baker, P. (October 2, 2014). Some blacks see secret service as flawed shield for the president. *New York Times*.
Ball, E. (March 15, 2015). Slavery's enduring resonance. *New York Times*, Opinion section.
Beirich, H. & Schlatter, E. (October 1, 2013). The state of hate. https://mobilizingideas.wordpress.com/2013/10/01/the-state-of-hate/ (accessed October 24, 2017).
Boulanger, G. (2007). *Wounded by reality: Understanding and treating adult onset trauma*. Mahwah, NJ & London: The Analytic Press.
Caviness, Y.G. (May 2, 2015). What black moms know. *New York Times*, Sunday Review Opinion.
Coates, T. (2015). *Between the world and me*. New York: Spiegel and Grau.
Cobb, J. (October 2, 2014). Barack Obama's safety. *The New Yorker*, www.newyorker.com/news/daily-comment/barack-obamas-safety (accessed October 24, 2017).
Du Bois, W.E.B. (1903/1986). The souls of black folk. In *Writings*. New York: The Library of America College Editions.
E.J.I. (Equal Justice Initiative) (2015). Lynching in America: Confronting the legacy of racial terror. www.eji.org/lynchinginamerica (accessed October 24, 2017).
Feuer, A. (June 4, 2015). Former store detectives sue CVS, accusing it of discrimination. *New York Times*.
Gardner, D. (February 11, 2008). Clinton sacks campaign manager as Obama surges ahead after weekend wins. *The Daily Mail*.
Harnden, T. (April 3, 2008). Martin Luther King anniversary stokes black fears of Barack Obama assassination. *The Telegraph*.

Holmes, D.E. (2006). The wrecking effects of race and social class on self and success. *Psychoanalytic Quarterly, 75*: 215–235.

Jackson, L.C. (2000). The new multiculturalism and psychodynamic theory: Psychodynamic psychotherapy and African American women. In Jackson, L.C. & Greene, B. (Eds.), *Psychotherapy with African American women: Innovations in psychodynamic perspectives and practice* (pp. 1–14). New York: Guilford Press.

Jacobs, H.A. (1861/2000). Incidents in the life of a slave girl. Written by herself. In Child, L.M. (Ed.), *Slave narratives*. New York: Library Classics of the U.S., Inc.

Jefferson, T. (1787/1984). Notes on the State of Virginia. In *Thomas Jefferson Writings*. New York: The Library of America

Krystal, H. (Ed.) (1968). *Massive psychic trauma*. New York: International Universities Press, Inc.

Levine, L.W. (1977/2007). *Black culture and black consciousness: Afro-American folk thought from slavery to freedom*. Oxford & New York: Oxford University Press.

Litwack, L.F. (1980). *Been in the storm so long: The aftermath of slavery*. New York: Vintage Books.

McPherson, J.M. (2015). The fugitives who changed America. *New York Review of Books*, Vol. LXII, No. 10.

Rankine, C. (2014). *Citizen: An American lyric*. Minneapolis, MN: Graywolf Press.

Robertson, C. (May 29, 2015). On the trail of a Creole pioneer, struck down, but alive in song. *New York Times*.

Thompson, C.L. (2012). The African-American patient in psychodynamic treatment. In Akhtar, S. (Ed.), *The African American experience: Psychoanalytic perspectives* (pp. 337–361). Lanham, MD: Rowman and Littlefield.

Toobin, J. (May 11, 2015). The Milwaukee experiment: What can one prosecutor do about the mass incarceration of African-Americans? *The New Yorker*, 24–32.

Vaughans, K.C. (2014a). Disavowed fragments of the intergenerational transmission of trauma from slavery among African Americans. In Vaughans, K.C. & Spielberg, W. (Eds.), *The psychology of black boys and adolescents*, Vol. 2 (pp. 563–575). Santa Barbara, CA: Praeger.

Vaughans, K. (2014b). Disavowed fragments of the intergenerational transmission of trauma from slavery among African Americans. Paper presented at Division 39 meetings, New York City.

Wilkerson, I. (2010). *The warmth of other suns: The epic story of America's great migration*. New York: Random House.

Williams, K. (July 11, 2015). Racial harassment suit filed over noose. *San Francisco Chronicle*.

4 Identity and the Discovery of "Race"

Grappling with Black Identity

Ta-Nehisi Coates (2015) writes that "race is the child of racism, not the father" (p. 7). Born out of racism, black as a race is not neutral; it is formed by an "ism," an ideological cudgel, and from the first awareness of being identified as an African American, a child begins a process of increasing comprehension of expectations white society holds for all who are grouped under this racial label. Racism inevitably affects the development of all Americans' senses of self, but my focus here will be its impact on African American consciousness, and how that impact has revealed itself in my consulting room. White racism relies on a mythology of black inferiority, with its variety of disparaging stereotypes, and has functioned from the start to justify and facilitate the theft and exploitation of black labor. An added "bonus" has been that by granting white workers psychological compensation for poor pay and working conditions in the form of belief in their superiority over blacks, it has often successfully discouraged working-class cooperation across color lines. Some of the elements of that mythology were outlined in Chapter 3, such as the myth of the ex-slaves' laziness, one element of the extensive, entangled imagery and set of stereotypes that make up the fable of black inferiority.

At its foundation in slavery, the myths embedded in ideas of white superiority functioned on the plantation in a way comparable to how a rigid mythology can govern an emotionally fragile family, with its members serving roles that often have nothing to do with their core being, but everything to do with the needs of one or both parents to maintain the family system. This similarity of plantation life to life in a dysfunctional family, I believe, contributed to the ability of the mythology of white supremacy to survive as a cultural force that has reproduced itself since its birth in what President Obama referred to as our national "original sin" in his eulogy for slain Charleston pastor Clementa Pinckney in June 2015 (Obama, 2015). Over the years there have been significant shifts, and many, if not most, Euro-Americans have worked to shed the prejudices with which they were raised, both individually and institutionally. But despite their best intentions, both white and black Americans have been insistently influenced by stereotypes, purveyed both consciously and unconsciously for generations, and enacted to undermine African Americans.

We get our first recorded accounts of the effects of the internalization of racist ideology by African Americans in reports of the mix of feelings with which former slaves reacted to Emancipation, which seems to have generated diverse and confused reactions among and within the freed slaves. Even at the moment of Emancipation, beneath the jubilation at what seemed like their prayers come true, many of the freed slaves were also aware of a sense of confusion as to what their new status meant about their identities. In part because of the paternalistic nature of the relationship between slave and master, in part due to this ideology of black inferiority maintained by white society, the emotional reactions of the freedmen and -women were ambivalent and complicated (Genovese, 1976, pp. 140–149; Litwack, 1980, pp. 171–178, 212–229). It may seem hard to believe that freed slaves would feel anything but elation at their liberation. Certainly that was one response, and the achievement of their hopes for freedom offered new feelings of well-being. One man, for example, is quoted as follows: "Don't hab me feelins hurt now. Used to hab me feelins hurt all the time. But don't hab em hurt now, no more" (Litwack, 1980, p. 228). But William Wells Brown voiced a different aspect of the experience of freedom. He had escaped slavery before the Civil War, and revealed to an interviewer his experience of the transition from bondage to independence. As a person who "could walk, talk, eat and sleep as a man, and no one could stand over me with the blood-clotted cowhide—all this *made me feel I was not myself*" (Litwack, 1980, pp. 219–220; emphasis added).

We know that these men, women, and children had experienced many forms of trauma during their lives in bondage, as well as in the devastating war just concluded; we know that the psychological residue of trauma does not go away with the removal of the traumatic stimuli. Like survivors of the Nazi camps, survivors of slavery must have been emotionally fragile for years following their emancipation and the war, if not for the rest of their lives. To a greater or lesser degree, each newly freed person had to confront a new life in this compromised psychological state. Furthermore, many of the oppressive features of their prior lives continued or, at best, died slowly. The psychological dynamics of the slave/master relationship and the angry responses of the masters to their sudden loss of authority (not to mention their financial loss) had complicated effects on the newly freed slaves. Antebellum masters and mistresses had convinced themselves that their slaves had looked up to them, so that when the ex-slaves chose to leave them, the loss was a shock and insult to their self-esteem. Missing the human connection the slaves provided, and facing the blow to the "enormous self-pride" many held in assuming the loyalty and attachment to them of their slaves, took a toll on the white slaveholders (Litwack, 1980, p. 301). The white reaction reflects a failure to imagine that slaves had private thoughts and desires that they did not choose to reveal to their masters and mistresses. A common response to these wounds was to angrily frame their former slaves' decisions to seek better lives for themselves as evidence of ingratitude and impertinence. The freedmen and -women likely dismissed these accusations, but they may also have had moments of self-doubt, remembering moments of kindness towards them on the part of their masters or mistresses.

Even as the chaos of the Civil War began to undermine the power of the slaveholders, African Americans appear to have struggled with "conflict between fidelity to the master and the yearning for freedom," a conflict that left "a bewildered white South to ponder, for example, over the behavior of a body servant who risked his life to carry his wounded master to safety and then remounted the master's horse and fled to the Yankee lines" (Litwack, 1980, p. 41). Such bewilderment at the two seemingly contradictory actions of the servant reflects white self-deception about the nature of their slaves' feelings and a denial of the complexity of those feelings, revealing some whites' fantasy that their slaves genuinely felt the devotion that they mimicked in the obedience and subservience demanded of them. Relationships that had compelled the slaves to perform the roles of inferior, admiring, subservient possessions of their masters and mistresses created an enclosed world in which the dominant values become difficult to resist internalizing, for the slaves as well as for the whites—again, very similar to what happens to children or abused spouses in a dysfunctional family.

There were other kinds of conflictual feelings experienced by some slaves upon manumission. Many "recalled taking the day off, if only to think through the implications" (Litwack, 1980, p. 212). Some chose to test for themselves the parameters of their new lives, by taking steps like leaving "the plantation without a pass, to slow the pace of work, to haggle over wages and conditions, to refuse punishment, or to violate racial etiquette," while others "waited for the master to confirm their freedom, rather than to assert it independently" (pp. 224–227). These uncertain responses to their new freedom make sense in the context of a system in which masters had structured the conditions of their slaves' lives by constantly acting to render them helpless and dependent (pp. 185–186), thereby attempting to inculcate in their slaves a belief in their own inferiority and unsuitability for a life of independence and fulfillment. Furthermore, as described in Chapter 3, the labor regulations and constrictions placed on the freedmen, supported and enforced by the federal government (though soundly criticized by many African Americans at the time), served to perpetuate the same dependent position of the freedmen that had characterized the master/slave relationship (p. 377), therefore giving the former slaves little opportunity psychologically to envision themselves as autonomous, confident men and women.

The fear of the unknown after a life in which the "world ended at the boundaries of the plantation," as well as the loss of the assurance that the master would, no matter how minimally, provide for them, made liberation an ambiguous experience. What seems likely is that for many freed slaves, their experiences involved both conscious awareness of the falseness of the ideology of the white world in which they lived, and an unconscious belief in the undermining messages of their former masters and future bosses. With all of the hesitancy and fearfulness experienced by the freed slaves, we also read, for example, of the clear-sighted observation of George G. King, an ex-slave from South Carolina, who explained the situation thus: "The Master he says we are all free . . . but it don't mean we is white, and it don't mean we is equal" (Litwack, 1980, p. 224). Or the freedwoman who shared her caution about relating to white people: "You jes' let 'em 'lone, ma'am . . . Your never know which way a cat is going to jump" (p. 199).

A brilliant window into this confusion of emotions, and of the memory, experience, and pain that is the psychological legacy of American history for its black citizens, is through the works of Kara Walker. Born in 1969, Walker is best known for her black-on-white silhouette figures depicting fantastical, ambiguous, often pornographic or scatological scenes that portray, in almost Rorschach form, African American encounters with white domination in the claustrophobic world of the plantation. Her works, often covering entire walls or even whole rooms, are at once whimsical, horrifying, beautifully rendered, and profoundly disturbing. They portray images that defy all laws of physics and the natural world, such as an African American female figure in her 2001 paper-on-walls work, "Darkytown Rebellion," who is shown almost dancing while holding onto a tilted ship mast with a small sail over her head; yet the mast is floating, completely unattached to anything. In the same work, we see a flag-waving female whose slender body seems to incorporate the round shape of a horse's rear and its tail as she stands daintily on her toes. Next to her is a thin young male whose leg has been violently severed and is lying on the ground. He stands almost impassively, his penis pointing in front of him and one arm delicately extended behind him, with one fingertip touching what looks to be another penis, or possibly a bone, that points behind him (Berry et al., 2003, p. 78). The images are almost dream-like, uncanny, and powerfully ambiguous.

Many of Walker's paintings depict overlaying images of suckling—both as feeding and as erotic—or of a birthing that is melting into defecation, themes that are not unfamiliar in psychoanalytic theory, but which here are literally colored by the black/white power dynamics of American slavery and, implicitly, its aftermath. The very format of black figures that are visible only against a white background reminds the viewer that there is no such thing as black without white, and that there is no black race without white racism. Because Walker employs an anachronistic medium that evokes the distant past, along with what political scientist and American studies scholar Mark Reinhardt calls "perverse echoes of 'historical' figures"—strange, yet familiar, characters of antebellum America, we are drawn to think and feel about the "primal scenes in the psychodrama of American racism (that) still play out in our imaginations" (2003, p. 111). Walker works with the paradoxical interplay of white denigration and its shadow, white desire. Citing the vital role of minstrelsy in nineteenth-century American culture as an example of that ambivalence, Reinhardt draws on the work of Michael Rogin (1996) to propose that one way in which white domination continues to be expressed is, ironically, through "white desire to be, to be like, or to have the expressive powers and libidinal freedom associated with, the denigrated black Other" (Reinhardt, 2003, p. 117).

This overt denigration and covert longing for "the black Other" affects the African American people who are the objects of that ambivalence on various levels, consciously and unconsciously. In a 1998 interview, Walker describes some of that experience:

> ... there are times when ... you're not thinking about race for a brief moment. Then suddenly the entire history of the whole United States of America or the American South or post-Reconstruction comes crashing down on you and you say to yourself, "Hmm, [t]his reminds me of something. I'm not sure what it is, but it's vaguely familiar."
> (Hannahan in Wagner, 2003, p. 101)

Walker here describes what must be a common sensation among African Americans as they try to sort out the multi-layered messages and projections directed at them now. In much the same way that the freed slaves struggled to make sense of their new relationship to their white dominated world, and to define who they were as individuals, Walker's figures, often depicted in ambiguous relation to whites, force the viewer to engage in that same project. As this chapter continues, we will try to think, feel, and observe our way into the psychological inner world that Walker's art so powerfully suggests.

Becoming Black

"Who am I?" is a question with which every human grapples, at times with purpose and awareness, but mostly unconsciously. It is a question that often drives the process of psychotherapy, typically situated in the context of relationships with family. Who am I in relation to the important people in my life? What do I retain or reject of what my parents, siblings, and others have told me about myself and the world? Identity can be thought of as a delicate balance between ways of seeing oneself as unique and differentiated from family and social environment, and observing oneself to be like others in one's group, be it family, ethnic community, nationality. Throughout life, people accumulate group identities through conscious and unconscious connections with schools, neighborhoods, a basketball team, educational and professional colleagues, unions, political parties, gangs, religious congregations, and an infinite number of subsections within those groups. But in the early stages of developing a sense of identity, caregivers, usually family, structure this process, inevitably transmitting messages based on their experiences in the social world in their interactions with the child and introducing the child into the territory of cultural attitudes and the "isms"—sexism, of course, and racism.

An African American child's first impressions about racism are thus understood through his or her parents and their historical realities. Eventually, once the child ventures out into the majority white world, racism is experienced in an unmediated way, directly through encounters with white people. Because "black" as a descriptor exists only in relationship to people called "white," that person may apprehend for the first time his or her membership in a group called "black." For many African Americans, this encounter begins a process of awareness, a turning point in the realization of an aspect of identity that presages much about how his or her life will develop.

W.E.B. Du Bois (1903/1986) begins *The Souls of Black Folk* with his recollection of the first discovery of his race, when, as he put it, "the shadow swept across me" (p. 363). When he was a young child in a small town in Massachusetts, the children in his "wee wooden schoolhouse" decided to buy and exchange visiting cards with one another. He recounts:

> The exchange was merry, till one girl, a tall newcomer, refused my card,— refused it peremptorily, with a glance. Then it dawned upon me with a certain suddenness that I was different from the others; or like, mayhap, in heart and life and longing, but shut out from their world by a vast veil.
> (Du Bois, 1903/1986, p. 364)

The "shadow swept across" Glenda about 90 years later. She was born and raised in an African American community in Oakland, and, like Du Bois, was also a young child at the time: "I remember my mother and I coming back from visiting relatives in the South, and we had to sit in the back of the bus, but I didn't know why, and my mother did not explain. Somehow, though, I knew it related to the fact that we were black." Whatever information about racial difference Glenda or Du Bois may have internalized at younger ages, the moment of consciousness about the meaning of the difference did not find articulation until a later stage. However, the fact that both Glenda and Du Bois intuited, without having an adult explain their experiences to them, that their brown skin was the issue, suggests that something about their group identity had slipped into their developing sense of differences that had significance well before the remembered moments of discovery. For Glenda, however, even the incident on the bus did not consciously hit her with the force that Du Bois' experience seems to have struck him; she immediately followed her recollection by adding, "But my first awareness of racism was really at my job. Other than that, I honestly thought some people were just mean."

Research into the acquisition of racial awareness in African American children reveals the complexity of the process, encompassing cognitive development, gender, parental influence, and environment. A 1970 study of skin color dynamics among preschoolers found that children may perceive skin color differences before they are 18 months old. Hamer (2002) concludes that skin color then becomes one of those physical differences that, for the developing child, can generate "anxieties about the separateness and 'otherness' of others' bodies," slipping into the child's growing awareness of differences that have significance as they experience those differences in the world around them (p. 1222). Some research suggests that preschool-age children seem to assimilate racial prejudices even before they develop the ability to accurately classify the physical features of race, which tends to happen by about seven years old (Quintana, 1998, p. 29).

Surprisingly, multiple studies indicate that although young children may absorb negative attitudes directed towards their ethnic group, their self-esteem does not seem to suffer (Quintana, 1998, p. 27), and that "African American preschoolers can have both a Eurocentric preference and a high self-concept" (Swanson et al., 2009, p. 271). Quintana speculates that children at that age do not integrate their perception of physical differences in racial categories with their affective understanding of the meaning of those differences (p. 30). In fact, researchers discovered that when African American parents tried to educate their preschoolers with positive attitudes about African Americans, they heightened their children's sensitivity towards racial differences and introduced them to the "reality that members of society hold prejudicial and negative views toward African Americans," thereby inadvertently sabotaging their best intentions (Quintana, 1998, p. 31). These results correspond to a separate finding that small children do not take on their parents' attitudes about ethnicity and race, absorbing society's racial prejudice while remaining "immune" to their parents' "direct ethnic socialization when it runs counter to the attitudes prevalent within the society" (p. 30). Bolstering these observations are reviews of research about children's racial attitudes conducted before, during, and after the Civil Rights Movement of the 1960s. As the Civil Rights Movement progressed, these studies showed that African American children began to express more positive racial attitudes about their own group, and while the researchers are not clear as to how that change took place, it seemed to confirm that young children are remarkably sensitive to a general social ethos as opposed to specific and conscious family messages (p. 31).

The idea that small children respond more to broad social cues than to their parents' messages seems counterintuitive, but makes sense if we consider the power of unconscious communication. An African American parent may try heroically to provide a child with confidence and pride in being black, yet his or her own immediate experience in the world, internalizations of negative projections by whites, and struggles with institutional racism, may generate feelings and attitudes that are difficult to conceal, and to which the child, so attuned to his or her caregiver, is subtly exposed. Similarly, a parent's optimism and greater sense of freedom at seeing change for the better in the social world would likely be expressed both verbally and nonverbally in ways the parent may not even notice.

By age 8, a child already understands the concept of racial difference, and by 10, children grasp the social stereotypes that are associated with racial groups (Swanson et al., 2009, p. 271). With increased cognitive maturity, children not only encounter and notice stereotyping at school, but also are now more likely to internalize these stereotyped messages. It is at around this age, middle childhood, that researchers find greater variability among African American children in the effects of contact with social stereotypes on their personal identities. At this age, self-esteem in the context of racial identity can be helped by parents who discuss with their children the history of racism and positive values in their own culture. Thus, while parents' educational interventions with their preschoolers about black history and positive black values often proved counterproductive, for grade-school children these interactions, including the parents' own relationships to their racial identities, can have positive effects (pp. 271–274).

The meaning that Glenda attributed to her awareness of belonging to a racial group was affected by several factors. For one thing, growing up in an African American neighborhood provided her with some insulation from experiences of racism. Frantz Fanon (1952/1967), the militant black psychiatrist from Martinique, writes that in a black environment, the "black man" is a person: "As long as the black man is among his own, he will have no occasion, except in minor internal conflicts, to experience his being through others" (p. 109). But Glenda is an American and a child of the Great Migration, the mass exodus from 1910 to 1970 of six million African Americans out of the South. Glenda's parents, like others of their generation, were reluctant to talk about the traumas of the lives they had left behind, yet she certainly sensed the emotional current running under her parents' silences. She is a feisty woman, who tends to ignore interpersonal red flags, an issue we have been working on in her treatment. One piece of that particular symptom is, I believe, a loyalty to her parents' need to honor silences, to "forget" the dangers of their pasts, and to believe that leaving the South provided not only safety from the frightening environment from which they escaped, but also a fair and level playing field for their daughter, despite signs to the contrary.

Eventually the signs could not be ignored, and Glenda faced racism in the work world. In the case of Ms. Brown, Holmes (2006) tells of her African American patient's experience of her first-grade teacher believing a white girl over her, and how

> ... her early exposure to racism contributed in an essential way to her failure to develop an adequate sense of self. She came to know and to internalize the view that a little black girl's reality and belongings were not her own; that another's power and definition of reality would be substituted for her own; and that if she protested, she would be declared a liar and a thief.
>
> (Holmes, 2006, p. 227)

Opening his remarkable memoir, *Beneath the Underdog* (1971/1991), American jazz musician and composer Charles Mingus grapples with the multiplicity of his identity and his blackness:

> "... I am three. One man stands forever in the middle, unconcerned, unmoved, watching, waiting to be allowed to express what he sees to the other two. The second man is like a frightened animal that attacks for being attacked. Then there's the over-loving gentle person who lets people

into the uttermost sacred temple of his being and he'll take insults and be trusting and sign contracts without reading them and get talked down to working cheap or for nothing, and when he realizes what's been done to him he feels like killing and destroying everything around him including himself for being so stupid. But he can't—he goes back inside himself."
(1971/1991, p. 3)

Though these words are Mingus' own, written in a work billed as a memoir, they are here placed inside quotes. As if to underscore the meaning of his opening paragraph, the author refers to himself in the third person throughout the book, seeming to find it difficult to embrace his direct subjectivity. He is thus the man who "stands forever in the middle . . . watching." The unnamed narrator in Darryl Pinckney's novel, *High Cotton*, describes his experience of his black subjectivity:

The ledger of how to be simultaneously yourself and everyone else who might observe you, the captain's log of travel in the dual consciousness, the white world as the deceptive sea and the black world as the armed galley, gave me the comic feeling that I was living alongside myself, that there was a me and a ventriloquist's replica of me on my lap, and that both of us awaited the intervention of the third me, the disembodied me, before we could begin the charade of dialogue.
(Pinckney, 1992, p. 220)

Pinckney's naming of the "dual consciousness" is not his own. Attempting to sort out for himself the same experience, Du Bois, in an often quoted passage, wrote that the "Negro" is born into

. . . this American world,—a world which yields him no true self-consciousness, but only lets him see himself through the revelation of the other world. *It is a peculiar sensation, this double-consciousness, this sense of always looking at one's self through the eyes of others, of measuring one's soul by the tape of a world that looks on in amused contempt and pity.*
(Du Bois, 1903/1986, p. 364; emphasis added)

Hamer (2002) translates Du Bois' double consciousness to mean "the simultaneous awareness of self and of self-as-a-racial-other" (p. 1231).

Of course, trying to describe the psyches of a whole people in a few formulas can be dangerously reductive and insulting. Such generalization, therefore, must be made and handled with care, as we are talking about more than 400 years of black/white relationships that have been, and continue to be, affected by the mythology of white supremacy, but with innumerable generational and geographical adjustments, adaptations, and circumstances. Even Du Bois' double consciousness is not as neatly divided as the term might imply, as we will discuss later on in this chapter. Nevertheless it does provide a starting point to understanding an aspect of oppression with which African Americans are burdened as they manage their psychological lives.

The idea of race in American consciousness as a creation of the interaction of European Americans and the descendants of slaves means that there can be no such thing as a black person other than against a background of self-described white people. Leary (2000) describes race as a "complex negotiation within persons as well as a complex negotiation between persons" (p. 649). Similarly, Hamer (2002) writes, "Intrapsychic meanings of race exist in the borderland between the body and the social contexts within which the body is recognized and constructed" (p. 1222). Thus, to grasp the impact of race and racism on the psychological development of American blacks requires a commitment to an understanding of the psyche that incorporates the social environment beyond the confines of the nuclear family, including generations of often traumatic history. In *The Invisible Man*, Ellison claims that "the notion of the 'individual' is really illusory" (Cheng, 2010, p. 128). After all, the protagonist of the novel is not even given a name. Ellison, writes Cheng, "locates identity, not in uncompromising individualism, but in painful interpersonal negotiations" (p. 137). Leary (1997) offers a useful way to conceptualize racial identity, by placing it in "transitional space . . . located," she writes, "in the tensions among biological distinction, sociocultural fact, and future possibilities—a tension that may be difficult to sustain in either social or clinical life." She warns that this transitional space can collapse "whenever racial or gender experiences become either reified or wholly indeterminate" (p. 163). In the following section, we will look at Leary's transitional space of racial identity as it emerged for Barbara.

Racist Mythology: Alive and Well

As Du Bois put it, "There was one thing that the white South feared more than negro dishonesty, ignorance, and incompetency, and that was negro honesty, knowledge, and efficiency" (Litwack, 1980, p. 553). In the dysfunctional "family" of the plantation, the slaves were forced to play the role of dutiful, admiring workers who lacked the competence, moral strength, and intellect to survive on their own. In thinking about the ways in which a person internalizes the "family" mythology of a corrupt system, I found myself remembering Barbara.

You may remember that Barbara, in Chapter 2, continued to feel ashamed of being the descendant of slaves. One day a few years ago she sighed and said, "Everyone wants to be like white people." I asked if she was saying that she wants the same power that whites have in this society. She brushed my suggestion aside: "It's not about power. It's about striving to meet the white standards. White people set the standards throughout the world. It's like the white man was the daddy of us all. Only the Father is above him." I asked: "Are you thinking about any white man in particular?" She replied, "No, all sorts of people," but then was quiet as she thought for a minute. "I do feel relieved that

I don't have to heal people, like a doctor, or design bridges, because I know white people, the big white daddy, will take care of it." Her words shocked and rattled me. Barbara is an intelligent woman, in many ways a fighter, so I felt baffled and disheartened. How could I begin to explore this astounding assumption that only a white man could have the ability to do the kinds of intellectual work that people's lives depend on: healing the sick or building safe bridges? How could she so thoroughly have internalized racist beliefs in white superiority? Grasping for an answer, I recalled something she told me of her childhood, which I now shared with her: "I'm remembering what you told me about how, when you were a very young child, President Eisenhower sent in federal troops to protect blacks in the South, and how that gave you a positive feeling about the federal government. Do you think that experience gave you the idea that only white men can protect black people?" Barbara: "Yes, that's really interesting. I always thought of him as a big daddy. You know, Dwight D. Eisenhower, D.D.E.—sounds like daddy, doesn't it?"

She then continued with a report about the young son of a neighbor who had been diagnosed with autism, and her profound sadness at this news. "It breaks your heart," she said, and without a pause, said, "Like that boy that picked up the rifle and shot people," referring to a recent (and rare) news story of an African American perpetrator in a mass shooting. I noted that most people diagnosed with autism don't murder anyone, but she continued with her worry about the mental-health problems of members of her family, and seemed to calm herself only by reiterating the "love thy enemy" message of Martin Luther King, Jr., and by telling me about how she was up until 5 that morning cleaning her refrigerator.

Although race is front and center here, there is also the fact that Barbara has been unemployed for quite a while, and has lost confidence in herself as a competent and skilled woman. It only occurred to me later to consider the cleaning of her refrigerator as an expression of a wish to rid herself of old, rotting beliefs and memories that made her feel bad. At the time of that session, I failed to pursue the issue of her assumption that only white men have the competence to heal the sick and design bridges; nor did I make a link between that revelation and the subsequent material. But some months later, following my 10-day vacation, we returned to the subject in a different way. She began the session complaining about the utility company and her perception that it disregards the needs of her neighborhood, and then about unfair policies of her health plan. Right before she left for her session that morning, she says, her sister called and stated with frustration, "We are the only group to buy into what white people tell us." I asked her what she meant. Barbara: "We buy into the need white folks have to feel they're better. We try so hard to be like you, yet you kick us back." At this point I am taken by her use of the direct second-person pronoun, but she pushes on: "It's what makes us turn on each other." She had recently run into an old supervisor at work who had given her a hard time, almost costing Barbara her job: "And she was a black woman, too!" "And that made it more painful," I said. "Yes, it did, absolutely. Why can't we get it together as a group? We're so busy fighting each other. Other groups cohere." I directed her back to her use of "you" earlier. She replied that I "didn't seem to judge. I feel all right talking here." I persisted, "But I'm part of that group (who 'need to feel they're better,' and who 'kick us back'). It must be complicated for you to work with me."

Barbara: "Yes, it is. I feel you respect the truth, that it's complicated, but you're like me. I face the truth, no matter how uncomfortable it makes me. I want to act like white people. I want to have the same opinions that you have." Me: "Why?" Here I am feeling very uncomfortable and somewhat overwhelmed by what she is saying. Barbara: "I don't know. Whites got the best system, except when it comes to dealing with race. You're a little different. But with whites, everything that's good and traditional goes out the window when they are dealing with blacks."

I asked if something had recently happened that brought these thoughts to mind. She said that her sister's comment in the phone call that morning about "how we're the only ones who buy into how whites do things, and how you guys see us and keep kicking us. I get how, when the economy is tight, people retreat to their own." I commented that she seems to be saying that this bad relationship with whites gets played out among African Americans. Barbara: "Yes, like that old supervisor. As soon as she has a little power she takes it out on someone like me." I noted how sad it is to not feel safety within your own community. Barbara: "Other groups don't buy into the white rules. They band together."

With the advantage of hindsight, I believe that Barbara is sharing with me in these two sessions a picture of how the racist mythology of white superiority is embedded not only in her everyday interactions in society, but even more insidiously in her inner psychological world. The economic and emotional stress that racism placed on her parents left them unable to protect her or to provide her with a sense of security in Jim Crow America that would have enabled her to develop some much needed healthy narcissism. Compared with President Eisenhower and his federal troops, her African American family and community seemed ineffectual in defending itself against the hostile and unjust white world in which they lived. It seemed natural to Barbara, then, that she would want to be like a white person. It appears she is not alone here. Holmes (1992) tells of her patient, Ms. B, who grew up with abusive parents in an environment of deprivation and seemed to equate whiteness "with safety, goodness, and abundance." Holmes speculates that a black patient might "be inclined to experience the whiteness of the therapist as a prized representation of an idealized lost, or never-achieved, object" (p. 9), a dynamic that has, at times, played out in Barbara's transference to me.

However, that idealization of the "safety, goodness, and abundance" of whiteness readily collapses for Barbara. As much as she would like to adopt the "good and traditional" ways with which white people negotiate the world, these very same idealized white people lose their good values when it comes to black people, and she ends up being "kicked" by the very group with which she wants to identify. She has been squeezed into an untenable situation, and sees other African Americans in the same boat—torn between the racism-induced low sense of self-worth as members of a denigrated group, and rage at those who do the denigrating. The lonely end result for Barbara has been that she has been mainly unable to find sisterhood or camaraderie with other African American women (i.e. her old supervisor). There is another layer to this position in which she finds herself: her own troubled relationship with her critical and unreliable mother, whom she loves and yearns for, while also feeling "kicked" by her. She is deprived by the very person with whom she would like to identify, so that she is primed to experience racism as a natural and expectable reproduction of her relationship with her mother, placing her in the same bind of impossible emotional choices. This ambivalence plays out in her relationship with me. Despite her denial that I, her therapist, am "a little different," and her wish to share my opinions, I think the angry "*you* kick us back" reflected some anger towards me, possibly exacerbated by my recent 10-day vacation; but it is an anger with which she is deeply uncomfortable and is unwilling to explore. The subject of this anger will be taken up in more detail later in the book.

Barbara's frustration at the lack of connection she craves with other black women is not peculiar to her. Glenda, who has a less troubled relationship with her mother and less sense of herself as a denigrated, dark-skinned woman, has expressed a belief that "we black people don't partner up to save each other." She complained of observing Asian co-workers banding together to start a little business, "but with our people they hold their money tighter. I believe it's a distrust factor. I can't understand how it passes on from generation to generation, where black people don't trust one another."

Feeling Racism

There is ample testimony by African Americans about experiences of racism, whether cell phone videos of police brutality against black citizens, the lyrics of hip hop artists, or reminiscences by our African American former attorney general and president, playwrights, poets, or athletes. The stories may vary but all confirm a sad truth: no African American seems to escape racism's sickening power. In her prose poem *Citizen: An American Lyric* (2014), Claudia Rankine, the Jamaican-born American playwright and poet, recounts the story of African American champion Serena Williams' encounters with racism on the tennis court, and describes the experience: "the daily diminishment is a low flame, a constant drip" (p. 32). These words could equally refer to the struggles many less visible black citizens face. In his letter to his nephew, James Baldwin talks about his friends

> . . . lost, and unable to say what it was that oppressed them, except that they knew it was "the man"—the white man. And there seemed to be no way whatever to remove the cloud that stood between them and the sun,

between them and love and life and power, between them and whatever it was that they wanted.

(Baldwin, 1962, pp. 31–32)

More than 50 years later, Ta-Nehisi Coates picks up where Baldwin left off in his own letter to his son, *Between the World and Me*. For him, racism is experienced through his fear of its power to attack or destroy his body. He describes his childhood in Baltimore:

> Fear ruled everything around me, and I knew, as all black people do, that this fear was connected to the Dream out there, to the unworried [white] boys, to pie and pot roast, to the white fences and green lawns nightly beamed into our television sets.
>
> (Coates, 2015, p. 29)

Coates says he heard the fear in the "boom boxes full of grand boast and bluster" and saw it in the "loud laughter . . . brutal language and hard gaze" of the girls (2015, p. 15). Yet another definition of racism came from President Obama, in his eulogy for the murdered minister and state senator from South Carolina, Clementa Pinckney, on June 26, 2015 (Obama, 2015). He described it as the "impulse to call Johnny back for an interview, but not Jamal."

Presumed Guilty

One of the most pernicious building blocks of racism's edifice is the presumption of African American criminality, which is regularly projected on law-abiding black citizens. Chris Rock described the emotional impact of being the object of these projections: "Sometimes I hate life because I was born a suspect. All black men are born suspects. When I come out of my mother, right away, if anything happened within a three-block radius, I was a suspect" (Watkins, 2002, p. 338). Many examples of those experiences of being assumed to be dishonest have come up over the years in sessions with my patients. I will be discussing this phenomenon regarding one patient in detail in Chapter 5, but for now I will share two short vignettes to illustrate.

Loretta, a 50-year-old African American patient with a sly sense of humor, says: "After I leave here I'm gonna go mess with that lady at the clothing store down the street."

RF: What do you mean?
LORETTA: She don't want me shopping there.
RF: Really! How did you figure that out?
LORETTA: She was real rude when I stopped in last week. (pause) She ought to watch for them *white* women who steal.

When I asked how she planned to "mess with" her, she said she was planning to go back to the store and again look through the "bargain basket" to see if there was something for her to buy, ignoring the woman's clear displeasure and mistrust. Loretta had not told me of her encounter with the woman at the shop before, and this material came up at the end of our session, yet the encounter clearly had angered her. She comes from an outwardly successful, but profoundly dysfunctional, family, and due to the effects of childhood sexual abuse and alcoholism, she has led a difficult life. It has been important to her to cling to her identity as a product of a privileged and respected family, so that her experience of being treated as the stereotyped potential thief evokes defiance, which she plans to mobilize into an enacted denial of the shopkeeper's wishes for her to be intimidated into staying away. When asked how the woman's attitude felt to her, she shrugged and said, "It's nothing new. You get used to it." I replied, "Maybe, but it's still pretty painful."

Barbara is about to have her first meeting with a new vocational rehabilitation counselor, whom she knows to be a white man. His office is near where she lives. She says, "It's not a good sign if most of his clients are from Oakland."

She responds to my puzzled look: "In plain English, people have perceptions about people who live in Oakland, 'Cokeland,' and you tend to group people together. Often it's fighting an uphill battle getting people to see me as an individual. People assume the worst." I ask what she is thinking when she thinks about "assuming the worst."

BARBARA: He may expect me to scheme him. It could be uncomfortable. I'm just wary.
RF: That makes sense, given your experience. How could you not be wary?
BARBARA: I'm glad to know my thinking is not off the wall.
RF: It's also important to be able to keep open to the possibility that he might be able to see you and help you.

Her anxiety about meeting the counselor is focused on her expectation that he will not see her for who she is, but rather as one of a mass of local African Americans, the stereotype of whom is that they are drug users ("Cokeland") and/or "schemers," someone not to be trusted. She follows up by speaking of her own distrust of men, in particular, "white men with power. It's the way I was brought up in the South." She speaks further about her fear of white men, although she is puzzled by her reaction, since the people who oppressed her most at her job were women, and she feels warmly towards two older white men who helped her during her life. When I ask if anyone comes to mind, then, she associates to an African American ex-boyfriend. They had gotten along fairly well until the day he hit her for the first time. With the second incident, she was out the door.

Barbara's vignette demonstrates how racism and racial history can interweave with individual experience. We saw earlier that she holds some idealized ideas of whites and particularly of white men. The two men who have helped her the most in her life, a mentor when she was a student and her previous psychotherapist, were white men. And, as it turned out, she quickly discovered she liked and valued the vocational rehabilitation worker about whom she was so worried. But growing up in the Jim Crow South and living in post-Civil Rights Movement California, with its more covert racism, Barbara knows that behind the forces that hinder her life and limit her success is a system dominated by white males and intent on negating her as an African American woman. In the context of her worry about being misrecognized and discriminated against by the vocational counselor, her association is to the man who caused her genuine fear, her black ex-boyfriend. Her reaction to those experiences of physical vulnerability, powerlessness, and degradation are momentarily confounded with the alertness she now mobilizes to deal with systemic racism as the source of her woes, embodied in the figure of the white man. Years earlier, Barbara's spirit had been badly wounded at her job by failing to register and confront the reality of some anti-black discrimination that was directed at her, wishfully hoping that by ignoring it and being competent and nice she could make it go away. I suspect that there are moments when she becomes especially vigilant to the threats of racist harm, determined never to succumb to the denial that had caused her so much pain in the past.

Loretta shrugs off her anger and responds with a bit of mischievous defiance. Barbara discovers her counselor seems to treat her with respect. On the surface, these incidents seem relatively benign. They are anything but. Barbara and Loretta both want to be seen for who they are—honorable, worthwhile women—and to be dissociated from the racist stereotype of black criminality.

However, some years after the session described above, Barbara seemed to suggest that the stereotype had nestled in her consciousness. She recounted a story of a corrupt African American businessman, and said to me, "I hate to say this, but my people have a lot of crooks." When I reminded her that most of the Enron executives, to my knowledge, were white, as were Bernie Madoff and Al Capone, she laughed. But we also explored more seriously the interesting observation that she seemed to believe that she belonged to an ethnicity that had more dishonest people than other groups, and that somehow this belief reflected on her ("my people"). The real issue, she realized, was the worry that a crooked African American makes life more difficult for her, confirming negative stereotypes that are already ingrained in white Americans.

The concept of "racial microaggressions" was introduced in the 1970s by Chester M. Pierce, an African American professor of education and psychiatry at Harvard Medical School. These are defined as "brief and commonplace daily verbal, behavioral, or environmental indignities, whether intentional or unintentional, that communicate hostile, derogatory, or negative racial slights and insults toward people of color" (Sue et al., 2007, p. 271). Leary hones in on one particularly hurtful aspect of this construct, that of the experience of being misrecognized. There is something very basic about being seen accurately, being read and understood, if not perfectly, then at least with a sincere attempt to look at a person with benign intentions, without blinders, and with genuine interest. Racial misrecognitions are ubiquitous in the lives of African Americans, ranging from a failure to see that Loretta is no more likely to shoplift than a white shopper, to literally failing to recognize the difference between one black woman met at a conference and one of the few other black women at the same meeting, as reported by Leary (2000, p. 641). Leary adds that at the same conference she found herself committing her own misrecognition by speaking particularly slowly to an Asian colleague, despite her knowledge that the colleague was highly fluent in English. Misrecognitions such as these, she maintains, can, over time, "erode the self, as a self that goes unrecognized or that is consistently misconstructed is made narcissistically vulnerable" (p. 641).

"For the recipient of a microaggression, however, there is always a nagging question of whether it really happened" (Sue et al., 2007, p. 275). Sadly, experiences that are so frequent as to become normalized, and that are so often denied by the "perpetrator," accumulate in toxicity and are psychologically corrosive. When a recipient of a microaggression cannot recognize the defensiveness behind the "color blindness" fiction, the invalidating response can wear away at that person's confidence in his or her own judgment. People, of course, develop protective coping mechanisms, but a lifetime of such experiences can, according to a 2000 study of microaggressions and African Americans, "be quite devastating," resulting in "a negative racial climate and emotions of self-doubt, frustration, and isolation on the part of the victims" (p. 279). Part of what makes these microaggressions so destructive is that their very nature leaves their objects with few tenable means of responding. For one thing, the person who inflicts the microaggression typically denies having done so, leaving the object of the microaggression confused, as described above.[1] Also, responding with negative affect typically ends badly for the indignant victim. But as Sue correctly writes, "not doing anything has the potential to result in psychological harm. It may mean a denial of one's experiential reality, dealing with a loss of integration, or experiencing pent-up anger and frustration likely to take psychological and physical tolls" (p. 279).

The two vignettes above each reflect two common microaggressions or misrecognitions inflicted on African Americans: the insulting presumption of dishonesty and criminality. In Loretta's case, she quickly translates the shopkeeper's "rude" look as racially based, because Loretta saw herself as a potential customer whose behavior would not otherwise cause someone wanting to make a sale to look so disapprovingly at her presence. She also instantly assumed, very possibly correctly, that the woman's attitude was based on a fear that because Loretta was African American, she was a likely thief. The woman's reaction may well have been automatic, and if questioned, it is also likely that she would be shocked at the idea that anyone would see her behavior as racist. Were Loretta to openly confront her, it is hard to imagine a satisfying outcome, so that Loretta's technique of silent defiance protects her self-esteem and provides a safe, small measure of relief. Althea, on the other hand, protects herself from the familiar microaggression by planning ahead for her regular shopping for hair products, returning to the same store where, she tells me, she knows exactly which aisle has what she is looking for. This way, she explains, she avoids the ordeal of being surveilled by nervous salespeople.

Almost every one of my African American patients has reported to me at some time during our work together incidents of being treated with suspicion as they shop. None has ever been found shoplifting or ever told me of having shoplifted. Barbara's fear of being seen as a schemer by the vocational counselor is not an actual instance of a microaggression, as the activity is all taking place within her thoughts; yet it illustrates her familiarity with experience of being treated not as "Barbara," but as a black woman. She knows that in situations in which she is one of a group of African Americans, it is more likely that she will be seen in a stereotyped way, and treated according to those stereotyped expectations. Since this particular context—vocational rehabilitation—involved the workers' compensation insurance company paying for her counseling, the particular stereotype she predicted was that she would be a "schemer."

Similarly, another African American patient patronizes a health center further from her home, where there are few other African American patients, because she discovered that she gets better care and is treated more respectfully when she is not lumped in with her stereotyped ethnic group. Often mistrust is a significant part of the stereotype, to the point that it can compromise health care, such as when the patient is dealing with medications treating chronic pain or anxiety, which can be addictive and also sold on the streets. Additionally, workers' compensation claimants of all ethnicities are typically treated as though they may be malingering, lying in order to get something for nothing, a topic that will be discussed in more detail in the next chapter. But, as we noted in Chapter 3, there is a long history of African Americans, especially those from the South, feeling burdened with the need to prove they are not shirkers, as former slave owners defensively asserted when their emancipated slaves left them. Thus Barbara was about to meet with a white counselor while anticipating that he would begin by viewing her through the lens of two negative stereotypes, both of which she hoped to dispel in order to allow her to receive the assistance she so desperately wanted. Steele (2010) writes, "Disproving a stereotype is a Sisyphean task; something you have to do over and over again as long as you are in the domain where the stereotype applies" (p. 111). It has been a humbling experience for me over the years of my work with Barbara, Loretta, Althea, and others to understand the level of privilege I possess by being white, not the least of which is my freedom to shop without assuming that I am under guard, an object of suspicion, and presumed guilty.

Black and Blue

The idea of race/racism in America has always been announced by using skin color as the primary descriptor of the denigrated other. As of this writing, Washington, D.C.'s professional football team astonishingly retains the name "Redskins," despite protests against this derogatory term.[2] Of course, skin color has been the marker, often used as almost a metaphor, for African Americans.

It was a move of political, but also psychological, genius for activists in the 1960s to reject the labels "Negroes" and "colored people"—names given by whites—and proudly embrace the label "black", thus taking a color that was meant to be an aspersion and turning its associations on their heads. But renaming and asserting pride in dark skin, as empowering as that change was and is, has not erased the ambivalent and complicated feelings about skin tone that many black Americans have experienced since their early days in this country, and which they continue to experience, if only because the white majority with whom African Americans must interact, and who dominate their material world, continues to attribute positive qualities to people with the lightest skin, and negative traits to those with the darkest. Yet color is not just a matter of black and white—far from it. People identified as African Americans represent many variations of features, reflecting original differences in their origins in Africa, intermixtures with other ethnicities there, centuries of relationships with other Americans, most obviously, the non-consensual relationships with white slaveholders, but also voluntary intermarriages with native Americans, European Americans, Asian Americans, and Latinos, so that the variety of skin tones and other features among "black" Americans is infinite. Since long before Emancipation, African Americans have grappled with the meanings of their respective skin tones, and these struggles represent for many aspects of their sense of themselves as people.

A selection of lyrics from a hit song recorded by Ethel Waters in 1930, and again by Louis Armstrong in 1955, gives a sense of the psychological pain that can accompany skin tone. Entitled "What Did I Do to Be So Black and Blue?" it includes the following lines:

> . . .'cause I'm black I'm blue.
> Browns and yellers, all have fellers,
> Gentlemen prefer them light,
> Wish I could fade,
> Can't make the grade,
> Nothing but dark days in sight.
> . . .
> 'Cause you're black,
> Folks think you lack.
> They laugh at you,
> And scorn you too.
> What did I do, to be so black and blue?
>
> (Razaf, 1929)

In fact, many blues songs of the early to mid-twentieth century reflect not only the black/white dichotomy, but several shades each of black, brown, and lighter hues, including the most commonly mentioned: "yellow"—the word used since the nineteenth century to denote people of African descent who have visible Caucasian ancestry. In a reflection of the attitude of white culture, predictably dark black was often the least desirable. But according to Levine (1977/2007), attitudes in these songs towards "yellow" skin were ambivalent, sometimes favored, but often not, with brown most commonly preferred. Of course, the range of blues lyrics is huge, and none of these generalizations are true across the board (pp. 285–287). I bring up this example of African American cultural history because it may help to understand not only the pervasiveness of awareness of skin color, but also its role in determining a person's experiences in the world, and consequently its effect on a person's self-image. Mingus recounts his childhood education about color. His father, he writes

> ... taught race prejudice to his children—said they were better than others because they were lighter in color. Grace [his sister] was hurt when Daddy said this and she cried and complained that by his teaching she was the lowest one in the family because she was the darkest.

But then one afternoon, slipping back into third person, he writes, "Two Mexican boys, not much older than he" yelled at him:

> "Get out of here NIGGER!" . . . My boy was shocked. Daddy'd warned him about playing with "them little black nigger yaps" down the street, so how could he be one too? Hadn't those greasers noticed his light color? For the first time it came to him that whatever shade he was, he was going to be nothing but a nigger to some people.
> (Mingus, 1971/1991, p. 27)

Singer and actor Lena Horne described the trials of her childhood as a light-skinned girl:

> I was often called a little yellow bastard because I had no visible, immediate family. I was always being asked why I was so light . . . To some Negroes light color is far from being a status symbol; in fact it's quite the opposite. It is evidence that your lineage has been corrupted by the white people.
> (Levine, 1977/2007, p. 290)

She later noted the irony of money spent on hair straighteners etc., yet "you were put down for being naturally closer to the prevailing ideal of beauty. I did not know whether I was supposed to be proud of my color or ashamed of it" (p. 290).

This last statement of Horne's is particularly wrenching to read. The idea that the subtle coloration of one's skin should be a reason for either pride or shame is a significant emotional burden to carry. Most, if not all, children have, at some point growing up, negative feelings about their physical appearances: my hair is too straight or too curly; I hate my freckles; I wish I had freckles; I'm too tall/short, and so on. But those traits are rarely linked to a group identity, especially one associated with the shame that Horne is describing here. The child who hates being short may grow up to be a short adult, and may well have to contend with unconscious biases favoring tall people. But he or she does not have to contend with a world that groups all short adults together and attributes to them a whole list of negative character traits, stereotypes that create real obstacles to their success in the adult world. Sadly, this is not the case with skin color.

In his work with other African Americans, psychoanalyst Forrest Hamer has "been impressed with how frequently shades of skin color approach the significance of racial difference" (2002, p. 1222). C.L. Thompson (1995), for instance, writes of a patient's distress about a long-held family narrative that as a baby she did not like darker-skinned people. This "fact" was based on their report that she would cry whenever a friend or relative with darker skin tried to hold her. Through their work together, she and the patient realized that the baby was most likely experiencing age-appropriate stranger anxiety, which had been misinterpreted within the context of a family in which color was registered along a value scale, generating competitive responses (pp. 537–538). Sometimes, the particular hue within the range of "being black" becomes almost as significant in the person's life experience as it is simply to be black in white-dominated America.

A fair-skinned African American woman in my patient's neighborhood behaved badly, doing things that the patient and others judged to be degrading. "But it didn't matter what she did," the patient reports. "It had no bearing on her status. She was light-skinned, and that gives her a pass in my community." Another patient mentions that her friends at work constantly talk about what she calls "color shading." During one lunch time, this patient and her friends were talking about the actress Halle Berry, sharing their views of how talented and beautiful she was. But one young woman in their group dismissed Berry, proclaiming her "totally overrated." The patient suggested to me that because her dissenting friend was dark-skinned, she probably envied Berry's fair complexion.

It was several years into our work together that Althea began to talk about her relationship to her mother, and it was in that context that, for the first time, she also began to talk about her skin shade. Althea, by her report, has the darkest skin of anyone in her family, and that difference plays a significant role in how she experiences herself in her encounters with not only the white world but, significantly, her African American family and community. She explains, "My [light-skinned] grandmother loved fair-skinned people. My grandfather was dark-skinned, and he couldn't do enough for her. Darker men work harder for fair-skinned women. I knew she *loved* white people, and I knew she had no interest in me." Althea's mother carried on the preference for lighter-skinned people, and her daughter believed that it was Althea's darker skin that was responsible for her mother's failure to demonstrate love towards her. Frustrated, she said, "I can't understand why I was so black, because my mother and father weren't!" Over the long term, her therapy has included attempts to understand her mother, to help her evaluate her belief that her mother's consistent failure to enable Althea to feel loved and valued was because of her skin color. Was her mother really a better parent to Althea's lighter-skinned brother and sister, as Althea believed, or were they also suffering from the deprivation of maternal caring? She was surprised a few years ago to hear her brother complain that he was not "one of those high yellow guys," a fact he felt had held him back professionally. She indignantly barked back at him, saying, "You're not as dark as me, and no one gave me anything." She added, "You know the dark people of this world always gonna have a harder time." I cannot dismiss Althea's sense of her reality, yet I have worked with her to examine her belief in her mother's failings as due only to Althea's skin color. She is now able to see signs that her brother and sister did not fare quite as well as she had imagined as the beneficiaries of their mother's preference for lighter-skinned children. No, her mother does not seem to be particularly nurturing, even as a grandmother, to any of her children or grandchildren. Exploring her mother's history has enabled us to see that her mother's own traumatic childhood may have had more to do with her lack of attachment to Althea and her other two children than other factors. But it is certainly true that her mother expresses ongoing preference for people who look more like Caucasians.

This sense of being victimized because of her darker skin has become generalized by Althea and her experience of her color within her family now extends to the larger world. While job hunting one day, she spoke of preparing for an interview: "I have to think when I meet with white people that they do tend to accept lighter skinned African Americans more easily." Can I assume her expectation is unrealistic, based solely on family dynamics? I cannot, but I was able to help her consider how that expectation might affect how she feels about herself as she approached the interview. On one occasion, as Althea was reflecting back on the struggles she had experienced in her last job, she found herself remembering a particularly painful moment when her supervisor scolded her for having taken a long lunch, and threatened to report her if she did so again. Althea was already feeling in danger of losing her job, so the experience was distressing. She concludes, "And on top of it, she's another dark black woman like me!" I ask, "and that made it worse?" "Of course," she answered. "Yes, she was like me, and I'd never do that to someone knowing the hard times we have in life." In this case, her anger at what she felt to be the supervisor's betrayal deflected her attention from her anger at herself for being late in getting back to work.

I share the above vignettes because a therapist who is not African American may have little awareness of the depth to which skin tone seeps into relationships within black families and communities, dramatically affecting the self-images of many African American individuals. For some of my patients, by the way, the issue has never come up at all. Whether silence on this issue is transference-related, an inhibition in response to my ethnicity, or if it reflects simply a variation in the level of importance the matter of shade holds in each person's consciousness, or a combination of both, I have not been able to determine. Some of the depth and complexity of this issue can be grasped in a report of an extensive study by social psychologists (Coard et al., 2001) of African American undergraduate and graduate students of various skin shades. The research was designed to measure many factors: self-esteem, self-perceived color, and preferred color for self, opposite sex, peers, and family. The results were interesting in unexpected ways. Participants preferred a "medium tone" of skin color over either dark or light skin, a finding that was consistent across all skin colors. While this finding confirms earlier studies, it also flies in the face of some commonly held beliefs of solid preference for lighter coloring. African American male students believed that women preferred darker-skinned men, while they preferred for themselves lighter-skinned women. Furthermore, their family members, they reported, found darker skin most attractive. Women, on the other hand, apparently accurately believed men preferred light-skinned women and thought that other women found darker women more attractive. They believed their family members preferred lighter skin (p. 2267), as was the case for Althea. For those subjects with lighter skin, their preferences for and perceptions of lighter skin related to skin tones they observed as being idealized within the family (p. 2268).

One paradoxical outcome regarding dark-skinned male subjects was a significant positive correlation between higher level of satisfaction with their skin color and lower overall self-esteem. The authors offer a few speculations as to how this counter-intuitive correlation can be understood. One possibility proposed is that these men were expressing a denial of the inner conflict about the known history of dark skin in this country. Another idea was that darker-skinned male subjects were more affected by family and opposite gender attitudes, so that if these significant others in their lives were not as satisfied with darker skin as the subject is, these men may suffer from lower self-esteem. A third possibility is that the seemingly conflictual responses reflect the "overall experiences of Black males in the United States (i.e., the lower value placed on Black males in this society)." In other words, within their close circle, or with family or girlfriends, their dark skin may have a positive value, yet in the world at large that same valued feature is viewed as negative, leaving them feeling unsuccessful and undesirable (Coard et al., 2001, p. 2269).

Taken as a whole, the study illustrates two facts. First, skin tone plays an important role in African American sense of self, but there is no simple formula that explains how black self-esteem relates to feelings about skin color, or even how African Americans respond to skin tone (Coard et al., 2001, p. 2271). And secondly, family attitudes play a significant role in determining "the importance and impact of skin-color variations in individuals" (p. 2269), a phenomenon reflected in Althea's experience, as described in the vignette above.

As I hope this chapter has demonstrated, there are many pressures imposed by white racism on African Americans that take their psychological toll, albeit in different ways and to differing degrees. Racism intrudes on relationships within families; it compromises people's abilities to make sense of their experiences; and it can greatly frustrate their capacities to be who they want to be. These realities must be taken into account when treating an African American patient, especially when the therapist is not African American. In the next chapter, I will focus on one of the effects on people of dealing with racism that can be most challenging for them, and therefore for their therapists: the anger generated by lifetimes of enduring racism, and of the accumulation of daily microaggressions.

Notes

1 The myth of "color blindness" will be explored further in Chapter 6.
2 Coincidentally, in 1962, the "Redskins" became America's last football team to agree to integrate its roster.

References

Baldwin, J. (1962) *The fire next time*. New York: Bantam Doubleday Dell Publishing Group, Inc.
Berry, I., English, D., Patterson, V., & Reinhardt, M. (2003). *Kara Walker: Narratives of a Negress*. Cambridge, MA: MIT Press.
Cheng, A.A. (2010). Ralph Ellison: Melancholic visibility and the crisis of American civil rights. *Journal of Law, Philosophy and Culture*, V, (1): 119–139.
Coard, S.I., Breland, A.M., & Raskin, P. (2001). Perceptions and preferences for skin color, black racial identity and self-esteem among African Americans. *Journal of Applied Social Psychology*, 31 (11): 2256–2274.
Coates, T. (2015). *Between the world and me*. New York: Spiegel and Grau.
Du Bois, W.E.B. (1903/1986). *The souls of black folk*. In *Writings*. New York: The Library of America College Editions.
Fanon, F. (1952/1967). *Black skin, white masks*. New York: Grove Press.
Genovese, E.D. (1976). *Roll, Jordan, roll: The world the slaves made*. New York: Vintage Books.
Hamer, F.M. (2002). Guards at the gate: Race, resistance and psychic reality. *Journal of the American Psychoanalytic Association*, 50: 1219–1237.
Holmes, D. (1992). Race and transference in psychoanalysis in psychoanalysis and psychotherapy. *International Journal of Applied Psychoanalysis*, 73: 1–12.
Holmes, D.E. (2006). The wrecking effects of race and social class on self and success. *Psychoanalytic Quarterly*, 75: 215–235.
Leary, K. (1997). Race in psychoanalytic space. *Gender and Psychoanalysis*, 2: 157–172.
Leary, K. (2000). Racial enactments in dynamic treatment. *Psychoanalytic Dialogues*, 10: 639–653.
Levine, L.W. (1977/2007). *Black culture and black consciousness: Afro-American folk thought from slavery to freedom*. Oxford, UK & New York: Oxford University Press.
Litwack, L.F. (1980). *Been in the storm so long: The aftermath of slavery*. New York: Vintage Books.
Mingus, C. (1971/1991). *Beneath the underdog: His world as composed by Mingus*, King, N. (Ed.). New York: Vintage Books.
Obama, B. (2015). Eulogy for Clementa Pinckney, Charleston, South Carolina, June 26. *The Washington Post*, www.washingtonpost.com/news/post-nation/wp/

2015/06/26/transcript-obama-delivers-eulogy-for-charleston-pastor-the-rev-clementa-pinckney/?utm_term=.dcea2edb41ca (accessed October 24, 2017).

Pinckney, D. (1992). *High cotton*. New York & London: Penguin Books.

Quintana, S.M. (1998). Children's developmental understanding of ethnicity and race. *Applied and Preventive Psychology, 7*: 27–45.

Rankine, C. (2014). *Citizen: An American lyric*. Minneapolis, MN: Graywolf Press.

Razaf, A. (lyrics) (1929). "What Did I Do to Be So Black and Blue?" Music by Waller, T. (Fats), and Brooks, H., Santly Brothers, Inc.

Reinhardt, M. (2003). The art of racial profiling. In Berry, I., English, D., Patterson, V., & Reinhardt, M. (Eds.), *Kara Walker: Narratives of a Negress*. Cambridge, MA: MIT Press.

Rogin, M. (1996). *Blackface, white noise: Jewish immigrants in the Hollywood melting pot*. Berkeley: University of California Press.

Steele, C.M. (2010). *Whistling Vivaldi: How stereotypes affect us and what we can do*. New York & London: Norton.

Sue, D.W., Capodilupo, C.M., Torino, G.C., Bucceri, J.M., Holder, A.M.B., Nadal, K.L., & Esquilin, M. (2007). Racial microaggressions in everyday life: Implications for clinical practice. *American Psychologist, 62* (4): 271–286.

Swanson, D.P., Cunningham, M., Youngblood, J., & Spencer, M.B. (2009). Racial identity development during childhood. University of Pennsylvania Scholarly Commons, http://repository.upenn.edu/gse_pubs/198: 269-281 (accessed October 24, 2017).

Thompson, C.L. (1995). Self-definition by opposition: A consequence of minority status. *Psychoanalytic Psychology 12*: 533–545.

Wagner, A.M. (2003). Kara Walker: The black-white relation. In Berry, I., English, D., Patterson, V., & Reinhardt, M. (Eds.), *Kara Walker: Narratives of a Negress*. Cambridge, MA: MIT Press.

Watkins, M. (Ed.) (2002). *African American humor: The best black comedy from slavery to today*. Chicago, IL: Lawrence Hill Books.

5 "Black Rage" Revisited

Under Control and Paying the Price

In this chapter, we are going to look at the psychological challenge posed by anger in the face of injustice. Surprisingly, not much has been written in the psychoanalytic literature about anger per se, although the topic of aggression has long been of interest in psychoanalytic thought. Initially viewed as innate, aggression was described as an instinct comparable to sexual drive. Analysts working within an object relations model rethought the meaning of aggression, seeing it as a "dynamic personal pattern of behavior" and not, like sex, a biologically determined instinct (Guntrip, 1971, p. 37). For Guntrip, anger is a "result of fear of some danger," which, like aggression, stimulates "biochemical changes in the body." He defines aggression as "a personal meaningful reaction to bad-object relations, to a threat to the ego, aroused initially by fear." He speculates that aggression "is a defensive anger in a situation in which the menace is not too great for us to cope with," when, in other words, the person can see a way to manage and survive the danger. But when the menace appears to be too powerful and overwhelming, aggression, he explains, mutates into "frustrated rage, hate, fear, and flight" (p. 37). My clinical experience confirms that, behind anger, one often discovers fear. Sometimes fear is generated by experiencing injustice. At those times, aggression may be too dangerous a response for the victim of what he or she sees as an unfair and irrational world, so that the emotional response (anger) must be suppressed and the fearsome and/or unjust object internalized.

Earlier, Fairbairn (1952) postulated a process whereby children, when frustrated or disappointed by caregivers, internalize bad parental objects, taking the parental badness inside themselves. By doing so, they are able to preserve their parents as good objects. Referring to this process as the "moral defense against bad objects," he explained the reasoning behind this unconscious decision:

> Outer security is thus purchased at the price of inner insecurity; and his [the child's] ego is henceforth left at the mercy of a band of internal fifth columnists or persecutors, against which defenses have to be, first hastily erected, and later laboriously consolidated.
>
> (Fairbairn, 1952, p. 65)

Thus the individual, when faced with hurt and frustration inflicted by those with power in his or her life, will opt to believe that he or she is bad and the world is just and benign, rather than confront the terrifying idea of living in "a world ruled by the Devil." Doing so means relinquishing the anger that would accompany the hurt and frustration that must now be denied. Even if one were to "escape the badness of being a sinner," that person would experience himself to be "bad because the world around him is bad" (Fairbairn, 1952, p. 67). Repression of anger, therefore, seems the preferable, if unconscious, choice.

Surviving racism and its inherent injustices means having to grapple with a steady pressure of dysphoric emotions. Being repeatedly misrecognized, seen primarily through the lens of racial stereotype, leaves a person demoralized at having been unable to accurately communicate who he or she is, frustrated at the seeming futility of trying to dodge hurtful rejection and deprivation, and often fearfully aware of the danger of trying to freely live one's life. Frustration and fear coalesce into anger, and, given how pervasive anti-black racism is in this country, most African Americans are given plenty of reason to be angry, often whether because of direct, personal challenges to an individual's integrity or worthiness or, by extrapolation and identification, when learning of a racist outrage perpetuated on a fellow person of color. Yet, obviously, millions of African American men, women, and children carry on their daily lives, raise families, go to school, fall in love, perform their jobs, form friendships, create art, apparently able to avoid being derailed by chronic frustration and righteous anger. In many cases, the will to live decent lives involves a conscious choice to "let things go," while not ignoring the realities of the "things" of which they must "let go." Whether conscious or unconscious, the awareness that survival in this country depends on reining in anger leads to massive repression of anger among African Americans, a decision that carries its own risks. The evidence of the toll this repressed anger is taking is generally invisible, subsumed under stress-related physical ailments, depression, or coping strategies that involve suppression of healthy aggression and assertion and, in reproducing an adaptation technique from slavery, repressing awareness of anger and adopting a "false self" in order to appear non-threatening to the white people encountered by African Americans in their daily lives.

One consequence of fearfully repressed anger, as conceptualized by both Guntrip and Fairbairn, is that the individual loses the advantages that awareness of one's anger provides. One such advantage is that noting one's anger gives a clue that something important is not right. Analyst Kathleen White, in talking about African American skittishness regarding psychotherapy, confirms the power of knowing one's anger, relating an "old prejudice that, if you go messing around in my mind, you're going to take my anger away: Black men have said this to me so many times . . . 'My anger is what helps me survive'" (Winograd, 2014). With a different perspective, one of my patients reported having felt very anxious one morning, only to discover that her "anxiety went down when I got angry. Then I turned up the music and blasted it, to not think. I don't like myself like this." But another African American female patient,

Althea, repressed her anger at the slights and microaggressions by co-workers and supervisors at her "dream job," and thereby deprived herself of vital information that could have mobilized her to confront a threatening situation, even if doing so led her to decide to look for a new job before the psychological toll on her made that solution impossible. Repressing anger over time is hard mental work, and drains creative energy. The confluence of feelings of powerlessness, fear, and anger can engender a pervasive, depressive sense of helplessness and resignation. It can also have profound effects on the body.

In a 1992–1993 study involving about 4,000 white and African American subjects between the ages of 25 and 37, both "working class" and "professional," researchers looked at self-reports of unfair treatment, numbers and types of experiences of racial discrimination, and how the participants responded to those incidents (Krieger & Sidney, 1996). They then tabulated these factors along with the subjects' blood pressures. Experiences of racial discrimination were reported by 80 percent of the 1,974 black participants, and the researchers concluded that overall, "racial discrimination shapes patterns of blood pressure among the U.S. Black population and Black-White differences in blood pressure." This linking of blood pressure with the experience of living as an African American is not surprising, but there were other intriguing findings. Researchers also discovered that those African Americans who reported no experiences of racial discrimination had elevated blood pressure on a par with those reporting more than average number of experiences of racism. Krieger and Sidney speculate that the former are underreporting. Furthermore, the two groups with the highest blood pressure were working-class African American women who responded to unfair treatment by seeing it as "a fact of life" and did not talk about it, and working-class African American men who also accepted incidents of racial discrimination against them, even though they, unlike their female counterparts, did talk about them with others. Also among those with the highest blood pressure were working-class black men who experienced racial discrimination in three or more different situations (pp. 1373–1376).

So what are we to make of these data? Taken together, it would seem that, for those who repressed, shrugged off, or kept silent about their experiences of racism, their unexpressed or unacknowledged dysphoric reactions found their way into the systoles and diastoles of their cardiovascular systems. Thus, the people who presented themselves to the outside, and particularly white, world as the least troubled by racism, the least angered by being treated unfairly, were putting the most stress on their bodies. Yet in order not to have to do battle with employers, co-workers, store clerks, highway patrol officers, or just strangers on the street—in other words, to remain safe—they had concluded, either consciously or unconsciously, that anger or hurt must be kept in check. According to Krieger and Sidney, "blood pressure differences we observed associated with reported experiences of racial discrimination, in conjunction with response to unfair treatment are on par with or exceed those associated with other cardiovascular risk factors," such as lack of exercise, smoking, and poor diet (1996, p. 1376). Is it any wonder that, as of 2004, the average life expectancy for African Americans was approximately 69 years, compared to 75–76 years for whites (Feagin, 2004, p. 57)? This is a heavy price to pay for having to make such terrible choices.

We met Loretta in Chapter 4, when she dealt with the insult of being the object of suspicion by a shop clerk. Her response, we recall, was a mixture of shrugging the behavior off as a normal experience for African Americans, while nevertheless deciding quietly to defy the woman's racism and to hunt for an attractive bargain for herself in the shop despite the clerk's obvious attempt to discourage her. Although I had worked with Loretta for several years, this was the first time she had reported to me an incident of racial profiling, most likely, I believe, because of the threat to her fragile self-esteem posed by this profiling. She has held back on the subject with me, but I would not be surprised if she also had tried to not notice it when she was confronted by it in the past. Denial is a critical part of her defensive repertoire, something we work on quite a bit, especially regarding interpersonal relationships and her obliviousness to their danger signals. Her low self-esteem derives primarily from a terrible childhood of incest and maternal abandonment, reinforced by community indifference; so the added insult of racism is all the more difficult to sustain. Nevertheless, she is intelligent and, in the incident at the shop, able to employ humor to resolve the conflict among the forces of her anger, her realistic concern about consequences of voicing her anger, and her pride. While she had not told me of the incident immediately, and recounted it in an offhand manner, it seems that she did want me to know about it. Perhaps she also wanted to test my reaction: would I challenge her interpretation of the clerk's behavior, or appropriate her outrage for my own? I often wonder in moments such as this whether my African American patients derive a particular kind of gratification in educating me about the realities of their lives in a world dominated by my fellow whites, and maybe more importantly, by receiving confirmation that their therapist has received their attempts to teach in an affirmative way, is willing to hear about white racism, and therefore will not invalidate their experiences.

Tracy, whose case will be the focus of the second part of this chapter, talks of how she had always been so proud of herself as someone who could "deal with that stuff." In fact, she says that when she encountered racial profiling that resulted in unfair treatment, she had no trouble articulating the situation, demanding to speak to a manager and so forth, and if she was not able to resolve the issue, working off her frustration by lifting weights or taking a long and arduous bicycle ride. Unlike the participants in the Krieger and Sidney study, who shrugged off racial discrimination and mainly kept it to themselves, or denied even noticing it, she typically was able to channel her anger by taking steps to try to rectify the situation. Even when she was successful in her response, she still needed to follow these encounters with intense physical activity, suggesting that her anger had not evaporated. Yet in her mind, and to all appearances, she was handling the racist world in which she lived very well.

It is not, I believe, a coincidence that Loretta and Tracy shared similar responses to the June 2015 murders by a young white supremacist of nine African Americans at a historic black church in Charleston, South Carolina. Although this was an event that shook the nation profoundly, when I mentioned it in their sessions, to my surprise, each of them denied feeling particularly affected, frightened, or shocked. Loretta, raised in Kentucky after the formal end of Jim Crow, shrugged and reminded me that "that's the South." Tracy, whose parents migrated from the Deep South before she was born, similarly expressed that she was not surprised: "Happens all the time down there," she said and reminded me of the story she had told me about an African American high school student from her relatives' rural area in the South who had recently been shot and killed as he was walking to a "white party," to which he had been invited. "That's how it is down there," she said placidly. Both women had decided that the division between the dangerous South and the rest of the country—or at least California—was such that they inhabited different worlds from that of the nine victims. Whatever intense feelings of fear or outrage they may have felt were deposited in South Carolina, and their shadows of personal threat and horror repressed.

One setting that has consistently figured in African American encounters with racism and the dilemmas of responding has been the workplace. In his argument for reparations for African Americans, Feagin (2004) found in his focus group that "racially hostile" or "unsupportive" workplaces, where participants encountered racist epithets or other forms of derogatory treatment, left them angry and often stymied about how to handle their anger. Such experiences "can lead to inner turmoil, emotional withdrawal, or serious physical problems" (p. 58). One middle-class African American social services coordinator who participated in Feagin's focus group described how unexpressed anger at being devalued at work may turn into headaches, hyperventilation, and chest pains. Sometimes, though, it can erupt:

> . . . well you know, if [white] people are constantly watching you . . . make you look like you just don't know anything . . . and even though you know you're competent . . . Sometimes, you come out, and lash out, and you almost validate what they're trying to say about you, because you feel outnumbered! . . . So, you begin to doubt yourself . . . it can take a toll on you, and I think it takes more of a psychological toll on us than we even care to admit.
>
> (Feagin, 2004, p. 58)

Former NFL offensive tackle Jonathan Martin left the Miami Dolphins in 2013 as a result of merciless bullying at the hands of a few teammates. Martin's comments about his experiences growing up demonstrate how he adapted early on to life as a young African American son of successful parents, who himself, from prep school to Stanford, went on to academic achievement as well as obvious athletic success. "You learn," he wrote on his Facebook page

... to tone down your size and blackness by becoming shy, introverted, friendly, so you won't scare the little rich white kids or their parents. Neither black nor white people accept you because they don't understand you. It takes away your self-confidence, your self-worth, your sanity.

(Dator, 2015)

Martin's path illustrates how he understood that to succeed he needed to not be offended by misrecognition and to suppress any potentially intimidating display of anger or aggression. But the fact that he left not only the team that was the scene of his traumatic ordeal, but within a short time the NFL as well, demonstrates that his practice of concealing himself did not make him less vulnerable to the effects of mistreatment. If anything, the anger revealed in his essay with, for example, the line, "so you won't scare the little rich white kids or their parents," shows that when the injustice of harassment became excessive, Martin was no longer willing or able to continue to suppress the pain of years of not being seen for who he was.

One day Althea described a painful experience at a job counseling agency, where she had shown up for an appointment with a counselor, an Asian man, only to have him tell her that she did not have an appointment with him. Confused and frustrated, she approached another counselor, who checked the schedule and reported that her appointment was "right there on the computer." Althea told me what she had learned: "Apparently, he's experienced trauma with black people. The counselor said, 'I told him you were a nice person.' I know I can relate to that. I can forget it. Except last night . . ." She then tells me that the night before this session she found a memo relating to her old job where she had been harassed. She then immediately returned to the topic of the Asian counselor: "He really didn't recognize me. On the phone he was personable. I wouldn't want his job jeopardized, but they shouldn't assign him to black people. He had some trauma face to face with a black person. I can relate." She sighs, "All's well that ends well. I'll be reassigned to another counselor."

All's well that ends well? She moves on to talk about the story of a local African American journalist recently murdered while investigating a corrupt African American business enterprise. Noting to myself the passage from topic to topic, I wanted to explore with her what it felt like to tell me about the experience at the job counseling agency, so I asked how she was doing.

ALTHEA: I'll keep on till I get so feeble I won't feel like getting up. Sometimes I feel really bad. I know why there are so many murders and mayhem. Even inside me at times I can feel such rage. That old company did me wrong.
RF: And then having people in your world, like the job counselor, today that . . .
ALTHEA: Some days are too much. I get labeled, pushed out of the system. I get so mad at my mother, but she is who she is. Dr. Fallenbaum, what bothers me is I talk to you, but nothing would have happened to you like it did to me.

RF: That I've been protected by not being black.
ALTHEA: Really frustrates me that they did so obviously, yet intellectually, I can't tell if I prefer that to doing it subtly.

Althea's abrupt shifts in this vignette illustrate the psychological complexities of trying to live with repetitive experiences of injustice and devaluation. Althea ferociously had denied anger, considering it to be almost sinful, but she is challenged here by its emergence into consciousness. She wants to cling to a rationalized explanation of the counselor's behavior ("I can relate" and "I don't want his job jeopardized"), to forget the insult and move on ("I can forget that" and "All's well that ends well"), and to "keep on" until she no longer feels like getting up. She tries to bypass her anger at the Asian counselor and her former white employer, but images of murder crop up, including the killing of the black journalist and the ongoing "murder and mayhem." Both reactions represent a depressive response to the injustices of her life, her vision of her muted and "feeble" self, in a context of an African American community that she views destructively turning against itself, a view that also mirrors her own internal battles with bad objects.

And finally, two other women appear in her narrative. First, Althea makes a quick and seemingly unrelated reference to her anger at her mother, by whom she feels so undervalued. In keeping with her aversion to acknowledging angry feelings, she cannot finish the sentence without an ameliorating "but she is who she is." And finally comes another problematic angry feeling: her awareness that while she describes the humiliations she has to endure, I have been spared such experiences, protected by my white identity. She completes her train of thought with her sense of confusion about her experiences of racism, wondering whether she would rather be mistreated openly or subtly. It is as if she is also contrasting my freedom from discrimination with her "choice" between open or subtle mistreatment, but mistreatment nonetheless.

Several years later, in 2013, Althea's relationship with anger emerged again, this time in a slightly different way. Between February 3rd and 12th of that year, a man named Christopher Dorner murdered four people, setting off a massive man-hunt that ended in his fiery death in a mountain cabin. You may remember the story. He was an African American police officer in Los Angeles who had been fired from his job after having accused a colleague of using excessive force on a citizen. In his rambling "manifesto," he declared a one-man war on police officers and their families. He obsessively detailed his attempts to go through channels to prove his charges, vindicate himself, and win back his job. After failing in all appeals, he plotted his revenge. "I am a man who has lost complete faith in the system, when the system betrayed, slandered, and libeled me," he wrote. Claiming, "The Department has not changed since the Rampart and Rodney King days," alluding to the L.A.P.D.'s notorious scandals of racism. He repeatedly defended his murderous plan as his only hope to achieve justice. "What would you do to clear your name?" he asked at one point. "A man is nothing but his name," he asserted again and again. "It's not JUST US," he wrote, "It's JUSTICE!!!" Dorner's "manifesto" notwithstanding, we will never truly know the full picture of the psychological pressures and conflicts that drove this man to his rampage.

After describing what she perceived to be racially based mistreatment by her bank the previous day, Althea mentioned, "I'm also down because of that police officer who went bonkers in L.A. How dangerous it is for black people in L.A.! Seems like black people (are) walking around with a bull's eye painted on them. My sister says 'The only thing black people should be thinking about is laying down and dying.'" She goes on to discuss her niece's recent firing from a job she had held for five years. Following a year of noticing the departures of African American co-workers, her niece had been called on the carpet for raising a safety issue, and was promptly fired. When I commented to Althea that she was talking about incidents of injustice in her life right now, with racism as a consistent current, she nodded and said, "I worry about my grandchildren one day having to feel this pain and disappointment." A few minutes later she added, "I've been thinking about Dorner. How was I able to hold on to my sanity? If I didn't have God, I can't say I wouldn't have blown up, myself."

As noted above, Althea does not approve of anger, believing that it is un-Christian. She no longer attends church, but nevertheless believes in a very personal and active God, who is present for her in her daily life, whom she credits for all the good things in her life, but who also acts as a reliable rein against any temptation to express anger in response to injustice. It was at that moment in the session that the faith to which she had often referred became concrete in a way that I had not yet understood. (It is worth mentioning that, in his manifesto, Dorner states that he is "not a Christian," and that he is not religious.) In a life filled with injustices big and small, Althea, like other African Americans in my practice, feels herself to be contained by a belief in an omniscient, stern, but loving figure to keep her steady. These two vignettes from Althea's therapy reflect internal struggles with anger that plague many African Americans who are trying to live their lives with some degree of safety and satisfaction by muffling any assertiveness that could "scare the little white kids and their parents."

Amok

In the documentary *Black Psychoanalysts Speak*, Kathleen White says:

> Microaggressions have a way of building up ... you just don't pay any attention, they're so small. Why should you be oversensitive? ... They build up and become, in my opinion, rage. And, like, oh my God, that was such a small thing. Why did I go off? Well, it's like you've been eating microaggressions for a diet, and the diet is killing you.
>
> (Winograd, 2014)

For some African Americans, the psychological toll of containing the pain and anger of racial discrimination becomes unbearable, and the struggle to negotiate life in the face of racist obstacles and provocations derails them. Sometimes it can even derail a whole community. In either case, the catalyzing incident can seem relatively ordinary compared with the eruption that follows.

The summer of 1965 saw what seemed like sudden and contagious explosions of "black rage" in the major cities of the United States, beginning with the 1965 "riot" in Watts, an African American neighborhood in Los Angeles. The violence in Watts was ostensibly triggered by the arrest by a white police officer of a young African American man named Marquette Frye for driving while intoxicated, but the community anger that exploded that day and the days that followed took Los Angeles and the country by surprise. White America wanted to know why this was happening, especially given the timing. Only the year before had seen the passage of groundbreaking federal civil rights legislation, barring discrimination in hiring and public accommodations; the very day before Frye's arrest and the Watts outbreak, August 10, 1965, Congress had passed the Voting Rights Act. So why now?

The country should not have been so surprised. In recent years, cell phone videos and social media have confronted the public with audio-visual evidence of police shooting and beating unarmed African American men and women, giving force to the Black Lives Matter movement. Yet American cities and rural areas have had a long history of police harassment and abuse of African American citizens, so that black suspicion of the police action against Frye and others at the scene was inevitable. Furthermore, despite achievements at the federal level, the incident took place months after the passage by California voters of Proposition 14. A classic example of white backlash, Proposition 14 effectively repealed the state's 1963 Rumford Fair Housing Act, which had for the first time prohibited housing discrimination in sales and rentals. The voters, in passing Proposition 14, amended the state constitution to grant landlords and realtors the absolute right to refuse to rent or sell to whomever they chose, legally guaranteeing the perpetuation of racial segregation in housing. The amendment eventually was to be overturned, first by the California Supreme Court, and finally, decisively in 1967 by the U.S. Supreme Court. But in June, 1965, Los Angeles' African Americans, having been again consigned to live in the state's urban ghettos, were, by vote of their non-black fellow Californians, blocked by both written covenants and unwritten agreements from moving into white neighborhoods. To what degree might the experience of backlash have stoked the frustration and anger of some of Watts' residents? What was happening psychologically to explain the ferocity of the unleashed aggression that appeared on the evening news?

In 1968, African American psychiatrists William Grier and Price Cobbs published *Black Rage* in an attempt to answer that question. They drew on their clinical experience with African American patients and on their own thoughts and observations in order to describe and explain the effects of social and historical forces on the psychological developments of black Americans. Their style was simple and direct as they tried to make sense of the seemingly sudden, uncontained aggression that was flooding America's cities. Such a book runs the danger of over-generalizing, yet much of what they describe, while particular to the moment at which it was written, remains applicable today. Reading the book, I sensed I was witnessing the authors' own constructively directed anger, the positive use of assertiveness and aggression that tries to rectify injustice through verbal communication, education, and professional discipline.

As discussed earlier, African Americans, and especially black men, have always had to manage their aggression so as not to threaten whites. One way they managed to do so, wrote Grier and Cobbs, was by developing the style of "playing it cool" so as to rein in any eruption of repressed feelings, most dangerous of which was anger against white society, something that was sure to bring quick and potentially deadly punishment (1968/1992, p. 68). Beginning in her son's childhood, the African American mother, Grier and Cobbs suggested, "must intuitively cut off and blunt his masculine assertiveness and aggression lest these put the boy's life in jeopardy." Consciously or unconsciously, these mothers parent their sons by preparing them to take subordinate places in the world, a consequence of which, the writers claim, leads the men "to develop considerable hostility toward black women as the inhibiting instruments of an oppressive system" (pp. 62–63). Rosenblatt (2014), in discussing Toni Morrison's *The Bluest Eye*, and the male character Cholly, who has been humiliated and traumatized by white men, writes of "feelings of rage that grow as they are augmented by the humiliations, frustrations, deprivations, defeats, and other harsh experiences that come with being an African American man in the racist system." He asks, "What to do with the rage? . . . his [the man's] wife becomes a readily available target . . . a much safer target than the racist society . . ." (p. 62). Together these writers speculate that some African American men, squelched by their protective mothers in the home and by white society outside, focus their anger on the women in their lives. Grier and Cobbs tell of another possible outcome of being compelled into this stance of blunted assertiveness, exemplified by a figure with a long history in folklore and slave legends they call the "bad nigger," the docile man who bursts into anger and goes berserk because, they write, "he has been required to renounce his manhood to save his life" (p. 65). The Dorner story certainly approximated this paradigm in Althea's eyes.

I am now going to describe how suppressed anger can give way to rage by looking at my work with one African American woman. This case is one in which the misfortune of a disabling work injury and the effects of racism have blended together in a toxic and psychologically ruinous mixture, and in which the problem of rage that cannot be repressed is central. The story of Tracy, the "workaholic" whom we met in Chapter 3, and her treatment are in many ways exceptional in the virulence of her symptoms, the severity of her physical injury, and decisions I have made in the course of our work together; yet it is in the very extremity of her case that both the destructive nature of racism in its least overt form, and the challenge of psychotherapeutic healing, may be instructive. At least, I hope so.

Tracy: The Relationship Between Trauma, Injustice, and Rage

At our first session, Tracy told me that she had been referred for therapy because she was informed by a relative that she seemed to be depressed. Her relative observed that Tracy spent most of her time alone in her bedroom, was irritable, and was unlike the lively, compassionate person her friends and family had formerly known and relied on. When she came to see me, it was apparent that she was, in fact, grieving the loss of her ability to work or to be physically active following a devastating and disabling industrial injury. Hard work had been vital to her sense of self-worth, but now even minimally physical work was impossible. I have seen Tracy in individual twice-weekly therapy for about 15 years. Her treatment is paid for by workers' compensation, as she was diagnosed with severe depression caused by the work-related injury.

Tracy is a single African American woman who was in her mid-30s when she began treatment. She was in shock over the loss of her ability to be completely self-sufficient and to be the one to help others. She talked about how her plans for her future, of returning to school to study for a career, were now impossible as her disability made both the training and the practice of her dream job impossible. She also described how she had been an athlete, an avid runner, cyclist, and skier, all activities she enjoyed, but also relied on to manage the emotional ups and downs of her life. She cried in every session, reiterating her anger and sadness at the loss of her dreams, and expressing her sense of helplessness in the face of her constant pain. She seemed hungry and eager for my help, and when I would make a comment that she found useful or interesting, she would seem to take it in with relief and a sense of encouragement. And then it would be forgotten.

Forgetting was a huge part of her psychological functioning at that point. It seemed that it was only in her sessions with me that she allowed herself to approach acknowledging the level of her disability and extent of her injuries, so that forgetting served her need to not assimilate that information. This denial also manifested itself in doing physical activity that was clearly contraindicated until the pain became unbearable, sometimes sending her to the emergency room; or simply loading up on pain medications in order to do some housework, and suffering the consequences later; or, most astonishing to me, failing to report symptoms to her physician lest doing so might make them more real. The repetitive nature of her sessions, the grieving and the denial, impressed me with the sense that she was trapped in a state of melancholia that was preventing her from being able to mourn. As may have been expected, given this level of distress and denial, one area that I knew would be painful to approach was her belief about the accident that caused her injury, and self-reproach for having placed herself in a position that put her in the wrong place at the wrong time. After some time, she touched on the story of the accident, enabling us to look at her narrative of the event, and she was able to express some of her anger at herself, and entertain the idea of feeling some compassion for herself for what was essentially bad luck. While much of the content of her sessions continued unchanged, she seemed less completely awash in her grief, and as she came out of the acute phase of her depression, and perhaps as she developed trust in me and our relationship, she began to talk about something more frightening to her than her grief.

As described earlier, Tracy had always prided herself in being well able to handle the injustices of the world with reasoning, creativity, and a cool head. As a worker, she had often negotiated for co-workers whom she felt needed someone to advocate for them. She ministered to the lost souls she encountered in her community who were undone by drugs or despair, and took in children who needed a steady home, seeing that they were cared for, did their homework, and stayed out of trouble. She shunned alcohol and drugs, a decision she made as a teenager, when she watched as friends succumbed to them. She had decided that, when able, she would go to college and pursue a career, and that to do so required her to resist those temptations. As mentioned earlier, if she had encountered discriminatory treatment at a store or business, she responded calmly with authority and clarity, met with managers, wrote letters. Her aim, as she described it, was to educate, as well as to right wrongs. In her depression, she had become withdrawn, but it was an event that took place some time after her injury that she said destroyed the disciplined and wise person she had been. The residual effects of that traumatic incident has been the focus of much of our work together.

The Making of a Trauma

Tracy was off work and at home, trying to cope with her pain and awaiting word from her doctor that the surgery he recommended had been authorized by the workers' compensation insurance company. Her expectation was to go through the surgery, recover, and get back to work. One afternoon, she received a phone call from a woman identifying herself as a claims examiner from workers' compensation, who, to Tracy's ear, sounded as though she was Caucasian. According to Tracy, the claims examiner immediately began to harangue her, angrily and falsely asserting that Tracy had refused to take modified work positions her employer had offered to her. That she could have rejected this offer of work was something that was unthinkable to this patient, the daughter of two workaholics and herself unable to tolerate idleness. Tracy was stunned, thinking, "These are lies. Why is she saying this?" As she tried to counter the woman's false accusations, the woman harshly interrupted and said, "So I'm not giving you the surgery. Just go back to work and good luck!" at which point she slammed down the phone. Tracy recounts what happened next as follows: "I found myself grabbing my car keys and saying, 'God, help me, or I'm gonna kill that bitch.'" The next thing she remembered was waking up on the floor of her room several hours later, with no memory of what had happened after grabbing her keys. While she has never been able to recapture those lost hours, the details of the phone call remain deeply etched into her memory.

Significantly, some weeks after the call—Tracy cannot remember when—she received notification that the surgery was, in fact, authorized, and it took place shortly thereafter. Even so, the impact of the call remained and remains intense, and she often cannot hold in her mind the fact that she did eventually get the surgery. As this story emerged, she began to report that she was finding herself unpredictably enraged in certain situations that she said would not have upset her in the past. These incidents now evoked a bodily reaction that completely bypassed thought. For example, she might find her fists clenched, ready to punch; or her face up close to someone who had angered her; or in her car following someone with a vague idea of confronting the person with his or her misdeeds. Sometimes, she was told later that she had been cursing and yelling at someone, when she had no recollection of doing so. At other times, she would return to the protective defense that took over the day of the phone call: she would simply fall asleep. The last thing she might remember, if she was lucky, was a physical sensation of rage, which she once described simply by waving her hand up the front of her body, breathing out the word "whooosh." More often than not, her first attempts at reflecting on a particular incident resulted in an instant recall of the phone call with the woman from workers' compensation, with all the accompanying distress associated with that memory. Tracy was clearly in the throes of dissociative experiences of traumatic recall that transported her back to the fear generated by the call. These were flashbacks, the frightening, confusing symptom so characteristic of posttraumatic stress disorder (PTSD), and as Boulanger succinctly puts it, "There is nothing integrating about the role memory plays in trauma" (2007, p. 29).

What was it about that phone call that took it from being an upsetting experience into the realm of trauma? Over the years of analyzing the details of the call, we have concluded that the traumatic nature of the call rested on the combination of four elements: 1. the caller's hostility and malice (Tracy's surgery had not, in fact, been denied); 2. the false accusation of malingering, implying both avoidance of work and dishonesty, thus negating the two values on which she most prided herself; 3. Tracy's belief that the caller was withholding much needed surgery, thus threatening her physical ability to live and work; and 4. the moment the caller hung up on her, denying Tracy an opportunity to defend herself. The combination of fear for her physical survival, the barely conscious awareness of the woman's irrational hostility towards her, and the sense of powerlessness in the face of being stereotyped as a malingerer who was trying to cheat the workers' compensation system—all of these experiences were playing and replaying in her mind and body, as if they had happened yesterday. Why had this woman, whom Tracy had never met, decided to lash out at her in this way, to threaten her physical recovery, to lie about her? Why pick on Tracy? Why make her out to be a shirker when she was anything but? One theory, of course, that could not be ruled out was racism.

Recently we have discovered a fifth trigger: we notice that she can become outraged at the exercise of a store clerk's discretionary power to rule on whether Tracy is entitled, for instance, to the discount as marked in a flyer or a service that she had previously been granted at the same store. Her association is quite naturally to the claims examiner's apparent arbitrary power to decide to withhold medical care recommended by Tracy's physician. The outcome for Tracy, in both cases, hangs on the attitude of the one who holds the power, a dynamic which can mean that Tracy's physical well-being can be compromised if the person with authority is having a bad day and/or if something about Tracy triggers a negative response, conscious or unconscious in nature. Of course, this situation is ripe for enactments based on both implicit and explicit racism. Because of our delicate work around the role that racism plays in her life, this particular trigger and its implications have emerged into consciousness later in the treatment and as Tracy's comfort in examining racism with me has expanded.

Thus much of our work in recent years has been to try to identify the triggers that have seemed, since the phone call, to lead to rage, sudden sleep, or other evidence of dissociation. While some of the incidents involve conflicts with people close to her, the ones generating the most virulent and frightening reactions occur in public and often are connected with the experience of being racially profiled. In Tracy's current life, racial profiling most often entails being eyed suspiciously and followed while shopping, although encounters with the medical profession can also turn into potentially racially charged incidents. Tracy claims repeatedly, with tremendous frustration, "But I used to deal with this stuff before the workers' comp lady! It never used to bother me!" She says she had been "taught to ignore it, to see it, know what it is, but know it's not what makes you." I remind her, as I mentioned earlier in the chapter, that she has told me that when she was physically fit she would deal with anger by engaging in demanding exercise, a coping strategy no longer available to her, and that, therefore, racial profiling probably did, in fact, bother her, but that she had felt able to divert her painful feelings. When the phone call, with its racial overtones, frightened and disempowered her, her tolerance for experiencing racism shrank dramatically. Although she can still handle racial profiling incidents, there has often come a point when, before she has any awareness of what she is feeling, she is pulled into her flashback rage. With the help of the work we have been doing with an EMDR (eye movement desensitization and reprocessing) therapist and her increased ability to think about her dissociated state and call herself back from it, there has been some improvement. But just as a woman cannot be a little bit pregnant, one cannot be partly safe from dissociative flashback experiences.

These incidents of dissociative rage horrify and frighten her, but only when she gains the distance and capacity to reflect on them. She has reported close calls in which her instantaneous belligerent behavior, which she characterizes as driven by an impulsive desire for "revenge," is halted by what she sees as a fortuitous intervention, although sometimes I suggest to her, perhaps wishfully on my part, that the intact reasoning side of herself plays a role. On those occasions, she might hear someone she knows urgently call her name, snapping her out of her trance; and sometimes, if she is completely alone, she will suddenly become very drowsy and fall into a deep sleep, thus rendering herself unable to do any harm. She is often not even aware of feeling angry before the eruption. But there have been times when she will report her behavior in a session, knowing that she had experienced the triggered rage, but oblivious until I point it out that her response had put her in serious danger. Her solution has been to restrict her contacts with human beings as much as she can, to avoid the danger of someone saying or doing something to make her angry. Sometimes we have phone sessions simply because, she says, she is afraid she will not go straight home after our session, so that it is safer to "meet" with her in the safety of her home.

That traumatic phone call took place several years ago now, but the fear of the rage that erupted in her that day persists, especially as she has become more conscious of it. She says that because of the call "something inside me broke into little pieces, the way glass shatters." Tracy believes firmly that it was only because God answered her plea that day that she did not drive to the insurance company, seek the claims examiner, and hurt her. Tracy strongly disapproves of the notion of revenge. "Vengeance," she tells herself, "is the Lord's." She has lived in fear that her luck will run out, and that one day she will actually hurt someone, get killed, or find herself behind bars, all eventualities she desperately wants to avoid. I have learned that her insistence on avoiding most gatherings, including family events and even church services, is partly because of the challenge posed by the violence-prone environment in which she lives. She has taught me that in her community confrontations do, at times, become physical. Anger does, at times, lead to acts of revenge. The possibility of resort to violence is all too real for her. For instance, Tracy has hesitated to talk to people she knows about her experiences with workers' compensation out of fear that one of them would decide to avenge her injustice. Even sharing the story with one friend or relative, she believes, could eventually lead it to the ears of someone who would set out to do harm. Similarly, being at a gathering at which one guest threatens or attacks another could trigger her rage reaction and find her in the middle of a fist fight or worse. I began to engage her in my own curiosity about why among her friends and family so many people are prone to either react violently or to behave in ways that trigger her own anger and that of others. In talking about one family barbecue, she said she left because she feared the situation was so volatile among some of her relatives that a moment's misunderstanding, perceived slight, or expression of impatience could cause a blow-up, possibly triggering her own explosion. With some more detailed examination, we realized that the primary sources of her concern were a few relatives whom we both knew to have suffered traumas of various kinds themselves. She found it helpful to realize that they, too, were operating on hair-trigger, traumatized response systems, and that while she knew that given her condition she needed to keep her distance, she could nevertheless view them with compassion. But for me the discovery of the psychological fragility of individuals in what would otherwise constitute her support system made me aware of an added obstacle to Tracy's recovery from her trauma: the absence of a close, healthy network into which she could reintegrate herself. The significance of her pre-injury role as the one on whom others relied, to whom others came for guidance and care, became clearer. Thus not only has Tracy been left out from the larger world of a white America with which she had previously devised a suitable *modus operandi*, but she also no longer has a satisfying role among her family and friends.

Tracy's story demonstrates the sad synergy of a severe workplace injury, the traumatic accumulation of misrecognitions, and the harmful effects of racism in ways that have taken me years to understand. This evolving understanding of the context of Tracy's narrative has created subtle shifts in the nature of our relationship and thus in the therapy. My work with Tracy has been informed, in large part, by my viewing the disarray of her psychological state as her response to trauma. In the treatment of adult-onset trauma, as we would describe Tracy's phone encounter with the workers' compensation examiner, Boulanger (2007) describes the therapeutic process as a movement towards facilitating the patient's development of a capacity to transform the viscerally held trauma into a manageable, verbal, mentalized narrative. This process is more easily named than achieved. Tracy had first to get to the point at which she was able to articulate *the wish to be able* to translate her visceral rage into the kind of workable, verbalized anger that had been second nature to her prior to the phone call. She and I are both encouraged to see significant progress in her increased ability to handle triggering incidents without dissociating. She is not yet confident about her ability to rein in her dissociated rage, and while she is able to remain more conscious during these distressing events, they take a heavy toll on her emotionally and physically. She often describes needing to sleep excessively afterwards or reports feeling upset and anxious for days, usually until she can process the incident in therapy.

Her traumatic experience and her resultant senses of disregulation and of no longer being herself leave her feeling very much alone. This feeling of isolation is all too familiar to other survivors of trauma who, like Tracy, believe that no one else can truly grasp the magnitude and strangeness of what they have experienced. Boulanger's description of her traumatized patient, Jonah, can apply to Tracy: like Jonah, she has been "deeply ashamed" of her "collapse," and baffled as to how "this dramatic change in his sense of self could really be attributed to" the assault that had traumatized her. Like Tracy, Jonah "believed he should have been able to rise above it" (2007, pp. 20–21). Furthermore, Tracy's massive efforts at avoiding remembering the trauma has led to a flattening of the emotional texture of her life and a sense of emotional distance from others. Tracy's isolation becomes all the more intense when the people in her environment find her account unbearable. Tracy's friends and family, as noted above, themselves feeling vulnerable and in need of care, have been often unable to accept the severity of her disabilities, both physical and psychological. Their denial serves to invalidate her experience, initially confusing her, but at this point infuriating her and enforcing her decision to keep distance from them. These invalidating experiences are common to many sufferers of PTSD. For Tracy, race provides an added challenge. White

American society, by and large, cannot seem to tolerate recognition of significant pieces of its racial history or the lingering effects of racial injustice and often acts as an invalidating presence in the lives of its minority population of African Americans, leaving them emotionally trapped between their memories, perceptions, and experiences and the invalidating, negating force of the white majority. Tracy's traumatic history has left her with a very low tolerance now for the kind of racist enactments that demonstrate such denial, invalidation, and failure to recognize her individuality.

Years ago, Tracy was referred by workers' compensation to a residential pain clinic just outside the Bay Area where she lives. Pleasantly surprised at the approval and authorization, she and I were both optimistic about the possibility of getting help in managing her pain without dependence on opioids, and were eager to see the results. The experience proved to be nothing short of torture, as the clinic was run by a fanatical director whose stated goal was to get patients' pain levels to "10" and then train them to bring those levels down. Even an ice bag was not allowed, and there seems to have been a sadistic element to the treatment. On what I calculated was precisely the tenth anniversary of her stay at the pain clinic, new material began to emerge about that experience that Tracy needed to process. One piece was the incident that terminated Tracy's stay at the clinic. On an afternoon of a particularly painful day for Tracy during her residence there, she was in an art therapy class. She said she'd made a point of complying and attending all classes, even if she was in too much pain to participate. This time, she asked if she could just observe as she was in too much pain to draw. The social worker, however, kept urging her to participate, repeating over and over that it didn't matter what she drew. Tracy, in a bad mood after a long day, drew a picture of a gun. The worker immediately summoned the director, a meeting was held, and Tracy was terminated from the program as a potentially dangerous and disruptive risk to the clinic. Tracy was shocked. She had always acknowledged the injustice she felt about the dismissal, but only recently did she remark, "Wow, it just dawned on me: what made them think I'd do *them* harm?" I had always suspected that the staff and possibly patients were mostly white, but now Tracy revealed that she was the only African American person in the clinic, either staff or patients, and that racism had likely played a role in the staff's viewing her picture as the sign of a violent and dangerous black person, rather than as a worrying indication of possible suicidal thoughts and her sense of hopelessness about her pain. Again, she was being misperceived and punished on the basis of a racist projection. No one, she said, asked her about her feelings about the drawing. It is interesting that during this same period in which we have been revisiting the stay at the clinic, she reported that in one of the classes she attended there, the patients were asked to give their goals: "I said, 'to comb my hair.' The teacher laughed and asked what I meant. So I said, 'I have African American hair, and it's thicker than yours.'" Justifiably, she felt insulted by the teacher's lack of comprehension and trivialization of her wish. Her unconscious experience of the racial dynamics of the clinic became clear when she was describing to me a morning of "excruciating" pain she felt there one day, when the staff were forbidden from helping to make a sling for her to ease the pressure she was feeling: "It was awful, Dr. Ruth. They were standing around, afraid to defy Lauren [the clinic director], and it was like they were pulling a noose tighter around my neck." A noose is not a typical image for pain, but it is a typical image for an African American targeted and tortured by a combination of sadistic and passive white people who have the power to dominate.

Tracy's relationship with workers' compensation has been an ongoing experience of unpredictable authorizations for treatment, denials, and untimely terminations of treatment, as well as frustrating and disrespectful interactions, often based on challenges to her or even her doctor's claims about what is happening in her body. Given her physical and financial dependence on this bureaucracy that behaved so irrationally, her environment has become dramatically less benign and manageable. Shay (1994), in explaining PTSD as it relates to American veterans of the Vietnam War, alludes to the "persistent expectation of betrayal and exploitation; the destruction of the capacity for social trust." (p. xx) In this context Tracy was no longer able to tolerate and negotiate encounters with racism that had been and continue to be a regular feature of her daily life.

Tracy: What is Therapeutic?

The psychotherapy with Tracy has seemed slow, but I believe that in part it has been hard to notice psychological progress because her physical pain and struggles to obtain health care have remained stubbornly frustrating. But in fact, slow as it has been, change has happened, and she has shared her belief that our relationship has played a significant and positive role in her life.

"The effective treatment of adult survivors of psychic trauma," writes Boulanger (2013), "rests on two therapeutic principles: containment and validation." (p. 41) In my experience with Tracy, these principles have been essential, not always easily achieved, yet often acting interdependently to push the treatment forward. There are multiple layers to the containing function of our work together. On the one hand, the fear of her overwhelming emotional states has, over the years, persisted, despite the therapeutic container which I have tried to provide. For a long time, working to understand why the words of the caller were so distressing and how her reaction makes sense were of great interest to Tracy, but did not reduce her rage at the nameless woman, nor the distress she felt when she became aware of her dissociative explosions. Likening the effects of the phone call to the traumatized response of a mugging victim or a war veteran had helped ground her, but again, had done nothing to assuage the anger. This situation was to change.

One aspect of my countertransference to the suffering Tracy brings to me has been to look for supplementary treatment in the hope that if we were able to chip away at some aspects of the burdens she carried, the emotional field would have a little more space in which she and I could work. My search for outside help also was driven by my uncertainty about my helpfulness, and possibly a wish to share the emotional weight of trying to mitigate Tracy's pain. I now also suspect I was trying to create a benign and even caring community to counteract the hostile one in which she lived, and of which as a white person I feel myself to be, albeit against my desires and largely unconscious, complicit. Thus in the course of our relationship I have referred Tracy for biofeedback for pain control (minimally useful), to a support group for chronic pain (very useful, until the group unfortunately disbanded), and to two psychiatrists at different times for evaluations for medication (unsuccessful since she feared that taking the medications could loosen the control she had over her anger), and have supported her referral to the residential pain clinic discussed above.

If a significant loss that occurs with trauma involves the disappearance of trust in the social world, my referrals both helped and undermined revival of that trust. On the one hand, Tracy's participation in the support group for chronic pain resulted in a positive shift inside her. She realized there were others who were going through something of what she was enduring and who listened to and understood what she had to say, thus creating a miniature institution in her world within which she could feel safe. The majority of the other members of the group were Caucasian. Unfortunately, her experience at the residential pain clinic confirmed her worst fears about making herself vulnerable and trusting in any institution. (A year or so after leaving the pain clinic, she inadvertently drove past it en route to a doctor's appointment. She reported to me that she noticed and recognized the building, and as she reached the next block became so sleepy that she had to pull over to the side of the road, where she slept for 20 minutes before waking and continuing on to her appointment.)

In the past four years, however, one of my searches for assistance for Tracy has proven genuinely helpful. She and I have together been meeting weekly for 90-minute sessions with a psychotherapist who employs EMDR with Tracy, specifically working on the traumatic phone call and its sequellae. Tracy and I then meet on another day in the week for our traditional one-on-one session. Since beginning this arrangement, Tracy has experienced incrementally noticeable diminution of her rage at the woman from workers' compensation and slightly increased control over her responses in situations that had been typically very problematic, a change which is exciting for all three of us. (It is beyond the scope of this book for me to discuss the various fascinating aspects of working in tandem with another therapist, who employs a very different style and modality. Teasing out the therapeutic elements in this complicated process is something I hope to explore down the road.)

There are other indications that her sessions, both the individual ones with me and the joint ones with Sue, have provided Tracy with a valued safe space in which to look at thoughts, feelings, and experiences that feel too explosive for her to allow into consciousness outside a session. For years she has remarked that she completely forgets what has been talked about in session once she leaves, while also becoming conscious of the fact and reporting that, once she leaves a session, she feels so stirred up that she takes herself to get something sweet to eat, or goes to a large store where she can sit in an electric shopping cart and move up and down the aisles, browsing and buying for hours at a stretch. On these shopping trips, we have now discovered, she is in a partially dissociated state, unaware of the passage of time. She also has advised relatives and friends that she needs to be alone on the days she has therapy, as she feels especially vulnerable to emotional loss of control in the hours following her sessions. Apparently, when she does interact with others at those times, the reactions she gets tell her that she has spoken with inappropriate irritability and ill temper. Yet despite what appears to be a sharp separation of her therapy hours from the rest of her life, it is clear that she has grown emotionally, and that on a less than fully conscious level she has been taking in something of the therapeutic experience. She takes satisfaction in the reawakening confidence in her ability to understand herself, her history, and her family dynamics, and to make sense of the pain and injustice in her life. A significant shift has been her willingness to connect the seemingly arbitrary withholding that characterizes workers' compensation with similar traits in her mother's personality, and we have increasingly been able to process those parallels and her attempts to manage the frustration and ambivalence of that relationship. In this past year, a very noticeable sign of progress is that she is increasingly able to remember and think about her sessions on her own, albeit not to the level she would want. She has become increasingly able to hold on to and remember ideas, such as the parallel of her condition to that of a traumatized veteran, and seems to be able to pull out of her dissociative states more quickly. Also, recently she has been able to laugh and share her merry sense of humor in sessions, as well as comment on moments of aesthetic beauty that she comes upon in her life.

The role of my validation of her experience has very much been in operation throughout our work together, and, I believe, has worked to ensure that therapy sessions are considered safe places for her to express, question, remember, and even forget. The idea of validation, or bearing witness, is an interesting phenomenon. Peskin (2012) explains the role of the therapist in this respect: "Essentially, we propose that the patient-survivor seeks to find in posttraumatic life, however reluctantly and ambivalently, the virtual witness of credibility who was not *there* nor allowed to be there to see what the victim endured in actual or psychic terror." He adds, significantly, "In this, the patient-survivor also searches for a listener who can be relied on to be *here* to witness the often concealed anguish of feeling disbelieved by self and others." (p. 199; original emphasis) Over the course of the first years, I believe one of the critical aspects of our work was my effort to hear, digest, and reflect for her the shocking and sad story she had to tell, events from which she felt no distance and hence no space in which to think and assimilate. She needed someone to be that witness "who was not *there*," but who could "be relied on to be *here* to witness" her experience.

Validation can be thought of as providing a confirmation that what the patient is telling you is understandable, and that even her reports of experiences of being the object of senseless and potentially unbelievable cruelty actually contain their own pathological logic, and are thus believable to another person. For instance, I decided to engage Tracy's curiosity about the person who called her, why what she said was so upsetting, and what kind of person might have done what she did. Doing so led to our naming the clear malice in the woman's language and tone. By interrogating the phone call, we realized that Tracy normally was notified of medical authorizations or denials by workers' compensation in writing or by the physician, and that, in fact, the insurance company had approved the surgery. We realized that the woman had made the call with its false claims gratuitously and that it was likely that she had done so specifically to lash out at Tracy. We realized that some of Tracy's fear surrounding that call was an understandable response to the caller's irrational hostility and violence, which Tracy understood but found too frightening to process. Making some sense of the experience as a real event that happened in real time, committed by a real, albeit disturbed, person did not alleviate her fear of her rage at the woman. But it did begin to re-establish her sense of her believability, something always endangered by traumatic experience, and to help Tracy remember that people who have been victims of all sorts of violence often have psychological reactions similar to hers. She was not, as she had come to believe, outside the human community.

In one sense, Peskin's reference to "posttraumatic life" is sadly not relevant to Tracy, and it is for that reason the healing has been more difficult than would be in a truly "posttraumatic life." Tracy's daily life continues to present her with elements of her trauma, whether incidents of misrecognition which often, but not always, stem from racism; or obstacles to obtaining appropriate medical treatment or medication, leaving her vulnerable to immobilizing pain and hopeless despair. In the sessions in which Tracy reported incidents in her daily life in which she was being treated as though she were under suspicion, initially it was usually I who, after listening to her account of the incident, raised the possibility that racism was involved. She inevitably confirmed her sense that that was the case. Now when recounting an event in which she believes race was an issue, she will name it as such, confident I am unlikely to defensively deny the reality that her life is affected by white racism. To get to this point, I believe it was and is important for me to learn what I can and make use of what I know historically and from my observations of life in the U.S., in order to understand as much as possible about the varieties of experiences on the other side of the racial divide. I have tried to make clear to Tracy both that I can tolerate hearing about her bad experiences with other white people without feeling threatened or skeptical, and that, hopefully, she need not live in fear of discovering that her therapist, upon whom she depends, holds racist beliefs, a discovery that would no doubt end the chance of a therapeutic relationship. Within the first months of treatment, Tracy put it this way: "It's a relief to hear that my experience makes sense."

But Tracy's experience as a black woman was not the only type of injustice she was facing. At the outset of treatment, she was clearly hurt and baffled by the obstacles she was encountering with workers' compensation. Why, she asked, would a program named to compensate workers seem to be doing what it could to avoid compensating her? Why did her claims examiner treat her injury and pain with suspicion and skepticism? Why did doctors, whom she assumed were motivated to take care of her, not behave in the ways she expected doctors to behave? Perhaps more like a social studies instructor than the psychotherapist I had been trained to be, I explained to her what I had learned about the history and structure of workers' compensation programs: that they were founded in nineteenth-century Germany by Otto von Bismarck to protect new factory owners from suits by injured workers, and that they function like any insurance company. Thus she, the employee, was not the client of the workers' compensation insurance; the paying client was the employer, and it was to the employer that the insurance company's primary allegiance went, after protecting its own financial interests. Both employers and their insurance companies have financial incentive to see claimants as people who probably are not entitled to the medical care or financial compensation they seek. Their employees serve on the front lines as their gatekeepers (Fallenbaum, 2003). Thus the claims examiner's skepticism towards her had little to do with her as a person or the medical realities of her injury. Similarly, when she was sent to the insurance company's doctor for an opinion of her condition, that doctor was being paid by the insurance company and was not acting as her treating physician.

This perspective was grounding for Tracy, enabling her to have a measure of intellectual control over her experience of negation and misrecognition. Sometime later I heard a National Public Radio series that featured a few injured workers and their similar experiences with workers' compensation. I printed out the transcripts and gave them to Tracy, explaining what they were about. Although reading and concentrating are now very difficult for her, she read one of the stories and expressed surprise and a sense of validation, as if, vicariously, her story was being told.

These two somewhat didactic and, I would maintain, political interventions are outside the realm of anything I was taught or was modeled for me during my psychodynamically oriented clinical training, yet I feel such interventions are crucial to my work with Tracy and other patients, in particular patients of color. Why do I consider these interventions political? In both instances, I am providing historical and political context for an experience that for Tracy is personal. To note and describe past or current events stems from and even creates a political position. My choice to "remember" and share the historical foundation of workers' compensation was designed to expose and demystify an institution that held a tremendous amount of power over Tracy's life. Without assistance, she did not have the tools to understand how the structure of workers' compensation was being played out in her relationship with that agency. Furthermore, it is in the nature of her traumatized mental state that it is difficult for her to have enough distance from the immediate, in-your-face imagery and bodily sensations to think, to take a distance and analyze a situation; often there is only the present moment that has collapsed into the experience of the past trauma. Tracy was suffering needlessly because she could not sort out what the workers' compensation employees' responses to her said about her and her relationship to the social and business world. It was a form of misrecognition that was not quite like the ones to which she was accustomed, even though it bore some of the familiar markings. I believe that my interpreting the bureaucracy's stance for her, while it did not take away the pain of that relationship, did enable her to take moments of relief and see herself as one of thousands of injured workers facing the same experiences of misrecognition, deprivation of needed care, and suspicion. Likewise, by selecting to focus her attention on the story of the other injured workers, I am connecting Tracy's experience to those of many others in this country, placing her treatment in a national political perspective, just as the information about the history of workers' compensation helped to contextualize that experience from a historical angle. As I recounted in Chapter 3, I also clipped a *New York Times* article about the class action suit filed by three non-white security guards working at a few large New York stores. They claimed that they had all been ordered by their employers to racially profile African American customers. Given how consistent her own experience was of being quietly harassed by retail security guards, I decided to share the contents of the article and gave her the clipping, emphasizing that this practice that she had been dealing with for years was now validated in a major newspaper; that it was real and widespread; and that these workers were taking action. "Wow," she said. "This is for real."

Perhaps another way of understanding these interventions as political is by seeing each one as a moment in which I am articulating a neglected piece of the relationship between Tracy and our shared social and historical moment in time, elaborating on the connections between Tracy's experience and our larger history, giving her narrative a different kind of depth, while demystifying what seemed like a personal and individual experience. Acknowledging that shared world and the therapist's more historically contextualized way of understanding the patient's experience creates a moment of intimate psychological contact between therapist and patient, as it both validates and provides the potential for gaining some distance and insight into the patient's perceptions and affects.

Not that long ago, Tracy reported on an instance of her dissociation that upset her, the likes of which had not happened in some time—possibly as long as a year. I am going to describe the sessions surrounding the incident because in some ways they demonstrate the interweaving of trauma, injustice, and rage. Tracy and I meet one-on-one every Monday in my office for 50 minutes, and every Thursday for 90 minutes with Sue, the EMDR specialist, at her office. One Monday, Tracy left a message requesting a phone session, a relatively frequent occurrence. She told me that she did not trust herself to leave home because of an incident that had occurred following our Thursday session with Sue. She recounted how a clerk at Home Depot refused her a service to which she knew she was entitled. "I tried to reason with him," she said, but to no avail, so she asked to speak to the manager. The manager backed up the clerk. Calmly, Tracy began to knock items off the nearest shelf, breaking some in the process, and walked out to her car, where she sat waiting for the manager to come to her. Without realizing it at the time, she remained in her car in the parking lot for seven hours. At some point, she recalls, she saw an African American man on a cell phone, giving her the idea of phoning the district manager to complain about the service she had received. She did so, apparently in a reasonable enough way that he confirmed that she was correct, and that the manager, who by then had left work, was in the wrong. He arranged for the relief manager to provide Tracy with the item and service she had wanted, but she was so angry she could not return—and has not to this day returned—to the store to take advantage of the changed situation. When we discussed her call, it was clear she had not realized the oddity of phoning to complain after she had just more or less vandalized the store. For most of this session I listened. I told her with genuinely felt sympathy, "I am so sorry for your rage and how badly you feel about what you did." She exclaimed, "But I used to be able to handle the degrading stuff!" She was unable to recall any thoughts or feelings she had during the hours in her car; nor could she recall anything of the session that had preceded the trip to Home Depot. I reminded her that we had talked about complications in trying to get authorization for a medical procedure requested by her doctor, that the memory of the traumatic phone call had erupted, and that she had become symptomatic. Even after some productive EMDR work with Sue, by the end of the session Tracy had returned to her memory of the phone call and complained of a terrible headache. Consequently, a sense of irrational forces depriving her of needed care that was her due was fresh when, without thinking, she had driven to Home Depot.

In the next session, we continued to process the store incident, this time with Sue. As we talked about the details of what she could recall, she reported an insight: "I think the trigger was that they said 'no' when they should have said 'yes.' It's like the workers' comp lady. If I could only recognize it at the time! I think I'm doing ok, we're talking reasonably, but then I go and knock those things off the shelves!" I ask, "Do you think you might feel some anger at us? After all, we often bring you back to thinking of these upsetting things." She replies quickly, "No, No!" Tracy has never allowed that she feels any anger towards me or to Sue, so this response is not unexpected.

Monday's session is another phone one, as she explains:

TRACY: I don't feel safe leaving. Still haven't gone back to Home Depot because I don't trust myself. I try to remind myself, "People will always lie."
RF: Lying to be unfair is really a trigger for you.
TRACY: This makes me sad, because I'm sure it happened all my life, but never stumped me.
RF: It's like your immune system for unfairness is shot.
TRACY: Yes, that feels right, but why?
RF: That phone call was the straw that broke the camel's back.

I explain once more the elements of the call and the Home Depot incident that reverberate and trigger her.

TRACY: I couldn't repeat what you said, but it made sense as I was hearing you. My heart is pounding, my hands are balling up to punch.
RF: Your fear and anger go straight to your body.
TRACY: (crying) I want to remember. I can't grab the words. You're saying what I can't put into words.
RF: That is what we're working towards, you being able to find your words at these moments, so that the experience of the phone call or the Home Depot incident can feel less in your face.

She's silent for a minute, and I ask her where she is.

TRACY: I want some Skittles.

I am jolted by the reference to Skittles, especially given that she has never mentioned a preference or desire for them before; nor did she ever talk about the Trayvon Martin case when it was in the news.

RF: What makes you pick Skittles?
TRACY: They're sweet. I want something sweet right now. I think of sorting the colors.
RF: Does anything come to mind as you say that?
TRACY: A rainbow of people, everyone different. When I was sitting in the car, a manager I know walked by, and I decided not to talk to him. This reminds me of the diversity of people.

I debate whether to introduce my own association to Skittles, and decide it is so blatantly iconic that her mention of it, even with her avoidance of the reference, cannot be chance.

RF: Well it makes me think of the awful story of Trayvon Martin, who was killed because he went to a store to get some Skittles.
TRACY: Oh yes. That's right. It's true that I'm afraid to go to the store to get something sweet, even though I crave a sweet right now. It could be dangerous.

In these brief scenes of her therapy Tracy reveals the painful contours of the rage she feels at the injustice of being treated as an object of suspicion and of hostility, a rage that has always been a force to contend with but which she no longer is able to reliably contain. I think it is significant that in her dissociated state at Home Depot it is the sight of another African American, the man on the cell phone, that returns her to her pre-traumatized self, the woman who will call the district manager when service has been unfair. She recalled that his expression was serious, and she had imagined him doing exactly what she proceeded to do, using reason and verbal skills to complain about poor treatment. The previous session, in which she reported yet another battle for her medical care with a seemingly impenetrable bureaucracy, ended before she could be returned to a state in which she felt more grounded in the present. Left feeling uncontained by Sue and me, and possibly, although she would deny it, angry at the experience of our abandonment, she was operating on a hair trigger by the time the clerk and manager at Home Depot said their "no's."

And finally, there is the bag of Skittles, a symbol that in our historical moment is as powerful as a noose in its ability to call up terror for black Americans, the reality that your life is always at the mercy of your white fellow citizens and the arbitrary nature of racism. Will wearing a hoodie seem suspicious? Will a package of candy be mistaken for a gun? Fear folds into anger, and the combination for an African American is dangerous. Tracy knows that in a state of vengeful dissociation, her loss of control is a matter of life and death. The only places she feels safe at that moment are in her home and in therapy, but since actually getting herself to my consulting room involves traveling between the two places, she is often stuck at home until her sense of danger has passed. Until then, the phone will have to do.

Recently Tracy has become more accepting of herself in spite of the dissociated Tracy by whom she is so appalled. She understands that she has a psychiatric condition, and tells herself, "It's just the PTSD," or what her one close friend calls her "condition." We are trying to develop techniques she can try to help keep her grounded when there is danger of her losing herself, and if her friend is with her when she seems to be moving into anger in public, they have discovered that by putting her finger to her lips, as if to say, "shhh," her friend can calm Tracy down. Grateful for this advance, she is nevertheless sad at "needing any outside control." I tell her that she is just borrowing us for now, to help her process her thoughts when she is triggered, and she says she finds that idea very reassuring. Shaking her head, she says, "I never knew how *deep* mental disability goes, how you really can't process in those states. I'm thinking about Mario Woods. He couldn't follow simple instructions." Here, she begins to cry. She is referring to a recent incident that had been in the local news. Mario Woods was a young black San Francisco man who was seen waving a knife and in an agitated state. Surrounded by several police officers, he failed to follow their shouted command to drop the knife, and was shot to death. She continued, "It's true. When I'm off track, simple instructions, like 'drop knife,' I can't process." I said, "So you know that in a state of fear and dissociation, surrounded by police, he couldn't hear and process and think." She agreed, still crying. "Yeah. There was a woman at my church. She was mentally ill and she was hanging out of her window. She believed the police were there to trap her. Only our pastor could talk her down."

My work with Tracy has been a reminder of the importance of long-term psychotherapy and the tragedy of its unavailability for most people who need it. The good fortune of Tracy's insurance coverage has allowed us to work solidly and consistently over time, so that real, albeit slow, progress is being made. In this context, signs of movement are exciting in much the same way as emerging blossoms in early spring can be thrilling.

One day, despite the persistence of her dissociative symptoms, Tracy reported the following dream: "I'm in a big, empty Victorian house. Someone is moving so there's no furniture. I'm on the bottom floor, waiting. It's spacious. I end up driving a U-Haul that got stranded in the snow. First, it's just the back wheels. I got out and saw six inches of snow, but from the side I saw the whole wheel had sunk into big holes. How did I do that? I should have seen that! Then all four wheels."

We discuss her associations to the images in the dream, and, as usual with dreams, various themes emerge. The house reminds her of her family home and leads her to think about the way in which her family's belief in work, especially physical work, as an urgent necessity to deal with every aspect of survival, led her to exacerbate her initial injury rather than allow herself to rest and possibly heal. "I should have seen that," she insists in the dream. The six inches of snow may refer to the six original members of her nuclear family. What about the snow? Tracy lives in a city that never sees snow, although she used to drive into the Sierra to ski over the cold, white landscape, taking pleasure in conquering the challenge. Now, hauling herself around in that same white environment, she gets stuck in it, blindsided by the dynamics of maneuvering in it with her impairment; again, "How did I do that? I should have seen that!" At this stage in her treatment, then, she has been able to symbolically represent her dilemma in the form of a dream rather than as an enactment. She can use it to understand and to represent change in herself over time, something that is so hard to achieve when in the throes of PTSD. The dream represents a bit of mental space that may be opening up in which we may be able to work.

References

Boulanger, G. (2007). *Wounded by reality: Understanding and treating adult onset trauma.* Mahwah, NJ & London: The Analytic Press.

Boulanger, G. (2013). Fearful symmetry: Shared trauma in New Orleans after Hurricane Katrina. *Psychoanalytic Dialogues,* 23: 33–44.

Dator, J.H. (August 26, 2015). Jonathan Martin posts powerful piece about his life and decision to retire from the NFL. www.sbnation.com/lookit20158/26/9211293/jonathan-martin-facebook-post-nfl-retirement-dolphins (accessed October 24, 2017).

Fairbairn, W.R.D. (1952). *Psychoanalytic studies of the personality.* London: Tavistock Publications, Ltd.

Fallenbaum, R. (2003). The injured worker. *Studies in Gender and Sexuality,* 4, (1): 72–92.

Feagin, J.R. (2004). Documenting the costs of slavery, segregation, and contemporary racism: Why reparations are in order for African Americans. *Harvard Blackletter Law Journal* 20: 49–81.

Grier, W.H. & Cobbs, P.M. (1968/1992). *Black rage.* New York: Basic Books.

Guntrip, H. (1971). *Psychoanalytic theory, therapy, and the self*. New York: Basic Books.

Krieger, N. & Sidney, S. (1996). Racial discrimination and blood pressure: The CARDIA study of young black and white adults. *American Journal of Public Health*, 86 (10): 1370–1378.

Peskin, H. (2012). "Man is a wolf to man": Disorders of dehumanization in psychoanalysis. *Psychoanalytic Dialogues, 22*: 190–205.

Rosenblatt, P.C. (2014). *The impact of racism on African American families: Literature as social science*. Farnham, UK & Burlington, VT: Ashgate Publishing Co.

Shay, J. (1994). *Achilles in Vietnam: Combat trauma and the undoing of character*. New York: Atheneum.

Winograd, B. (2014). *Black psychoanalysts speak*. PEP Video Grants, 1:1.

6 The Color of Psychotherapy

Something that nags at me even now is this question: how do my African American clients experience my whiteness, and how do those experiences affect their respective treatments? What about my identity as a psychotherapist, as a psychologist? What about differences of class? Whatever I have been able to learn from history, socio-politics, and psychoanalytic writing does not fully satisfy the mysterious specificity of one black person's response to one white psychotherapist with whom that person is in treatment. Tummala-Narra (2015) warns that the "culturally competent" psychotherapist must "bear the anxiety of not knowing or experiencing difference from the client's cultural identification" (p. 286). Yet there is always a desire to take the client's experience inside, to understand through identification. The persistence of my question stems from the unique depth and breadth of the racial divide and the emotional complexity it adds to the transference/countertransference relationship. If I bemoan the way in which America's racial history has invaded every nook and cranny of this country's life, it should come as no surprise that it intrudes into my consulting room and my therapeutic mind, leaving, as American racialism inevitably does, confusion and frustration wherever it lands. This is not to say that African American clients are universally mum on the subject of racial difference, or that none ever reveals their responses to their white therapists. Occasionally, of course, patients' thoughts and feelings about the therapist's Euro-American identity burst through or sometimes they just peak out, as I will describe below. But such moments can hint at the meaning of a therapist's racial identity within the wider transference relationship.[1]

In this chapter I will try to approach these questions from as many angles as I can, knowing that there are no definitive truths to be found. Instead what we will find is a *Rashomon*-type depiction of beliefs and expectations respectively of African American patients and Euro-American psychotherapists and the barely conscious mindsets of each that exist long before the first appointment has even been made or the treatment begun. Hopefully, assembling these assorted discoveries and reflections at least can help us to consider our biracial clinical encounters. When dealing with a population as diverse as Americans of African descent, it makes sense to view whatever we find as suggestive rather than definitive. Furthermore, as you will see, variations and contradictions abound, and those very variations can provide rich material for thought. I will first review some research into African American attitudes and responses to mental health professionals, and in particular to non-black therapists.

"Someone Who Can't Relate to You"

> I would say there are more White psychotherapists out there than Blacks. You know if you made an appointment to see a therapist, more likely than not you are going to be sitting down and talking to someone who can't relate to you.
>
> (Thompson et al., 2004, p. 23)[2]

Over a period of several months in 2000, researchers held a series of 24 focus groups designed to answer the question: how do African Americans perceive psychotherapy and psychotherapists? A total of 201 African American men and women (one of whom spoke the words cited above) met in 90-minute-long groups, each conducted by a female African American psychologist. The groups took place in a mid-western city and included people who had used mental health services, as well as family members of patients, and a number of people who had considered seeking psychotherapy but had decided against it (Thompson et al., 2004, pp. 20–21). The findings are illuminating.

The extra pressures African Americans face would lead us to expect a commensurate need for mental health services, at the very least to deal with the psychological repercussions of those burdens; yet, despite some mixed reports of increased willingness to do so (Office of the Surgeon General et al., 2001, Chapter 3), we know that, historically, African Americans have under-utilized such services. The same Surgeon General report reveals that by the end of the twentieth century, "only 16 percent of African Americans with a diagnosable mood disorder saw a mental health specialist, and fewer than one third consulted a health care provider of any kind" (pages unnumbered). What accounts for this gap between need and care? The report stated that two-and-a-half times more African Americans feared mental health treatment than whites, and that they were also "more likely than whites to describe stigma and spirituality as affecting their willingness to seek help." Althea has her opinion on the subject: in responding to a news story of a mass shooting by an African American man in 2013, she complained, "I can't talk about this with other black people. They don't believe in mental illness. They just say, 'That nigger, he just went off,' or 'He just lost it.'"

Feedback from participants in the Thompson et al. study also made clear that there were a number of barriers to seeking mental health services, including, but definitely not limited to, financial and logistical. A phone-based field experiment involving 320 New York psychologists who were members of an insurance panel recently revealed one obstacle faced by African Americans seeking mental health care: getting a first appointment. Kugelmass (2016) had both male and female actors leave messages on the therapists' voice mails indicating that they were seeking appointments and had insurance. The actors portrayed either middle- or working-class patients, half African American and half white. Each therapist received two calls: a white or black middle-class caller and a white or black working-class caller. Among those who posed as working class, only 8 percent were offered appointments, whether white or black. However, when it came to middle-class patients, race made a difference. Twenty-eight percent of white prospective patients were offered appointments, compared with 17 percent of the African American callers. Additionally, 18 percent of white middle-class callers got appointments at a time they had requested, while only 8 percent of the African American middle-class callers did. Thus class played a very significant role in the counter-transference responses of the therapists, but when class was more congruent with the psychologists' own status, race still played a significant role.

Most participants in the Thompson et al. study reported that they believed psychotherapy to be an "invasive" and "impersonal" process, although those who had been seen in long-term treatment allowed that, given time to develop trust and to form a relationship, they did experience "empathy" and "compassion" from their therapists. In a seemingly paradoxical finding, cited by Thompson et al., Diala et al. (2001) reported that "African Americans have comparable and, in most instances, more favorable attitudes toward seeking care for their mental illness than do their White counterparts" (p. 807); yet, once they had made contact with mental health professionals, they expressed more negative attitudes and were less likely to continue and use mental health services than were their white counterparts (Thompson et al., 2004, p. 19). The common finding here, then, is that initial contact with mental health professionals is more often unsatisfactory for African Americans seeking help than it is for whites. What the Thompson et al. findings indicate, however, is that if not faced with or deterred by early negative experiences, African Americans can develop the kinds of therapeutic alliances that enable them to feel understood and cared for by their therapists.

Group members thought that, when compared with social workers or counselors, psychologists tended to be "older White males, who were unsympathetic, uncaring, and unavailable."[3] As one participant put it, "You know it's just like 'I'm about to get paid . . . your hour is up.'" This perception was reiterated in reports of "experiencing and hearing about cold, condescending, arrogant interactions, and there were persistent complaints about the inability to make a connection." One cannot read these remarks or the statistics about people getting call-backs from psychologists without feeling distressed that people taking the difficult step of seeking help felt so rebuffed. I certainly have heard reports from patients describing earlier interactions with non-black therapists in ways that made the patients feel put down and turned off, or worse, as I will describe later in the chapter. However, it is also possible that there are times when an African American patient already comes to his or her new caregiver with trepidation and ambivalence, and from that position may interpret a reserved style or the routines of the 50-minute hour as rejecting, cold, and uncaring. The August 2001 Surgeon General report also comments on black wariness of mental health professionals: "Historical and contemporary negative treatment have led to mistrust of authorities, many of whom are not seen as having the best interests of African Americans in mind" (Chapter 3). Looking at history, this assessment could be seen as quite an understatement. Probably no single confirmation of African Americans' worst fears about doctors has been as dramatic and unambiguous as the infamous Tuskegee syphilis study.

In 1932, the U.S. Public Health Service designed and implemented a study to learn how syphilis, when left untreated, progresses. For subjects, the researchers used 600 impoverished African American sharecroppers from Georgia, many of whom were diagnosed with syphilis. The men were recruited with the promise that, in exchange for meals, free medical care and burial insurance, they would be treated for a condition the researchers called "bad blood." They were not informed about their real diagnoses and were given placebo treatments while researchers observed and recorded the progressions of their syphilis. In the 1940s, when penicillin was found to be successful in treating syphilis, researchers not only continued to conceal the men's diagnoses from them, but also withheld penicillin, even though the researchers knew the infected men could be cured by the drug. As a result, not only did many of the subjects die of the illness, but 40 of their wives were unknowingly infected, and 19 children were born with congenital syphilis. It was only when a whistleblower leaked the story to the press *in 1972* that the study was terminated. It must be noted that African American researchers at Tuskegee were, from the beginning, involved in the study, so that the betrayal of medical ethics, while directed by white researchers, was not limited to whites (https://en.wikipedia.org/wiki/Tuskegee_syphilis_experiment).

What must have been the effect on African Americans of reading or hearing the story of the Tuskegee study when it finally became public in 1972, and has that history relevance now, about 45 years since its revelation? One study (Katz et al., 2008, abstract) sheds some light on the question of the long-term impact of the story. Its findings indicate that, 35 years after the Tuskegee study was made public, African Americans were nearly four times as likely to have heard of it as were whites, and, interestingly, were more than twice as likely as whites to know that it was President Clinton who issued an apology for the study. Surprisingly, at least at first glance, Katz et al. also found that once all respondents, white and black, were told the story, African Americans were two to three times more willing to participate in biomedical research than were whites. The researchers surmise that because the information was newer and more shocking to whites, it had a greater immediate negative effect on their willingness to participate in such research than African Americans. Nevertheless the widespread knowledge among black Americans of the Tuskegee study and its disregard for the health and welfare, never mind dignity, of its subjects and their families suggests that the story has been passed on within black families and communities as a cautionary tale that continues to reside in the consciousnesses of today's African Americans, particularly when they are confronted with an ambiguous or less than satisfying experience with health care professionals. For African Americans, then, although the direct victims of the Tuskegee experiment were the 600 sharecroppers and their families, the psychological injury, once the story became known, was felt by black people throughout the country. The greater significance of President Clinton's apology for African Americans than for whites, as reflected in their higher likelihood of remembering it, suggests that President Clinton's attempt at reparation through public acknowledgment and apology for the injustice and inherent racism of the study's design and implementation were meaningful for the African American community as a whole. The importance of acknowledgment and apology will be discussed in greater detail in Chapter 8.

When Barbara began having medical symptoms that seemed to me to warrant attention, she began to report that her physician was brushing her off, preoccupied with making sure she was not just trying to get prescriptions for pain medications, when what Barbara really wanted was a diagnosis of her pains and appropriate treatment.[4] She often complained about feeling judged by her doctor, but laughingly brushed her feelings off, saying Dr. Z was "just bossy." After thus accepting this inadequate treatment for a while, she finally decided to find another doctor, this time an African American woman in whom she hoped she could have more confidence. But as time went on, it became clear to me that damage had been done by her first doctor, and her belief in the good intentions of physicians, even a black doctor, was gone. She was suspicious of the doctor's advice and rarely followed up on her recommendations.

One day Barbara was talking about her health problems and a recent appointment with Dr. Y, when it became clear to me that during her appointment with her doctor not only had Barbara's anxiety impeded her remembering clearly what had been said to her, but also she had failed to ask important questions—questions she and I had discussed in a session prior to the appointment. Hence she was no less in the dark about her medical condition than she had been before the appointment. Eventually, she sighed and said, "Because you're white, you think you're entitled to these explanations." I asked, "What about being black disqualifies you from having them?" She replied, "The world tells me I'm not entitled. I get that from my mom. She and her friends say, 'Doctors ain't interested in black people.'" As time went on and Barbara's condition worsened, she began to reveal to me her suspicions that her treating physicians were experimenting on her, and at times even voiced a belief that her health insurance company probably wanted her to die, so that they would no longer have to cover her care. While this highly intelligent woman seemed to be in the process of cognitive deterioration of organic etiology, the idea of being an involuntary and unwitting subject of medical experimentation was readily available in her menu of possibilities.

Marion, Alabama, is a city of fewer than 3,600 people, of whom approximately 63 percent are African American. Between January 2014 and January 2016, it suffered an outbreak of tuberculosis "so severe that it posted an incidence rate about 100 times greater than the state's and worse than in many developing countries" (Blinder, 2016, p. A9). Authorities blamed the dramatic incidence of the contagious disease on the reluctance of those affected to respond to public health officials, often explaining, "I don't want nobody knowing my business." Some, however, linked their reluctance to the Tuskegee experiment. According to Blinder, many said "they knew little about what happened in Tuskegee, but they often said their wariness of medical professionals had been passed on through generations" (p. A14). They may not have known the details of the story, but, by their reactions of "wariness of medical professionals," they knew something bad had been done to African Americans by medical professionals at Tuskegee, bad enough to warrant avoiding doctors at all costs.

Loretta consulted with me one session about a friend who appeared to be suffering from hallucinations and paranoia while struggling to hold onto her job. In instances when a desperate relative managed to drag her to see a psychiatrist in her health plan, the friend would inevitably refuse to accept the doctor's prescriptions for medication, not uncommon behavior seen with people suffering from psychosis. Loretta told me with a sad sigh, "Even when she was well, she's always believed all medication is a white man's drug, designed to destroy us. She won't even take her blood pressure pills." In *The Immortal Life of Henrietta Lacks* (2010/2011), Rebecca Skloot recounts the history of a young African American wife, mother, and tobacco farmer, dying of cancer in the early 1950s. Her doctors at Johns Hopkins decided to harvest her cancer cells for research purposes, a decision that was to have far-reaching consequences. Ms. Lacks was never informed of either the removal or the fate of her cells. Nor did she give consent to be part of the research. But perhaps most disturbing was the fact that, in the decades following her death, Ms. Lacks' cells, which the researchers named "Hela cells" after the first two letters of her names, traveled to laboratories worldwide and became one of the most important tools of twentieth-century medical research—all while her children and grandchildren struggled with poverty and inadequate health care, oblivious to the ongoing story of their late mother's invaluable contribution. In the early 1970s, researchers contacted Ms. Lacks' children to ask for blood samples—again, without revealing their reasons for doing so. At that time, the history of the Tuskegee study had recently appeared in *Jet* magazine, so that when contacted for the blood sample, Ms. Lacks' daughter, Deborah, was frightened. Furthermore, she had heard "the stories about [Johns] Hopkins snatching black people for research," and "started wondering if instead of testing the Lacks children for cancer, the researchers were actually injecting them with the same bad blood that had killed their mother" (p. 186).

The children of Henrietta Lacks, Loretta's psychotic friend, the citizens of Marion, Alabama, and Barbara demonstrate the damage done to black Americans by generations of ill-treatment, deception, and/or exploitation of African Americans by the medical profession. This historically bad relationship with the health care system generates in many African Americans significant anxiety when it comes to encountering health care professionals, sometimes preventing them from taking advantage of medical treatment that is available to them, and in the case of Marion, possibly endangering a whole community. A few years ago, a young African American girl appeared to have died following a routine tonsillectomy at a locally renowned children's hospital in Oakland. Although the doctors declared her brain-dead and advocated ending the life support systems, the child's parents insisted she was still alive and sued to have the life supports maintained. Tracy mentioned the case one session: "Like the girl on TV. Who knows if she's really dead? My experience with the doctors was they lied to me. I don't trust those doctors." Loretta's friend's fear of the "white man's drug" left her afraid of her blood pressure medication, a fear that could be life-threatening. Although she may be an extreme case, particularly given her mental illness, I believe she is reflective of a worry that may form a latent layer of expectation for many other African Americans, an expectation that can be especially stimulated when encountering doctors with their own racialized expectations of their African American patients and who unreflectively enact microaggressions in response to those expectations. While I cannot know the full story of Dr. Z's interactions with Barbara, it is possible that he had stereotyped her as prone to drug abuse because she was a black woman. It should be no surprise, then, that wariness of the medical profession affects how many African Americans approach mental health practitioners.

Skepticism about psychotherapists places those African Americans who need mental health services in the uncomfortable position of needing to figure out how to negotiate their worries. The Thompson et al. study to which I alluded earlier recorded a reluctance in black men and women "to trust professions not active in the African American community and activities directed toward community well-being" (2004, p. 33), which may reflect a strategy of selecting practitioners whom they hopefully predict will approach their black patients with reduced negative bias. Participants in this study also talked of attempts to assess whether to trust a therapist by looking for "subtle cues," such as the type of reading material available in the waiting room, "diversity of art," presence of minorities working for the therapist or the clinic, and, when in session, the therapist's "reactions to financial, legal, employment, and discrimination issues" (p. 25). Taken together, this feedback indicates that before making themselves vulnerable to the intimacy of the psychotherapeutic relationship, these potential clients were looking for assurance that their prospective therapists had a minimal level of familiarity with African Americans and the challenges they face in their daily lives, and had demonstrated a will to combat internalized racism. One African American psychologist with whom I spoke told of his own method of assessing white psychotherapists with whom he was considering entering treatment: "I look for a comment that lets me know he is getting a sense of my narrative and if he can make some feeling statement about the conflicts." Like detectives worthy of Sherlock Holmes, African American psychotherapy clients watch for the subtlest visual and verbal clues to decide not only whether to begin treatment with a white therapist, but perhaps more critically, how open they feel they can be with that therapist.

In a rare moment quite late in her treatment, Althea revealed her own early expectations of working with me. She was talking about the declining membership in her all-black church, and I responded somehow in a way that had resonated with her. She had concurred and said, "You know, sometimes I almost forget you're not a black therapist. I never expected to be so comfortable with you. It wasn't that it was *un*-comfortable, but I didn't think you'd understand." I replied: "That I'd not be able to see you as an individual with your own stories?" Althea: "Yes! Given time, everybody's a human being, underlying it all, with so many emotions common to all humans, so that I guess it's possible. But I worried about how would you deal with a person who couldn't deal with not feeling superior? If I were working with a white person—it's true—I want to feel I'm better than somebody who'd stoop to do anything for a dollar bill. In my day there were white girls who wanted to seem superior. They wouldn't dare hold a conversation with you, and would look right through you. Very snooty." Before discussing this exchange, some history is important. Prior to beginning to work with me, Althea had had a very positive therapeutic relationship with another white therapist, an older man who had died suddenly, necessitating her transfer to a new therapist, me. In talking about the meaning of his loss during the first months of our work together, she told me: "It was really terrible. I don't like or trust men much, so it surprised me that we hit it off. But he let me know he'd experienced hard times. Told me he was Jewish and had suffered discrimination, and he wasn't ashamed to say it. I saw that not all white men have had the best lives, so it made me trust him."

These two sets of comments are telling when considering both content and the stage of our relationship. In the material about her former therapist, when we were in the opening stages of the therapy, she opened by talking about her therapist's sex as a potential barrier, yet only later did she proceed to refer to his past suffering based on his ethnic identity, leading her to conclude that "not all white men have had the best lives." In other words, she moved from introducing the less loaded gender gap between them to noting their racial difference, which she diffused and *defused* into a difference in ethnic identity. Seeing him as having "suffered discrimination" due to his ethnicity, she was able to minimize the racial divide between them, thereby, she maintains, enabling her to trust him. At the time of the comments about her expectations of me, the emphasis was on her surprise that I could understand her feelings as they related to her identity as an African American woman and church-goer. However, her immediate association to my unexpected ability to understand her was to her expectation that as a white woman I would need to feel superior to her, as did the "snooty" white girls of her day. This earlier belief that I would need to see her as inferior to me conformed to a role she had been accustomed to fulfill as what she assessed to be a condition of employment. Of course, the background to these expressions of racial aspects of her transference are complicated, as they pertain to her direct experiences with the white world, but are deeply rooted in and routed through her problematic relationship with her very critical mother; that is, her mother's "snooty" attitude to her daughter, which maintained a tight grip on Althea, despite her conscious wishes to the contrary.

Over the years of our work together, then, something happened between us that enabled Althea to open up about her feelings about me, and particularly about her feelings about our racial difference. In reflecting on the cues and criteria for trust expressed by the research group participants and their relevance to Althea's relationship with me, I am aware that in some ways she was able to be satisfied that I was non-racist enough to be open to her experience as she lived and expressed it. This shift was made possible in part by the passage of time and the routine of our weekly sessions. But I believe that the emergence of Althea's confidence that she could talk about and struggle with issues of race with me grew out of two things I brought to the table besides my clinical training: history and politics. I grew up with the Civil Rights Movement and maintained an interest in the evolving politics of African American struggles. By my reactions to her initially tentative references to the challenges of trying to live as a black woman and my familiarity with African American history and current events, Althea gradually discovered that I was comfortable with, and had feelings about, hearing her story. Once able to talk about her struggles with racism, Althea began to open up about another, perhaps more sensitive, area of her racism-infused experience.

One participant in the Thompson et al. study volunteered that she avoided talking to her therapist about "diversity" and "internalized racism" *among* African Americans. "We have the whole thing about shades," she explained, "and I don't think a White person could really comprehend what I was talking about" (2004, p. 24). McDonald (2006), in describing her work with an African American woman, recounts that the subject of race and racism within the family based on skin tone emerged only "gradually" as Mrs. T developed trust in the therapist to provide help in other areas of her life (pp. 93–116). In my own experience, it was only after being comfortable with my willingness to validate her encounters with racism of non-African Americans that Althea was able to open up about "the whole thing about shades," a topic that was discussed in more detail in Chapter 4.

While Althea had described the bond she had formed with her former therapist as based originally on his revelation of suffering discrimination as a Jew, Loretta had a slightly different response to her therapist. Apparently assuming, correctly, that I was Jewish (something Althea never mentioned or perhaps had not realized), she remarked in one session three years into her treatment: "When I come here and look at you, and you know what people have gone through, the holocaust, lots of holocausts, it makes it easier for me to deal with . . ." She trails off, and I ask where her thoughts went. She talks about war: "How come people could be so cruel and turn a blind eye to cruelty? What we have to do to survive!" I ask her, "Any thoughts about people turning blind eyes?" Loretta: (after a pause) "Shame, guilt, fear. Fear first. It seems my world is fear-based." Here Loretta, like Althea, takes comfort in her therapist's identity as one of a persecuted ethnic group; but for Loretta, the connection is based on identification with Jewish victims of the Holocaust. In her mind, perhaps my association with victims of Nazi brutality would enable me to understand her experiences of the cruelty of racial oppression as an African American woman.

Whereas Althea bonded with her former therapist through experiences of discrimination, Loretta's connections seems to be with a more dangerous and violent experience of persecution and war, representing the total breakdown of a socially constructed container. In fact, Loretta's life at home growing up was more immediately dangerous to her bodily integrity than was Althea's, as she was subjected to severe, ongoing sexual and physical abuse, and an honored family matriarch turned a blind eye. The traumas of war and Holocaust resonate with her own inner landscape, and her hope was that I could relate to the traumatized child inside her, as well as to the vulnerable African American woman she had become. Althea's childhood, by her account, was imbued with discrimination against her based on her dark color, both in her outside environment and within the family. Loretta did not apparently need to hear confirmation from me of my experience as a Jew to establish, at least in part, a positive transference to me based on her presumption. However, to put Loretta's relationship to me in perspective and to introduce another type of response to the challenge of dealing with a white therapist, in her third session she talked about women in her life who seemed unpredictable and unreliable, much like her outwardly successful but drug-addicted mother. I suggested, "Maybe you're trying to see if you can trust me." She replied, "Oh, I trust you. You have experience. And," she added, "you *have* to trust somebody." Or, as an African American psychotherapist I interviewed put it, "I ignored things in order to continue to enhance the therapist. We all want a good parent."

"A surprising majority of participants," according to the Thompson et al. study, "noted the historical expectation that life would be difficult and that African Americans as a cultural group could and would cope with all adversity," an expectation that tended to "inhibit help-seeking behaviors." This expectation was linked to another "surprising consensus" within the focus groups: that family concerns be resolved within the family (2004, p. 22). Bennett (2006) writes that, when he embarked on a graduate school course to become a psychologist, friends and family were shocked and puzzled by his decision: "They were coming from a tradition within certain segments of the African American community in which you do not air your dirty laundry in public[;] nor do you go to a stranger to consult about family issues," as opposed to a "trusted family member or a clergy person." Others wondered "how I could be a member of a system that oppressed African Americans and others" (p. 61). Holmes (1992) speculates that "a black patient may feel like a traitor for seeing a white therapist." But she looks a little deeper into why that might be so. "'Feeling like a traitor,'" she writes, "may represent the black patient's guilty feelings for having trespassed other boundaries for which the analyst's 'whiteness' is symbolic" (p. 9).

Subjects in Thompson et al. also expressed worries that white therapists would be influenced by racial stereotypes (2004, p. 25). In an article about microaggressions, Sue et al. (2007) confirm what seems obvious: that "the therapeutic alliance is likely to be weakened or terminated when clients of color perceive White therapists as biased, prejudiced, or unlikely to understand them as racial/cultural beings" (p. 280). Thompson et al. made this further observation: "Men and lower income participants were more likely to assert that race mattered," when it came to considering psychotherapy and psychotherapists (2004, p. 24). While the authors do not offer interpretations of these correlations, we can surmise that African American men of all classes, and poorer African Americans in general, tend to encounter more open expressions of white racism in their daily lives than do black middle-class or wealthy women whose resources and education may provide some added cushion from the kinds of direct expressions of racism that confront poor and African American males. When it comes to seeking psychotherapeutic treatment, who would want to open up to a therapist only to discover that he or she harbors racist attitudes?

The dangers of speaking honestly about intense feelings to a non-black psychotherapist can be real. Participants in the Thompson et al. study expressed the belief that psychologists were more likely to see African Americans as "crazy," and to pathologize their emotional expressiveness (2004, p. 23). Disturbingly, this belief, it turns out, is well founded and was confirmed by the Surgeon General's report: "African Americans are more likely to be incorrectly diagnosed than white Americans" (Office of the Surgeon General et al., 2001, Chapter 3). Black clients tended to be incorrectly diagnosed with schizophrenia, and incorrectly not diagnosed with affect disorders. In other words, as was voiced by the focus group members, African Americans were more likely to be seen as "crazy" when they were not, and less likely to be seen as suffering from, for instance, major depression, when they actually were. Again, according to the Surgeon General, a 2000 study found that both black and white clinicians applied different decision rules in diagnosing African American and white patients, resulting in more diagnoses of schizophrenia in the former group than in the latter. Correspondingly, African Americans who presented at psychiatric emergency rooms and were diagnosed with schizophrenia were more likely to be prescribed "both more and higher doses of oral and injectable antipsychotic medications" than were whites, this despite longstanding knowledge that African Americans tend to have higher sensitivity to some of these medications due to metabolic differences. Conversely, another 2000 study cited in the Surgeon General's report found that 27 percent of African Americans were prescribed antidepressants when their depression was first diagnosed, compared with 44 percent of white patients. Furthermore African Americans were less likely to be given SSRIs, then newer and more effective, than were white patients (Chapter 3). Another study in the report provides further bad news: "African American youth were four times more likely than whites to be physically restrained after acting in similarly aggressive ways" (Chapter 2).

Dwayne, an intelligent but highly anxious middle-aged African American man whom I have seen intermittently for a few years, was suffering from posttraumatic stress disorder as a result of having witnessed the accidental death of a co-worker under circumstances he felt were caused by negligence of their employer. He was having conflicts with supervisors at work, almost exclusively about safety issues, found himself drinking too much, and eventually had taken himself to a psychotherapist covered by his health plan. When Dwayne told the therapist of his frustration with his workplace, and said that there were times he felt so angry at a supervisor he "felt like smashing the guy," the therapist immediately heard the statement as a real threat and, without further exploration of the comment, had Dwayne transported to a psychiatric facility for an involuntary 72-hour evaluation. This experience, itself, was traumatizing. When Dwayne came to see me, referred by a friend, a month or so later, he cried, "I was just using that as an expression to say how mad I was! Don't people always say things like that, and not mean they plan to *do* it?" His question seemed rhetorical but also reflective of his genuine bewilderment at what had happened. My suspicion, although we did not discuss this together, is that an angry black man seemed dangerous to the white therapist in a way that he might not have seemed had he been Euro-American, even using the exact same words with similar affect.

Similarly, we remember Tracy's experience at the chronic pain management program. When she drew, among other images, a gun she was immediately expelled from the program on the basis of her "violent" drawing. The experience represented an added trauma to her reservoir of pain, and, like Dwayne, she expressed frustration and bewilderment at how she was treated. Again, would such a drawing done by a white, middle-class woman at this primarily white facility have generated the same response? I suspect not. Experiences such as these are embedded in the memories not only of the clients themselves, but also of their friends and family as they recount their stories, deepening community mistrust of psychotherapists.

One of the difficulties faced by white therapists wanting to learn how their African American patients are experiencing the biracial nature of the relationship is the reality that patients do not always report everything that they think, particularly thoughts about their therapists. It appears that for African Americans self-censorship may be even more prevalent. Focus group participants said that they had avoided discussing with their therapists problems they encountered with racism, financial insecurity, and "exposure to community trauma," citing "fears therapists would not understand" (Thompson et al., 2004, p. 24). Althea's expectation that I would not understand things about her related to race is congruent with this finding, and I have found that almost every African American patient with whom I have worked over the years has been reticent in identifying conflictual encounters as racially driven, even when they clearly are. As I have described elsewhere, it has usually required my naming of the situation initially for the patient to acknowledge to me a problem with racism in her or his life. Even when later probed about their apparent shyness in uttering the word "racism," they have generally been hesitant to voice their concerns about doing so. One African American therapist, Dr. A, discussed this phenomenon at some length, having noticed himself measuring what and how much of his experience he could safely reveal to his white therapist. "Whites can only tolerate so much before you'll say something very upsetting," he remarked. He added, "Many black people feel that one thing that comes with [white] privilege is not being used to disturbing conversations."

What is this "upsetting" and "disturbing" material to which Dr. A is referring? He recounts an experience with a white therapist: "I wondered how much history will be allowed to be expressed in the hour. Most experiences that African Americans have are not tolerated as topics for therapy. In my experience there's never been a conversation about the terror of slavery." He suggests that, when African Americans honestly talk of racism and complain about its impact on their lives and the life of their community, whites listening will feel guilt or shame and, in that discomfort, they will fall into any one of a number of attitudes—defensiveness, anger, remorse—any of which will rebound negatively on the patient and his or her therapy. He reminded me that some therapy patients feel a need to protect their therapists, much like their compulsion to protect fragile parents, in order to ensure that they (therapists and parents) can assume their roles of caring for their patients/children. But, he states, this dynamic "is amplified with blacks." He continues, "Blacks are often measuring whites, to see how much they can take and not feel bad. We're not supposed to make whites uncomfortable, so we end up taking care of the therapist."

Sometimes, despite the black patient's efforts to protect the therapeutic alliance, a troubling interaction around race may erupt, possibly without the therapist's awareness. In Sue et al.'s view, because of the inherent power differential in the therapy/client relationship, "clients may be less likely to confront their therapists and more likely to question their own perceptions in the event of a microaggression" (2007, p. 281).

According to Jackson (2000), many African Americans also do not bring up racial trauma with their psychotherapists because "the experience of racism is often so implicit that one is not completely sure whether it is racism or not" (p. 8). That uncertainty in the face of a possibly skeptical white therapist could make speaking of racial trauma too risky. How could someone feel comfortable in a treatment with a therapist who cannot come to terms with the reality of racism and its traumatic effects in people's lives? Daniel (2000) also describes how African American women in therapy may censor themselves when it comes to disclosing memories of any trauma, either out of a wish to protect their white therapists from the discomfort of anger, guilt, or shame, or out of concern not to reinforce white negative stereotypes of African Americans, if the trauma involves abuse perpetrated by another African American (p. 129). Thus it is not surprising that Thompson et al. found that their research subjects were more comfortable "when therapists did not appear overwhelmed by their [patients'] problems and issues" and were able to show "genuine concern" and "ask appropriate questions" (p. 23).

What is suggested by these findings is the African American patient's worry of eliciting from his or her white therapist a comment or remark that will reveal the therapist's insensitivity to the reality of racism—a form of racism, itself—thereby shattering the therapeutic relationship. Thus, in a field dominated by non-black practitioners, avoiding the subject may be the price a client pays for obtaining psychotherapeutic help. "The prize," said Dr. A, "is worth what you have to put up with."

Whiteness

Psychotherapy is a treatment modality, but it is also, of course, a relationship; hence there is no such thing as a transference without a countertransference. The therapist who is not African American also brings his or her own internalized version of America's racial pathology to a first session, particularly one with a black client. The therapist's whiteness, itself, is a presence. If there is no such thing as a single, definable African American identity, whiteness is no less diverse. We saw earlier how, for instance, for Althea and Loretta their white therapists were "white, but Jewish," introducing a particular nuance to their respective transferences. I am also aware that, in talking about whiteness, I am participating in the racial compartmentalization that plagues us, because there are many therapists who are Asian American, Latina or Latino, or biracial. Unfortunately, much of the literature focuses on the black/white binary, and my experience is limited by my own racial identity.

So what is whiteness? To Miller and Josephs (2009), whiteness works "as a kind of forbidden secret identity that may exist outside the conscious awareness of the people who possess it" (p. 102). For many Euro-Americans, the word generates unease, as the only context in which the category of white exists is in relation to people of color, and that relationship is defined by the oppression of people of color by whites. Leary (1997) believes that this association of white identity with white supremacy prompts white Americans to hide from the concept, thereby losing the opportunity to explore this aspect of their identities (p. 180). Truth be told, the only people who proudly assert their whiteness are white supremacists, so reflecting on one's white identity can sound like a toxic enterprise. Leary writes elsewhere (1995) that psychodynamic authors, at least at the time of her article, seemed to assume that "race and ethnicity . . . were qualities possessed *only* by people of color and ignore the fact that White patients also have a race and an ethnicity" (p. 131; original emphasis).

That whites "also have a race and ethnicity" is a reminder that those two words, as used in our historical moment, are not synonymous. American whites may be very well aware of their individual ethnicities, such as Irish American, or the example discussed above of the Jewish therapists. It is their/our identities as white people that remain hidden in plain sight. At the heart of white identity is a factor that can often remain unacknowledged and disavowed by those who possess it, but that is rarely much of a mystery to those who do not: that of white privilege. Miller and Josephs take up this gap in white consciousness to push deeper into the notion of whiteness and the denial of those who possess it, pointing out that "the analysis of white racial identity seldom goes beyond the touchy issue of white racism into the analysis of white privilege and the deeper dread of losing it" (2009, p. 103).

Some weeks following the exchange I described earlier in this chapter, Barbara reported to me that a physician had finally expressed concern about her worrisome symptoms and wanted her to follow up with her primary care doctor. She seemed ambivalent about doing so, expressing doubt that her doctor would take action. Barbara's health, as is probably evident by now, had me distressed and worried. Frustrated, I reminded her, "You are entitled to the same top-quality medical care as everyone else in that waiting room." Barbara, smiling, replied, "You make good points, and you're usually right, but white lady expectations are not the same as black lady expectations." I asked, "Say a little more." Barbara laughed and said, "You talk about medical conditions that are 'preventable, treatable, or curable.'" I asked about her laugh. Barbara said, "You say, 'I expect,' and I say, 'I hope.'" I suggested "Well then, maybe it's a good thing that I'm bringing you my white lady expectations." Barbara nodded: "Yes, it is. I'm fired up now, and will call my doctor." This exchange demonstrates the interaction between my unquestioned acceptance of privilege, my "white lady expectations," and Barbara's astute awareness of that privilege. She is clear both in this session and the one described earlier that she needs to remind me of my entitlement in order for us to work together to sort out her thoughts and feelings about her health care.

Made aware of my entitlement, I instantly recognize its truth. On a given day, I am probably more aware of my age or my clothing as they define my presence in the world than I am of my whiteness—which seems strange, given the respective impact of each on my life. My obliviousness is a testimony to the depth of that privilege. Like most people, I grapple with idiosyncratic questions about my place in the world and my right to expect or demand what I want of that world. These insecurities can be annoying and self-limiting, to be sure; but I am mostly confident that my doubts are internal, and that within reason I can "pass" for a woman who is entitled to much of what society has to offer, and that my skin color renders me neutral in the eyes of the police, store clerks, physicians, and strangers on the street—so confident, in fact, that the thought of my color does not even enter my calculus, or evolve into a conscious thought. Aside from encounters I have described in my consulting room, the one exception to this state of unawareness is that I live in a neighborhood and city with a significant, though dwindling, African American population, so that I am reminded in daily interactions that despite our friendly smiles at the farmers' market or the local cafe, or waiting for the light to change, I know there is a gap. Because I am white, I am aware that I am free to go about my life with little fear that someone will say something demeaning to me, or that a store clerk will eye me with suspicion, or that a stranger will frown at my exuberant child skipping down the street, or recoil in angry fear at my teenage son and his buddies in their jeans and hoodies as they wander, seemingly aimlessly, down the street for slices of pizza. Thus it is mainly when I am confronted with the experience of a person of color in my environment that I awaken to my racial identity. Barbara's analysis of our differing positions is as unarguable as it is ugly. She and I are sharing geographic space, language, and nationality, but we are actually living in two different countries.

My experience, I assume, is not very different from that of other Caucasians who make their careers as psychotherapists. We are parts of an emotionally intense and dysfunctional national relationship, and when we provide treatment to African American clients we inevitably carry into our work our socially white selves. Leary (1997) is probably correct when she writes that it is "inevitable that all of us—patients and analysts—will have racial thoughts and feelings that are libidinally and aggressively tinged" (pp. 167–168). Thus it becomes the responsibility of the white therapist to become on close terms with his or her particular relationship to American "whiteness."

J. Bonovitz (2001), in describing her work as a white analyst with African American patients, urges fellow white analysts to try to understand the role of "race in everyday life." She writes that this effort "is not an easy undertaking and we cannot expect to come through the struggle with our narcissism unscathed" (p. 402). Straker (2004), a psychoanalyst who emigrated from apartheid-era South Africa, writes that becoming aware of her automatic benefit from being white "was what bothered me most; it was a feeling that carried with it shame and racial melancholia" (p. 420). If Bonovitz refers to the assaults to our narcissism inherent in self-examination, Straker, with admirable honesty, gives a personal example. She was a member of an anti-apartheid group of activists that "would give enormous energy and time to taking on minority-group individuals as our special projects and then subtly and unconsciously expect them to affirm us, feeling affronted when they did not." She interprets this need for affirmation as representative of the group's "unconscious intention to deny and cover up our own powerlessness concerning our government's enactment of values of exclusion and inequality." As she further points out, this dynamic between white "helper" and black "help-ee" risks transforming the minority person into a fetish, an "object to empower the white self in its group identification, in order to cover up its lack." Put differently, Straker writes, "'I am a good white; therefore all whites are not bad,' and whiteness as an ideal can be preserved" (p. 416).

What is this "whiteness as an ideal" to which Straker refers? Michael Rogin (1996) posited that American "whiteness" was invented in the context of the influx of European immigrants between the 1840s and the 1920s, enabling the newcomers to become Americans by virtue of their difference from being black and slaves. "History," he writes, "not biology, distinguishes ethnicity from race, making the former groups (in American usage) distinctive but assimilable, walling off the latter, legally, socially, and ideologically, to benefit those within the magic circle and protect the national body from contamination" (p. 12). Cheng (2001) affirms Rogin's contention: "Racialization in America may be said to operate through the institutional process of producing a dominant, standard, white national ideal, which is sustained by the exclusion-yet-retention of racialized others" (p. 10). What makes the contributions of Rogin and Cheng particularly important to our understanding of whiteness is that both emphasize that the development of "whiteness" was not solely an exclusionary process, but instead one that is a more conflicted and paradoxical arrangement of "exclusion-yet-retention." Cheng names this model for understanding "the fragility and bravado that haunt American national integrity," "racial melancholia" (p. xi).

"Like melancholia," Cheng writes, "racism is hardly ever a clear rejection of the other" (2001, p. 12). In melancholia, the bereaved incorporates into the ego the lost object, typically an object that is both hated and needed, or even loved; thus "racial melancholia" is an apt term. Cheng cites Julia Stern from the latter's 1997 work on novels of the American Federalist period, in which she describes the setting of the stage for this tragic dynamic. She says of the early nation's "noncitizens—women, the poor, Native Americans, African Americans, and aliens," that they were "prematurely interred beneath the great national edifice whose erection they actually enable," and who "provide an unquiet platform for the construction of republican privilege, disturbing the Federal monolith in powerful ways" (p. 13). This structure creates "internally fraught institutions not because they have eliminated the other but because they need the very thing they hate or fear" (p. 12). Whiteness in America, then, demands of itself a continual confrontation with "ghosts it can neither emit nor swallow," racial others whom it prefers remain invisible (p. 133). This unconscious ambivalence of whites towards the others whom they both "need" and "hate or fear" thus forces on the African American objects of that ambivalence to contend with these confused and confusing projections.

What makes this melancholic structure so difficult for whites—its pitfalls for nonwhites are obvious—is that "America is *founded* on the very ideals of freedom and liberty whose betrayals have been repeatedly covered over" (p. 10; original emphasis), as it fails to "live up to its own democratic and humanitarian ideals" (Straker, 2004, p. 409). Furthermore, despite indisputable privilege, few white people feel themselves to be genuinely powerful in the world. Straker warns that "the shock of this confrontation with de-idealized and castrated Whiteness" can engender a temptation to heal the wound of this loss by "using the minority group itself as a fetish," as one tries to separate from white identity, while in the process resorting to what amounts to "subtly enacted racism" (p. 415). The contradictions are all the greater, I suspect, for us white psychotherapists, who believe ourselves to be part of the helping professions, involved in clinics, professional associations, mental health programs, and insurance companies that are part of the dominant, white structure, yet want to be proud of our identities as healers, professional do-gooders.

Straker relates how her own response of the "shame" of being associated with de-idealized whiteness "involved going beyond ideals of equality in regard to the Other and casting the Other as superior," thereby creating an "idealized but stereotyped" view that denigrated the Other by homogenizing all blacks, and thus denying them their individuality and subjectivity (2004, p. 419). Here Straker is pointing to a particularly problematic vulnerability to which a consciously well-intended, anti-racist white person living in a white-dominated society may succumb. Furthermore, the paradox of this "solution" to the problem of "castrated Whiteness" is that by granting idealized status to the African American Other, one is automatically asserting dominant status by wielding the power to define and bestow elevated status. This process enables a person to have it all: "I am a good person. I am not a hostile racist. And I still have power." As Miller and Josephs suggest, "it is difficult to admit to sadistic/narcissistic pleasure in wishing to become and remain a member of a superior ruling class" (2009, p. 103); yet unexamined, these subtle forms of anti-racist racism may pose a significant threat to a biracial psychotherapeutic treatment, particularly one involving a white therapist and an African American client.

The hard truth is that in this country racism is unavoidable. To survive it demands heroic efforts on the part of its identified objects. To subvert its destructive power requires constant and conscious effort on the part of its beneficiaries, including tackling the kinds of projections and attitudes that lie beneath the surface of their/our awareness. Resistance to undertaking that task can be recognized in a tendency of some whites to brush off any idea that race could play a part in their relationships with people of color. These are people who describe themselves as color-blind. Leary (1997) writes about biracial treatment from the point of view of the African American therapist treating white patients and comments on the wish to dismiss the likelihood of race as a factor in transference:

> ... my experience has been that white patients respond nearly universally by saying the [racial] difference is "not a problem," although this is usually then followed by an implicit statement of exactly the problem that the patient expects will complicate the treatment, namely, the fear of saying something that would be perceived as racist or discriminatory.
> (Leary, 1997, p. 167)

This same unconscious conflict can occur when the Euro-American is the therapist in the biracial relationship as well.

Burkard and Knox (2004) decided to test the effects on the therapeutic relationship of the kind of denial Leary is describing. In their study on "therapist color-blindness," they surveyed 247 practicing psychologists and found "therapists' color-blindness (minimal awareness of racial issues) impedes their ability to empathize with clients, which may then lead to decreased sensitivity to cultural issues" (p. 16). Awareness of racial issues, conversely, was positively correlated to empathy. Interestingly, they also found that those therapists with this greater level of awareness of racial issues were more empathic towards all of their clients. Perhaps, speculate the authors, such therapists "may have a greater range of empathy, resulting in sensitivity to a wide range of client diversity, including racial-cultural diversity" (p. 17). Sue et al. (2007) also take on what can only be termed the "myth of color-blindness," writing that a "failure to acknowledge the significance of racism within and outside of the therapy session contributes to the breakdown of the alliance between therapist and client" (p. 281). They write that "color blind statements . . . may leave the client feeling misunderstood, negated, invalidated, and unimportant (especially if racial identity is important to the client)." They reject the idea that the therapist is "*capable* of not seeing race" and believe that a therapist who takes the color-blind stance imposes "a definition of racial reality on the client" (p. 281; original emphasis), a definition that distorts and mischaracterizes that racial reality and the client's experience.

One area of differentiation between the "color-blind" therapists and those who rated low on color-blindness concerned the attribution of responsibility of the client for solving problems. Not surprisingly, those who rated high on color-blindness—that is, those operating with a higher level of denial of the importance of race as a factor in relationships—placed greater responsibility on African American clients for their life problems than did those therapists who were less color-blind, while no difference was observed regarding European American patients (Sue et al., 2007, p. 18). The implications for this finding are important. Those psychotherapists who assert that race has no impact on their thoughts and attitudes towards people are likely to resist allowing themselves to acknowledge the burdens racism directly or indirectly imposes on their African American patients. African American patients of such clinicians may intuitively refrain from discussing problems in their lives, particularly those involving racism or racial conflict, sensing they will not be understood by their therapists. If they do bring up these problems, they run the risk of being confused and disappointed by their therapists' failure to demonstrate empathy for them. Instead of validation of their experiences, what they may hear are subtle suggestions that the blame for misfortune must lie with them. As we learned above, the African American therapy patients in the Thompson et al. study considered the therapist's "reactions to financial, legal, employment, and discrimination issues" (2004, p. 25) as important indicators in assessing whether to continue treatment. Many prospective black clients would consciously or even unconsciously avoid presenting such material in order to preserve the therapy relationship, knowing that discovering the therapist's lack of sensitivity would make continuing difficult, if not impossible.

The Question

One of the first questions that arises when discussing biracial psychotherapy is whether or not the therapist should introduce the topic of the racial difference between patient and therapist. My colleague Dr. A, speaking of his experiences as an African American client in treatment with a white psychologist, surprised me when he said that his therapist's question to him, "'How do you feel working with a white therapist?' just amplified the therapist's discomfort. It closed it down for me." When Dr. A told me this, I squirmed in my chair, and did not confess that not only have I posed that question at times, but, more disturbing to me, I had never considered what doing so might have conveyed. On consideration, it is likely that the question does, at times, arise out of a therapist's worry about how he or she is being experienced as a white person, more than in response to the individual patient and a particular moment in the treatment. Still, despite the clarity of Dr. A's position on that particular intervention, decisions about if, how, or when a white therapist should initiate discussion about race, racism, and racial difference are not that easy to make. Psychodynamic treatment should never be formulaic, and questions of technique regarding the subject at hand are no exception. What distinguishes therapist/client interactions about race from those involving other material that emerges in a given session is their uniquely heavy load of historical and racialized projections and identifications. For the therapist, realization of having made a misstep about race can feel more distressing than other problematic interventions, since it not only threatens a therapist's wish to be helpful and successful as a therapist, but also attacks the therapist's aspirations to be a decent person. Nevertheless, any psychotherapy is best served by relying on the fundamentals of psychoanalytically oriented treatment, a modality that rests upon curiosity about and respect for the client's individual inner world of meanings.

In fact, among the many topics touched upon by the Thompson et al. (2004) focus groups was the question of whether the white therapist should raise the topic of race with an African American patient. As if to prove how unsuitable prescriptive formulaic interventions are for dynamic treatment, the responses of the group members were perfectly inconsistent. Their positions broke down roughly into three groups. About one-third felt that therapists who bring up the topic of race reveal their "racism and discomfort." Another third said they would be "relieved and could speak honestly" were their therapists to raise the issue. The rest were "neutral" and said they felt it was unlikely "such a conversation would affect the course of therapy" (p. 24). One way to read these results is to realize that for about two-thirds of 201 African American subjects it would mean *something* for their therapist to raise the issue of race, but that there was no consensus on what that meaning would be.

A 2003 study by Knox et al. (2003) interviewed twelve therapists specifically about "their experiences of raising and not raising the topic of race in cross-racial dyads," including both European American therapist/African American client, and vice versa (p. 467). The results were also ambiguous. Seven therapists (three African American, four European American) felt that choosing not to discuss race was the right thing to do as a way of being respectful of the client's primary concerns. Three therapists (all European American) felt the decision to not discuss race produced a negative outcome, with one reporting that she felt confused as to whether race was her issue or her client's (p. 475). Both black and white therapists in the study felt that addressing or discussing race improved the therapeutic relationship; yet three of the twelve (one African American, two European American) reported negative outcomes, blaming the discussions for either "creating distance" or "increasing client anxiety" (p. 475). Perhaps these negative outcomes correspond to the respondents in the Thompson et al. study who interpreted therapists' decisions to introduce the topic as evidence of racism or, at the least, discomfort, thereby "creating distance" and "increasing client anxiety." The wealth of variables in a given psychotherapy session makes coming to a resolution that can be generalized impossible. Nevertheless there is value to exploring the question.

The Knox et al. study, for instance, did report that some white therapists said they addressed race "when clients were struggling with personal versus community expectations" something that did not emerge with the African American therapists in the sample (2003, p. 478). This finding illuminates an aspect of the biracial therapy relationship in which it is possible that the therapist's position as someone who is outside the black community does not pose a significant limitation to the treatment, and may actually facilitate a client's need to confront and explore conflicts between "personal" desires and "community expectations." By "community expectations," I understand the therapists in the study to refer to the people who most matter in the client's daily life—family, to be sure, but also friendship groups, neighborhood acquaintances, fellow congregants at a church, workplace friends. These are people whose disapproval a person tries to avoid, not merely for career reasons, but because of something more significant to the person's sense of self. One example of the constructive introduction of race by a white therapist with a black client is the following situation: a college senior is struggling with her desire to pursue her education by going to graduate school, as encouraged to do by her peers, rather than returning to her community to work in accordance with her family's wishes. As reported in Knox et al., the therapist gently raised the topic in such a way as to allow the client to explore her conflicted feelings. The patient expressed gratitude to the therapist for this intervention (p. 476). A similar dynamic was at work when Althea and I processed her inhibitions about demanding good health care. By talking about the contrast between my "white lady expectations" and the attitudes of her mother and her mother's friends ("community expectations"), I believe she was able to appropriate for herself, at least for a moment, some of my distance from those expectations and with that new angle to vow to proceed in her own way. The sample of the Knox et al. study is small, but the fact that no African American therapists reported similar interactions suggests that perhaps another aspect of "community" is that it refers exclusively to fellow African Americans, so that the black therapist becomes absorbed into the patient's internalized community, simply by virtue of being African American. The patient may then become more reticent about raising material about separation from or conflict with "community expectations" to someone perceived to be a member of the community with which the patient is in conflict.

The clinical decision to raise the topic of race with an African American patient must obviously be just that: a decision that emerges from the work the client is doing with the therapist. This idea seems simple but the confusion about whiteness and race, as we have seen above, makes relying on the psychodynamic instincts of the well-trained psychotherapist on this topic undependable. Hamer (2002) suggests that resistance to "easy and meaningful discussion of race is the fact that race implicates matters of domination and subjugation or submission between people, of potential conflict, and of the sexual attractions and fears coded within ideas of race" (p. 1225). Therapists may remain silent if they fear that to raise awareness of race and racial difference could lead them into a minefield of the sort that Hamer describes. Yet because, as Hamer writes, "race can mean more than one thing and more than one thing *at once*" (p. 1221; original emphasis), the therapist must try to help the client sort through and narrate those racial meanings for the treatment to be of significant help. Furthermore, Leary (1997) warns, "Clinical silence about race may be perceived—with some justification—as a commentary on the analyst's effort to stay out of the fray, to opt out of the tension that comes with open talk about race" (p. 167).

As a psychologist trained in a psychodynamic model, I am always most comfortable responding to material the patient raises, and least comfortable introducing a subject that has not been spoken or named, only doing so when the elephant in the room becomes too distracting for me to ignore. And for all the many reasons described above, my reticence was initially all the more inhibitory regarding racism and my African American patients. Of course, there have been the rare times when a client has brought the topic of race and our racial difference up to me more or less directly. But more often than not, such material is heavily veiled, and my tentative openings have been required even to allow simple acknowledgment of the reality of racism in the client's life. In some cases, such as that of Tracy, once I do name the "elephant," her response is relatively easy and one of relief. However, this has not been the case with everyone.

Cheryl, a light-skinned African American woman, lives and works in a town with a minute African American population. For a period during her treatment she was preoccupied with her job as an administrative assistant. She complained of feeling she was being treated with disrespect by her supervisor and passed over for promotions, despite the fact that her work performance and pleasant demeanor were praised by many in her company. I would ask her if she had any theories about what was going on, but she drew a blank. After many months of her focus on this topic I asked if she ever wondered if there was a racial element to her bosses' treatment of her. She more or less ignored the question. However, a year later, after she had abruptly quit her job over her "stress" there, she told me about hearing from a former co-worker, who updated her on the scene at her old job. "An African American was offered my old job," she had learned, "and my old manager went to her and said, 'Every time we hire someone for this job they're black.' She didn't say anything because she really needs the job. Now I know why he didn't like me. I didn't want to think that maybe that's why. I'm just as white as you are." As a light-skinned African American woman, Cheryl hoped that she could dodge the negative effects of white racism, and fervently did not want to contemplate the possibility of it affecting her. Even when this story threw racism in her face, the subject was one she did not want to discuss with me, despite my implicit invitation to do so.

As Hamer had pointed out, race "can mean more than one thing *at once*," and, for Cheryl, her relationship to her African American identity clearly was complicated. On the one hand, she clearly identified as a black woman from an African American family. However, she was also the object of envy by some in the family for her light skin and felt real anguish at feeling rejected and unprotected by family members. Her African American ex-husband, she revealed over time, was currently dating only Asian women, would refer to Cheryl as "ghetto" when mad at her, and constantly disparaged their dark-skinned daughter. She is angry and hurt by his rejection of the child, whom she adores. Yet somehow, Cheryl had been drawn to this man enough to marry and have a child with him. My sense is that there are feelings about her racial identity that are tangling her up, but about which she is quite skittish. I hope to find ways to enable her to begin to use psychotherapy to work through this tangle of identifications. Until now, I have proceeded by letting her know that I am aware of racism and notice that race and color are of significance in her life. Daniel writes, "Therapists who collude consciously or unconsciously with their patients in avoiding disclosure of life experiences with racial content or who deny the existence of racism will impede the healing process" (2000, p. 127). This is an impediment I struggle to avoid.

Notes

1. Obviously, a psychotherapist who is African American is not guaranteed the trust of African American patients any more than any white therapist is bound to be trusted by any white client. In fact, there may be problematic issues specific to that match. Black psychiatrist and psychoanalyst D.R. Powell (2012) writes, "Questions about my own cultural competence as an African American—a sort of 'whose side are you on'—make these experiences distinctly different from other patient-physician relationships at its inception" (p. 79). As if to confirm Powell's report, Dr. A, the African American psychologist, revealed his own experience with a black analyst: "I kept wondering what he had given up to get there." This topic, addressed by African American psychotherapists, is an important area and one which I cannot begin to explore here, but would refer readers to writings by Holmes, Leary, Jackson, Vaughans, and others.
2. Between 2005 and 2013, 3.6 percent of psychologists practicing in the U.S. were African American (ACS Files, U.S. Census), whereas 13.2 percent of the U.S. population as a whole were black (U.S. Census Bureau QuickFacts).
3. This perception is interesting as it does not match the statistical reality. Since the 1980s, women have made up an increasing percentage of U.S. psychologists, so that by 2005, nearly 72 percent of new doctoral-level psychology students and 75 percent of masters-level psychology students were women (Cynkar, 2007, p. 46).
4. In a 2016 article about the startling rise in drug overdose deaths among white Americans, a drug abuse expert claims that doctors "are much more reluctant to prescribe painkillers to minority patients, worrying that they might sell them or become addicted." He notes ironically "that racial stereotypes are protecting these patients from the addiction epidemic" (Kolata & Cohen, 2016).

References

Bennett, J.O. (2006). The analyst at the intersection of multiple cultures. *Psychoanalytic Perspectives*, 3: 55–63.

Blinder, A. (January 18, 2016). Outbreak is fueled by mistrust in Alabama: Reluctance to report tuberculosis in town. *New York Times*, pp. A9, A14.

Bonovitz, J. (2001). White analysts seeing black patients. In Akhtar, S. (Ed.), *The African American experience: Psychoanalytic perspectives* (pp. 377–402). Lanham, MD: Rowman and Littlefield.

Burkard, A. & Knox, S. (2004). Effect of therapist color-blindness on empathy and attributions in cross-cultural counseling. *Journal of Counseling Psychology*, 51 (4): 387–397.

Cheng, A.A. (2001). *The melancholy of race: Psychoanalysis, assimilation, and hidden grief*. Oxford: Oxford University Press.

Cynkar, A. (2007). The changing gender composition of psychology. *Monitor in Psychology*, 38 (6): 46.

Daniel, J.H. (2000). The courage to hear: African-American women's memories of racial trauma. In Jackson, L.C. & Greene, B. (Eds.), *Psychotherapy with African-American women* (pp. 126–144). New York & London: Guilford Press.

Diala, C.C., Muntaner, C., Walrath, C., Nickerson, K., LaVeist, T., & Leaf, P. (2001). Racial and ethnic differences and attitudes toward seeking professional mental health services. *American Journal of Public Health*, 91 (5): 805–807.

Hamer, F.M. (2002). Guards at the gate: Race, resistance and psychic reality. *Journal of the American Psychoanalytic Association*, 50: 1219–1237.

Holmes, D. (1992). Race and transference in psychoanalysis and psychotherapy. *International Journal of Psychoanalysis*, 73: 1–12.

Jackson, L.C. (2000). The new multiculturalism and psychodynamic theory: Psychodynamic psychotherapy and African American women. In Jackson, L.C. & Greene, B. (Eds.), *Psychotherapy with African American women: Innovations in psychodynamic perspectives and practice* (pp. 1–14). New York: Guilford Press.

Katz, R.V., Kegeles, S.S., Kressin, N.R., Green, B.L., James, S.A., Wang, M.Q., Russell, S.L., & Claudio, C. (2008). Awareness of the Tuskegee syphilis study and the U.S. presidential apology and the influence on minority participation in biomedical research. *American Journal of Public Health*, 98 (6): 1137–1142. www.ncbi.nlm.nih.gov/pmc/articles/PMC2377291/ (accessed October 24, 2017).

Knox, S., Burkard, A.W., Johnson, A.J., Suzuki, L.A., & Ponterotta, J.G. (2003). African American and European American therapists' experiences of addressing race in cross-racial psychotherapy dyads. *Journal of Counseling Psychology*, 50 (4): 466–481.

Kolata, G. & Cohen, S. (January 17, 2016). Drug overdoses propel rise in mortality rates of young whites. *New York Times*. www.nytimes.com/2016/01/17/science/drug-overdoses-propel-rise-in-mortality-rates-of-young-whites.html?_r=0 (accessed October 24, 2017).

Kugelmass, H. (2016). "Sorry I'm not accepting new patients": An audit study of access to mental health care. *Journal of Health and Social Behavior*, 52 (2): 1–16. http://journals.sagepub.com/doi/abs/10.1177/0022146516647098 (accessed October 24, 2017).

Leary, K. (1995). "Interpreting in the dark": Race and ethnicity in psychoanalytic psychotherapy. *Psychoanalytic Psychology*, 12: 127–140.

Leary, K. (1997). Race, self-disclosure, and "forbidden talk": Race and ethnicity in contemporary clinical practice. *The Psychoanalytic Quarterly, 66:* 163–189.

McDonald, J.A. (2006). Potential influence of racism and skin tone on early personality formation. *The Psychoanalytic Review, 93:* 93–116.

Miller, A.E. & Josephs, L. (2009). Whiteness as pathological narcissism. *Contemporary Psychoanalysis, 45:* 93–119.

Office of the Surgeon General (U.S.), Center for Mental Health Services (U.S.), & National Institute of Mental Health (U.S.) (2001). *Mental health: Culture, race, and ethnicity: A supplement to mental health: A report of the Surgeon General.* Rockville, MD: Substance Abuse and Mental Health Services Administration (U.S.); August. www.ncbi.nlm.nih.gov/books/NBK44243/ (accessed October 24, 2017).

Powell, D.R. (2012). Psychoanalysis and African Americans: Past, present, and future. In Akhtar, S. (Ed.), *The African American experience* (pp. 59–84). Lanham, MD: Rowman and Littlefield.

Rogin, M. (1996). *Blackface, white noise: Jewish immigrants in the Hollywood melting pot.* Berkeley: University of California Press.

Skloot, R. (2010/2011). *The immortal life of Henrietta Lacks.* New York: Broadway Books.

Straker, G. (2004). Race for cover: Castrated whiteness, perverse consequences. *Psychoanalytic Dialogues, 14:* 405–422.

Sue, D.W., Capodilupo, C.M., Torino, G.C., Bucceri, J.M., Holder, A.M.B., Nadal, K.L., & Esquilin, M. (2007). Racial microaggressions in everyday life: Implications for clinical practice. *American Psychologist, 62* (4): 271–286.

Thompson, V.L.S., Bazile, A., & Akbar, M. (2004). African Americans' perceptions of psychotherapy and psychotherapists. *Professional Psychology: Research & Practice, 35* (1): 19–26.

Tummala-Narra, P. (2015). Cultural competence as a core emphasis of psychoanalytic psychotherapy. *Psychoanalytic Psychology, 32* (2): 275–292.

7 In Session

Typically, our clients bring to their sessions their conflicts, confusion, and worries about love and about work, and how those difficulties affect their senses of themselves. The patients about whom I am writing here are no different, and although the specifics of their historical and sociological realities cannot help but infuse those human relationships, for the most part, Barbara, Althea, Glenda, Cheryl, Dwayne, Loretta, Francis, and Tracy mostly do not talk directly in their sessions about racism and their experiences as African Americans. While race and racism hum in the background, what preoccupies my patients are their daily struggles with jobs or unemployment, family conflict, health problems, financial worries, and the attempts to come to terms with their respective, and in some instances traumatic, childhoods. However, there are times when their racial identity and its role in their lives are at the forefront for them, and somehow find their way into the open in our work.

In this chapter I will talk about three issues that have cropped up in the treatments of some of my African American patients, issues that directly arise from having to navigate within a white and racist social world. The three issues are 1. the confusing nature of racism, 2. experiencing injustice, and 3. gaps in support. While these topics reflect only issues that have come to my attention within my practice, with all the limitations that this qualifier implies, I hope to suggest some approaches that other white therapists might want to consider in their own work with black patients. Finally, I will look at how racism especially challenges the white psychotherapist working with a black client to take an often uncomfortable account of countertransference.

What's Going On?

Claudia Rankine (2014), in describing the persistent pressure of racism that tennis champion Serena Williams has experienced during her career, writes, "Perhaps this is how racism feels no matter what the context—randomly the rules everyone gets to play by no longer apply to you, and to call this out . . . is to be called insane, crass, crazy" (p. 30). Put another way, (white) beneficiaries of a crazy system call a (black) person crazy for daring to say that the crazy system is crazy.

Encounters with non-African American people can often leave the black participants angry, sad, or frustrated; but there are also times when they find themselves just as troubled by their uncertainty about their perceptions, wishing they could know for sure whether or not the discomfort they are feeling is the effect of white racism: "This person has always been pleasant, but did he really say what I just thought I heard him say?" Or, "I was perfect for the job, felt I did well in the interview; but I was probably passed over because someone else was better qualified. Yet could it have been racial?" Or, "Am I just being too sensitive?" This kind of uncertainty imposes a persistent emotional strain on people whose success and even survival depend in large part on deciphering the white world around them. Grier and Cobbs (1968/1992) reported that, in their psychiatric practices, black patients "are preoccupied with determining just how many difficulties are a consequence of the prejudice of whites" (p. 29). For some people who struggle with family dynamics that have blended almost seamlessly with white racism, an example of which we saw in relation to skin shade in the cases of Barbara, Althea, and Cheryl, the challenge of sorting out their responses to life events is even more complex.

Glenda found herself in a situation that was, for her, unusual. She was taking part in a religious conference along with about a hundred people, ninety of whom, she estimated, were white. She rarely talks openly about race or racism with me, but this time she remarked, "One thing going through my mind was: out of all those people, there's still some prejudiced people. Don't know why. Yet I picked up none of it there." Glenda's fleeting observation provides a revealing angle of relations between blacks and whites in our country in the twenty-first century. She finds herself in an atypical situation, away from her ethnic community, and cannot help but consider the reality that there are people around her who are "still ... prejudiced." Yet, she comments, her antennae for racism have not detected signs of it. She is puzzled, perhaps a little uneasy. The youngest child of migrants from the South, Glenda was born and raised in northern California. She consciously seems to adhere to a faith that dangerous racism is, or was, a feature of life in the South, but that race is not much of a problem for her. In fact, that position suits her well as, in general, she tends to maintain a wishful expectation that people will behave rationally and do the right thing. Not surprisingly, Glenda is regularly disappointed when that expectation is not met. Her unwarranted optimism and its repercussions have been a recurrent subject of her psychotherapy. Nevertheless, despite her self-protective optimism, every once in a while, as in the above comment, her underlying doubts and worries peek through.

One of the frustrations of the subtle or covert forms that racism may take, in particular those instances in which the offending person is not conscious of his or her enactment, is that those who feel hurt are often in the position of trying to determine the true impulses and motivations behind the offending particular action or statement. Whether in the public sphere of the media or in the unrecorded daily lives of ordinary people, remarks or actions that offend

African Americans for their perceived demeaning and racist quality are often hotly contested by non-African Americans as to whether or not they do constitute racism. As detailed earlier in the book, microaggressions are stressful for their recipients, who are left to deal with the emotions stirred up in response, and are especially challenging when people have to deal with such situations repeatedly over the course of their lifetimes. One aspect of what makes microaggressions so difficult to handle psychologically is that often their ambiguity deprives their object of a resolution in the form of acknowledgment, validation, apology, and reparation.

People inevitably develop ways to cope with the repeated experience of this kind of ambiguity. Grier and Cobbs (1968/1992) describe one strategy: "For a black man survival in America depends in large measure on the development of 'healthy' cultural paranoia." However, they also suggest that the "frequency of paranoid symptoms is significantly greater among mentally ill blacks than it is among mentally ill whites" (p. 161). What they see, then, as a necessary element of resilience for blacks in America has its drawbacks.

Althea addressed the problem differently. When she moved to California from the Jim Crow South as a young teen, it had not taken long, she told me, before she realized that the overt racism with which she had contended in her home state had been replaced by an obfuscated form, one that was less virulent or physically dangerous, but every bit as real. It was a kind of racism that was elusive and more difficult for her to protect herself against. When she began psychotherapy for symptoms of a major depression following a prolonged period of harassment at her white-collar job, we focused on her experience at work. In that process, it became clear that after Althea's first years on the job the staff and mission at her workplace had changed, and that she had studiously avoided noticing that she was being both sidelined and harassed. That I came to that conclusion based solely on her narrative, while she had failed to register the meaning of what she was experiencing, observing, and reporting, was a central subject for our work, and she began to retrieve memories of her perceptions from that time that she had suppressed.

However, it took some months more before she was able to notice an additional aspect of the experience, that she had suspected that racism had played some role in the troubles she was having at work. Not long after that acknowledgment, she began to talk about the possibility of rejoining the workforce. She admitted her fears at the thought of doing so: "I'm scared I'll still be naive about job politics. I want to put it out of my mind, because it terrifies me. I was really scared for my sanity." I remarked that she had not talked to me before about how afraid she had been. She replied, "I didn't realize how scared I was." I said, "You feel that now you can acknowledge worries about the realities of racism and harassment." Althea: "I have to . . . I don't think it will bother me if they don't like blacks, if they have their private agendas. As long as they don't hurt me . . . Anyway, I don't think it was racial. They mistreat everyone." Althea's contradictory statements here about the relevance of racism in her work-related stress are important to understand.[1]

Unlike Glenda, who never lived outside her northern California city, Althea spent her childhood until her teens in the openly racist environment of the Jim Crow South in the 1950s. It was dangerous, to be sure, but it also was a place where the rules of engagement between blacks and whites were codified and relatively clear-cut. She knew how to maneuver in that world with appropriately visible humility and caution. The more ambiguous social arrangements of mid- and late twentieth-century California were both liberating and mystifying to her. And unlike Francis, whose political identification and engagement provided her with a conceptual framework for, and hyper-alertness to, racism, Althea adapted to the anxiety stimulated by her new, more ambiguous, situation by taking California at its overt assumption of non-racism, and tried as best she could to ignore or minimize indications to the contrary. As we see at the end of the above vignette, she has circled back to her position of comfort: "Anyway, I don't think it was racial. They mistreat everyone."

I was struck also by her comment that she had feared for her sanity. Her responses, while somewhat indirect, suggest an intense psychic conflict surrounding her terror of admitting she might be vulnerable to racism, her fear of the power of racism to harm her, her resulting wish to repress knowledge of danger, and, against all that, her worried awareness of her situation. The non-racist self-image held by the white population of the supposedly liberal city in which she lived contributed to her defensive denial and her confusion. Like Francis, she was well educated in the politics of race, civil rights, and backlash; but, unlike Francis, she found it difficult to apply what she knew to her own situation. And also like Francis, she brought her uncertainty and the pain surrounding it into her treatment, albeit in different ways. There are questions that resonate for both, as well as for other black clients who have brought in such material: How do I sort out my perceptions from my instinctive assumptions about racism? Can I trust my white therapist to hear my experience and to take seriously the reality of racism in my life? Can I trust my white therapist not to leap to the conclusion that just because I wonder if something was racist that it must have been? What do my perceptions mean about who I am? Of course, I have the same questions.

Althea had a hard time understanding her relationships with white people, but she had a struggle with one non-white supervisor whose ethnicity also was problematic for her. She complained that the woman, who was Asian American, "would talk to me like I was dirt under her feet. She had no respect for me or my people. So blatant. Frankly, I don't want to dwell on this. It gets confusing and jumbled." She paused briefly, then continued: "Another Asian woman once said to me, 'My father would disown me if I married a black man.' On top of everything else! She just looked at me and said it. But it bounces off you. It had no effect on my feelings towards her." I am skeptical about these last words. "Really, no effect on your feelings?" I ask. Althea responded, "I may have taken the attitude of not liking her back. But I couldn't believe she'd say that," and repeated the woman's statement in wonder. I said that she is reminding me of her past descriptions of childhood encounters with Asian Americans. Althea: "The Asian kids didn't even acknowledge our existence when we went to the dry cleaners. Now I know young black people can be cruel, so I can see how that contributes to the bad feelings. But it's enough that we were there." I say, "You are confused about how much to factor in racism. It's scary to believe it's there, but wearing blinders is also not realistic." She nodded and sighed and said, "I really feel better. I'm glad I came." In trying to understand what happened in this exchange that resulted in Althea's gratified conclusion, I believe that two factors were helpful. Being able to narrate some painful experiences of racism and my skeptical response to the possibility that they had no effect on her gave validation to the pain she was feeling. Also, she was able to articulate her process in sorting out the ambiguities about the negative attitudes of the "Asian kids" towards her and other African Americans, acknowledging the provocations of "cruel" youngsters. And finally, communicating my sense of how confusing white, or in this latter case Asian American, behavior towards African Americans can be, turned out to be helpful in naming something that had strained for articulation, and thereby validated Althea's perceptions.

Althea's "blinders" and her tendency to denial, which were so evident in the earlier vignette, became a central subject of our work together, and her avoidance of raising the subject of racism in her therapy gradually melted away. One aspect of her impulse to deny the experience of racial discrimination, an impulse I have encountered with some other African American patients, is rooted, I believe, in the longing to feel safe. Parents who made the migration out of the South often managed the effects of their traumatic histories by creating a sharp split between the bad "there" of the Jim Crow South with all of its deadly violence and the good, safe, "here" in California. This psychic strategy is one adopted by many immigrants, who strive to not fall into the trap of Lot's wife, who looked back at Sodom as the family fled to a better place and, in doing so, was turned to a pillar of salt. As Boulanger (2004) explains, this particular "solution," the attempt to cut off completely from home, has psychic costs and may not truly be achievable. But it is a seductive solution when home has been the site of terror and pain. The migrants who, unlike Lot's wife, had looked only ahead may have conveyed to their children the imperative that they must believe in the promise of this new land where they can live and do well, as long as they work hard and follow the rules. But we know about the long fuse of trauma. Their children were never completely cut off from feelings and memories their parents had repudiated. They absorbed them from stories they were told, from visits to relatives in the South, or most likely through silences coupled with the symptoms through which their parents expressed the traumatic histories from which they had fled.

As Boulanger describes, this splitting between past and present, there and here, creates a sense of discontinuity that can be quite damaging. Despite the sense of safety it may provide, there are troubling effects in wishing away the awareness of experiencing or witnessing acts of racism. One, as in the case of

Althea, is the way in which doing so deprives a person of information that she or he needs to recognize the reality of a situation and thereby be able successfully to navigate its dangers. But the other is that, if a situation is misinterpreted by ignoring its racist components, the person who is its victim is likely to take the blame for something he or she could not have controlled, that is, someone else's behavior, while unconsciously internalizing the denigrating messages of the denied racism. All of those outcomes were issues for Althea in her therapy, and working on them over a period of many years was to prove hugely gratifying for her as she developed a more complete sense of herself.

Another example of the impact of the mystification of racism's presence came up during a session with Barbara concerning her medical care. She presented an account of one of her many unsatisfactory interactions with her health care providers, this time regarding a physician who was requiring her to come in for a face-to-face appointment in order to have a medication prescription renewed. She saw this demand of her doctor's as an obstacle being thrown in her path to obtaining what she needed. I pointed out to her that she seemed to give up as soon as she encountered what feels like an obstacle, and proposed to her that she and I "try to figure this out." She replied, "When I run into obstacles, my sister will give some white folks credit for sympathy for minorities, but this is different." After a pause, she said, "A man on Bill Moyers' program said, 'Most racists are good white people.' Now, why am I bringing this up?"

RF: You were talking about obstacles to health care.
BARBARA: I don't believe they [the doctors] would require the same things of other people that they require of me.

I explained that the particular "obstacle" that she was describing actually was common, and had a legitimate, medically sound rationale. But, I added, "You've had bad experiences with some of your doctors, so your association to the man talking about nice white racists lets us know that you are feeling that racism is an obstacle here." She replied, "Yes, I guess I do . . . It's all over the black community that doctors don't care about black people."

I relate this vignette because I think it reflects the confusion generated by the perpetual question with which she grapples: is my African American identity affecting the "obstacle" that I am currently experiencing? "What is about me as Barbara, what is about me as an African American woman, and what just isn't about me at all?" My sense is that initially when presenting the problems she was having, she may have suspected racism, but attempted to suppress that notion, either out of desire, similar to Althea's, to feel safe from ill will on the part of her doctor, or out of worry about my potential white skepticism. However, as we have seen, she is unable to keep her concern down and, to her surprise, brings up the comment from the man on Bill Moyers' program. I heard in her story a medical protocol that makes complete sense from a physician's point of view, but which she sees only as an "obstacle" that she suspects has been inflicted on her by a racist medical system because she is African American. But to add another element of ambiguity, she may well be correct in perceiving that she is being racially profiled. Whatever the realities of the situation, her spontaneous mention of the man she heard on television also suggests that she felt on some level that her thoughts about racism were not off limits in her therapy, and that she and I could speak together about such things.

In another instance of the confusion with which racism taints interactions and relationships, Althea had occasionally talked about Jane, a white woman with whom she had worked several years earlier and who had become a good friend. Things changed, however, when she learned that the friend was "dating a black man. They like each other," she said, "But I never thought she was like that—would date a black man." Puzzled, I asked what it meant to her that her friend would date a black man. Her answer surprised me. "It makes me wonder about the basis of our friendship. Was it because she was trying to understand our people? She'd talk about him to me, and she'd ask questions about black men that had nothing to do with work, and I just had this terrible feeling of embarrassment. I just cannot figure it out. I feel embarrassed if that was her motive for befriending me." She began to back off her relationship with the woman, uncomfortable in the uncertainty she felt about whether or not she was being used as a cultural informant, a thought that "embarrassed" her because it made her think that she had fooled herself into believing her friend might have liked her for who she was.

While this internal debate speaks to her insecurities about herself as a lovable friend, it is doubly affected by the impact of racism. She is suspicious that her colleague befriended her in the context of establishing a romantic relationship with an African American man, speculating that spending time with, and getting close to, Althea would somehow assist her in her romance, thus reducing Althea to a generic black woman from whom she could pick up some helpful tips. Fear of racism destroyed a possibility that her friend may have felt both affection and curiosity. Furthermore, Althea's interpretation of this scenario reiterates the message she received both from her family and from her own observations of the world: that she, as a dark-skinned African American woman, would never be genuinely appreciated for who she is, especially by a white person. An added element may have been the realization that the African American male co-worker preferred a white woman, a pattern about which she had complained in the past. But most of all, her experience of the ambiguity of the situation destroyed her sense of trust in her friend, and without any real means of testing her speculations, she simply drifted away. As with Barbara's suspicions of racist undercurrents in her medical care, Althea may be correct in her guess about her friend's motivations. And, as is true in both cases, whatever racist attitudes might have been in play may well have been unconscious, would have been very risky to confront, and were unlikely to be either validated or disconfirmed.

As I noted, Althea's insecurity about her friendship found grounding in her sense of herself as devalued on the basis of her skin color, both within her family and outside in the white world. In her treatment, I have worked with her to see what she calls her family's, but is actually her mother's, devaluing of her as evidence of the power of white racism to bedevil the family's ability to have richer relationships with each other and with her, while at the same time breeding in her the expectation, probably often met, that white people will view her through the same critical lens her mother does. C.L. Thompson (1995) wrote of "racial surgery," a therapeutic intervention that aims to help "patients begin to discern the differences between those struggles that would be theirs regardless of ethnicity and those that appear complicated because of their race" (p. 536). Congruent negative projections can be fired at their objects from all directions, and psychotherapy can be of help in identifying their sources.

Layton (2013) describes the case of an African American woman in which, she felt, the family dynamics mimicked the racist enactments of the woman's public world, in this instance the central issue being her life-long, angry struggle with being experienced as invisible. As Layton put it, "Anger at being slighted and invisible is a legacy of her family history to be sure, but her family history is also inflected by a legacy of white racism that has historically made blacks invisible" (p. 284). Boulanger (2014) emphasizes the destructive power of invisibility: "When experience goes unwitnessed or unrecognized, personal credibility is always in doubt." But Layton, who is a white psychoanalyst, reflects on what looks to her to be the patient's significant progress over the course of her treatment. "She has analyzed her many failed attempts to be seen, she feels seen by me, and she has become proud of modulating her anger" (2013, p. 284).

The strength of the therapeutic relationship has relied, in part, on Layton's capacity to "see" her patient—not only to observe her, but also to offer her something precious: recognition. The patient's pride in her improved functioning also suggests the importance of Layton's observing her positive change and the hard work it took for her to achieve it. Layton's pleasure in her patient's achievement, however intangibly it is expressed, is part of that experience. Meares and Graham (2008) describe this aspect of the therapist's ability to help the patient as "a fundamental, yet subtle and complex task" (p. 443).

In some African American families, then, racist attitudes can be absorbed into parent/child relationships to the detriment of the child's development of healthy self-esteem and ability to feel confident, either within the family and ethnic group or in the dominant culture. At the same time, family loyalty may become confused with loyalty to one's racial community, so that separation from one becomes equivalent to separation from the other. This emotional tug of war is not exclusive to African Americans, but is a well-known phenomenon among the children of immigrants, who are torn between their drive to assimilate and succeed in the new country and the pulls of their ambivalent parents to adhere to cultural norms of their countries of origin, represented by family and religious values. Because of the long, uninterrupted history of oppression of African Americans in this country, this kind of conflict can be more ambiguous and less consciously available than it is among most immigrant groups. After all, black Americans are Americans, and have been for centuries, so that the sharp division between cultural norms of white and black Americans are not as clear-cut and generational as with immigrants. Sometimes the demarcation between what feel like family demands and the pressures of white-dominated culture is blurry.

We read, for instance, in Chapter 6 about the young woman who found psychotherapy useful in helping her to sort out her ambivalence about her ambitions and its relationship to a blend of family and community expectations. In the case of Dr. Green, Holmes (2006) describes the power of internalized racism within a family and community to disrupt the psychological equilibrium of those who try to resist its regressive pull. Dr. Green is an African American woman who had spectacularly outdistanced her family in achievement. Ultimately, her progress in her therapy, writes Holmes, "resulted from resolution of her internal representations of structured, institutional racist proscriptions against her success" (p. 224). Similarly, McDonald (2006) tells of work with Mrs. T., who talked about both family history and her day-to-day experiences with racism, increasingly realizing that her "deep-seated feelings about her lack of entitlement and her inability to realize she had options" reflected both her internalized repressive mother and the repressive, racist society in which she lived (p. 112). In both these instances, the clinicians observed how the therapeutic process, with its careful disentangling of emotional strings, enabled Dr. Green and Mrs. T. to become better able to understand themselves and the world in which they were living. Sadly, McDonald reveals, Mrs. T. terminated treatment at her mother's death, overwhelmed by the guilt she felt at having cut off her relationship with her mother two years earlier (p. 114). My work with Barbara, who had struggled to distance herself from the hurtful influence of her own mother over the course of several years, had a similar painful ending.

Understanding the roots of the repressive internalized prohibitions can play a significant role in enabling people to develop their understanding of these interwoven pressures. It can also help patients to maintain some compassion for the loved ones who seem to be holding them back, while feeling more secure in coming to their own conclusions about what makes sense for them in their own time and place. Tracy's treatment has concerned itself at times with ways in which some of her symptoms mirrored dysfunctional behaviors and attitudes of her mother. For the most part, Tracy had absorbed some of these styles to what felt like her advantage, and laughed off the ones she thought were parental quirks. However, once injured and traumatized, even attitudes that had worked well enough before now were problematic, and in some ways she began to exhibit a few attitudes that she had previously repudiated. An aspect of working with this material has involved placing her mother into the historical context of her traumatic youth in a dangerous Southern environment, where her approach to the world was structured around keeping herself safe and thus made perfect sense. Distinguishing between then and now has been important, and something that we return to over and over.

"That Wasn't Right"

"I dreamed that someday someone will say, 'That wasn't right.'" This quote comes from Barbara, but it could have come from anyone who has felt the sting of being treated unfairly. The desire for justice is universal. My black patients, their relatives, and their ancestors have all experienced these injustices and have all had to grapple with the psychological and material consequences of these injustices, each in his or her own ways, and given circumstances, including family dynamics, constitutional factors, geography, and chance. You will recall in Chapter 3, Vaughans' (2014) observation that the parents in their study of African American boys did not, as a rule, speak to their children about their own, or even their children's, experiences of racism. The two reasons parents gave for their silence were, "I don't want them to hate or dislike White people" and "I don't want them to be racist" (p. 570). The children may sense the deception in their parents' silence yet also take in the puzzling message, leaving them unable to understand clearly their experience, other than to sense that for some reason what they were reporting to their parents reflected badly on them (the children), and that they could avoid being treated unfairly if they behaved properly. A message communicated by this strategy, aimed at protecting their children, is that the unfairness and injustice visited upon African Americans cannot and should not be named, sadly complicating their children's capacities to understand their feelings and experiences. As reported earlier, black psychotherapy patients often resist talking openly about their experiences with racism, at least with their white therapists.

In my experience, when a patient has become comfortable not only reporting experiences of racism but also naming the experiences as unjust, she or he has taken an important therapeutic step.

To illustrate, I am going to return to Althea. What follows are three exchanges that took place over a period of a few months, in which I believe we can see subtle shifts in her response to racial injustice. In the first of these sessions she begins to accept and understand her defensive need to deny the power of racism: "It's so hard to accept that it's so bad out there," she said. "It's much worse to accept that than to think it's about me." She recognizes the fear behind her wish to deny the injustices she observes and her vulnerability to those injustices. It can be overwhelming to try to live your life feeling constantly under threat of hostile intent towards you. Better to think that the world is benign, and that the bad is within you, because even if that construction means that you are not a good person, at least it affords you some control. After all, maybe you can change yourself.

"I see now," she continued, "that I really didn't have a chance to make it, even with my education. My son is reluctant to go for anybody's education and has to hang by his fingertips for bottom-feeder jobs. It's almost enough to make you wish for an asteroid." The powerless anger in her vision of the catastrophe that destroys all as she speaks of the obstacles racism and its sequelae have thrown in her path evolves into resignation and despair, reflected in the loss of hope for even the next generation. In a sense, resignation and hopelessness substitute for feelings, serving as vacuums that suck up emotional response.

About a month later, however, something different emerges. Althea begins to touch on the possibility of having responses to injustice beyond resignation.

Watching a documentary about an impoverished woman in Latin America, she had noticed in the woman "that same glazed look I've seen in my mother's face." When asked to describe what she saw in those faces, she replied, "Just a place of emptiness, no feelings, nothing left, no hope. They [the woman in the documentary and her mother] escape to that place." A few minutes later she elaborates on her mother's affect: "That emptiness. They couldn't afford to have feelings. I think it was that poverty." She goes on to talk about the perennial centrality of food in her emotional life, stemming from those early worries about sustenance, and circles back again to her mother, and her new-found insight: "She can't afford to have feelings. But I was born during a period of hope and change. The first thing I had were feelings. In the '60s everything changed and you talked about your feelings." I commented, "The 1960s gave you permission to notice your feelings for the first time."

She then proceeded to reminisce about her political activism as a young woman at that time, a part of her past she had never revealed to me. Again, she recalled her mother's sad silence. "It's overwhelming, even for me, when I think about the unequal treatment . . . I don't really expect to be treated equal."

RF: Equal to what or whom?
ALTHEA: We all strive to be like white people.
RF: Or is what you want is to be treated like white people?
ALTHEA: Good question. I'd never thought about it.

She went on to describe a situation in which a family member was struggling against racism at work, and said to me, not for the first time, "When you speak, people will hear you." I responded by saying that what she is telling me is "unfortunately very real, very common, and really appalling," to which she replies, "I wouldn't go so far as to call it appalling."

RF: What makes it not appalling? In what way is it ok?
ALTHEA: Well, it's not ok, but, like you said, it's a constant. I don't want to be like my mother, just manipulative and thinking that the whiter the better. She's always putting out the message, "I'm the mama, the one with power."

In this session, her preoccupation is clearly her attempt at understanding her mother, and her increasing success in that task, in particular the deep depression that lurks beneath her mother's rejecting and manipulative behavior. She is able to connect the problematic and hurtful relationship she has with her mother with her mother's sense of futility at what feels to her to be the impossibility of obtaining security and comfort in her life. Remembering her own coming of age during a "period of hope and change," and her freedom to assert grievances at injustice during the heady days of protest in the 1960s, she can feel both compassion for her mother and a desire to take a separate path. Yet, in the same session, she mimics the very resignation that so saddened her in her mother, when she challenges my use of "appalling" to describe experiences of racial injustice. I should mention here that, at other moments in her treatment, Althea has revealed her resentment at the very "hope and change" that played such a significant role in her life, believing that her 1960s' youthful optimism merely set her up for the disappointments that were to follow, disappointments due in large part to the persistence of racism and its cycle of backlash, as described in Chapter 3. Her complaint of her mother's emphatic assertion that motherhood confers power upon her seemed initially to be a non sequitur, but I sense that on some level Althea brings it up here as a comment on her awareness of the compensatory nature of her powerless mother's claim.

By the following month, Althea was able to acknowledge something that had been very difficult for her to express before: anger, even rage. Catalyzed by the then current news about Christopher Dorner, the African American police officer who went on a shooting rampage described in Chapter 5, she is able to talk about the feeling of rage at persistent experiences of injustice, albeit in an unusual and roundabout way. "I know I've lived many lives before," she began. "I think it's the rage, mainly. I think I must have been a racist in my past life." She turns to the subject of "the police officer," Christopher Dorner, and says, "I know how he felt, and how . . . for me, when I was fired, I knew somewhere someone would hear me and understand how I'd been mistreated. The fact that I was in therapy continuously, without a break, was very important. There was one person who already knew."

Althea's style of speech can often be elliptical, as I think the above example suggests, but in her oblique way I believe she is letting me know that she feels comfortable enough to tell us both that today's Althea, in this life, does feel very angry at the racial injustice she sees and experiences in the world, hence her suspicion that she had been a racist in a previous incarnation and that being victimized by racism is a result of her bad karma. She is also sharing how important it is to her that "there was one person who already knew" about racism, someone whom she did not have to try to convince and who would not either minimize or delegitimize her perception and experience.

Loretta and Glenda have very different personalities and life histories, and their relationships to acknowledging racial injustice are also quite different. Glenda is a union activist and has been a blue-collar worker for most of her adult life, and will occasionally comment on issues about race and racism. Her enthusiasm for the first African American president took her to Washington to witness both inaugurations, despite her limited finances. Although she rarely spoke of current events in her sessions, she did volunteer her thoughts about the acquittal of George Zimmerman for the killing of Trayvon Martin. Talking about how she saw a program about corrupt judges, she said, "It reminds me of my case. And Trayvon Martin and 'stand your ground' — watching Zimmerman's acquittal. How does this boy buying Skittles get shot? It just doesn't stop." I ask if the idea of racism playing a role in her case ever crosses her mind, especially since she mentions that it reminds her of her case.

Glenda replies, "Yes, it does. The workers' comp judge, he only held your report for a minute."

I reminded her that the white attorney for the other side had referred to her as "the EEO (Equal Employment Opportunity) queen." This appellation has a history. When, in an earlier session, she had told me of the attorney's use of this term, presumably in reference to her having filed several claims, I had shared with her that the term made me think of Reagan's "welfare queen," and my sense of it as a coded racist slur. She had agreed. I noted, "It is so hard and painful to accept that this is what is going on." She seemed to ignore my remark and went into a report of a phone call related to the logistics of her case. Glenda is often able to consider and even talk about the impact of racism on her life and the lives of fellow African Americans, but she has not yet been able to talk about the feelings that she experiences surrounding the topic. Only once, and like Althea, during the week when the Dorner story was in the news, has Glenda conceded that she does experience significant anger in response to racial injustice, and that she believes it is only her relationship to her Christianity that keeps that anger in check. Glenda's proclivity to denial of red flags in her relationships with others could seem to contradict her vigilance as a union activist, but, in fact, it is consistent with her strenuous efforts to deny emotional reactions to experiences of injustice. Other than the anger that she says she manages through her faith, she has not confirmed any of the other feelings one might expect when a person is a victim of racism.

A day after the acquittal of George Zimmerman for killing Trayvon Martin, Loretta reported that she had seen the movie *Django Unchained*. She explains, "It's about a man gettin' paid to kill white folks. He killed the slave master and the Uncle Tom character." I remarked that the idea of racial killing reminded me of the Zimmerman verdict. "I'm anesthetized," she said. "Things like that gonna happen. I did not like the tearing up of downtown, and it pissed me off that the news only showed blacks doing that. My hostility is not to a race; just to a system. If you have money, you can get away with things. Some racist probably paid for his defense attorneys. Anyway, there's nothing I can do. Protesting is right, but damage just hurts." At this point, it is the end of the session, and as she is walking out, she says, "I love you. Don't think I ever told you that."

I have pondered the meanings of this exchange, particularly the significance and timing of Loretta's parting words that day. The juxtaposition of her spontaneous choice to recount a story of a deadly solution to racial injustice with her nonchalance about the injustice of Trayvon Martin's death and Zimmerman's acquittal suggests an unconscious compromise she has made to let me, or maybe herself, be aware of the rage that she does in fact feel about racism, and the racist structure of society, as expressed by the unchained Django. She introduces class into the calculation, noting that an expensive attorney can protect the George Zimmermans of the world, and supposes a racist paid for his successful legal defense. Actually, money is something that Loretta's family had, to a certain degree, when she was a child; but it is something she most certainly and almost deliberately does not have now. As a young girl, she suffered directly from the way money buffered her very dysfunctional family from any consequences for the sexual and physical abuse to which she was subjected throughout her childhood. She voices her sense of powerlessness in the face of the combined forces of money and racism, suggesting that "protesting is right," but is counterproductive when it becomes destructive, especially because "the news only showed blacks doing it."

At this point in her emotional development, she is very far from the idea of engagement in political action or protest. Her struggle to achieve some measure of mental health in the face of her traumatic history and to make a life for herself demands her full attention—her psychic plate is full. Furthermore, the suffering she has endured at the hands of family members who took out their bitterness and frustration on her has made a mess of her relationship to injustice, autonomy, assertiveness, and aggression. I discussed earlier her tendency to deny the power and prevalence of white racism as a reflection of a wish to not be overwhelmed with feelings of fear and powerlessness. Thus Loretta has her own approach to the challenge of racism in her world. Since the oppression she faced within her family as a child has created such devastating wounds, she has turned to immersing herself in catastrophic traumas from which she has been spared and from which she feels comfortably safe. I asked her once about her fascination with films and books relating to the Holocaust. She said, "I relate to the Holocaust and slavery, too. They're overwhelming compared to what I've gone through." She later added, "My struggles are nothing like the stuff going on in Iraq and Afghanistan." She also enjoys horror films for much the same reason, as they give her a sense of control over the revisiting of experiences of terror.

And what can we make of her parting lines at the end of the session? One possible interpretation is that she felt a need to reassure me that, whatever anger at white injustice she may have revealed, either in the discussion of the film or in her thoughts about the Zimmerman acquittal, was not directed at me. She had, after all, emphasized that her "hostility is not to a race; just to a system." I had been surprised early in her treatment when she asked one day, "When are you going to ditch me?" So was she wanting to be sure that I felt loved and valued so that I would not "ditch" her? Another possible understanding of this ending is that she found relief in being able to voice that mix of her feelings, including feelings about racism, to her white therapist without generating an unwelcome response from me. Of course, both interpretations might apply.

The "Village" Under Stress

When I first began working with African American clients, I was impressed by a kind of fluidity and generosity that I observed within their families and communities when it came to helping one another out with their children. You may recall that Tracy had raised any number of nieces, nephews, godchildren, and others when their parents were unable to do so. But even before I began to work with Tracy, I had already encountered more modest examples of this phenomenon. It got to the point that when I heard of any young person who was living with a non-parental relative, I just assumed, correctly, that the family was African American. A black teenager who was embroiled in struggles with a parent might be sent to live with an auntie for a while, or a godmother would take in a child when the mother had a medical or mental health crisis, or a youth might appear at a relative's or friend's door asking to stay while things cooled down at home. Sadly, at the height of the crack cocaine epidemic in the 1980s and 1990s, grandparents were often raising the children of their own sons and daughters, who were collapsing under the combination of addiction and the accompanying movement to mass incarceration for African Americans. A few patients reminisced about their childhoods prior to that time, when neighbors kept informal watch on them, reprimanding them if their manners did not pass muster, or reporting to parents if there was cause to worry. I would not want to romanticize the past or create a myth of a golden age in which the village it supposedly takes to raise a child was intact and available. These arrangements were not always ideal. Some children, for instance, were shuffled between relatives whenever they became too troublesome, with predictably damaging effects on them.

I recall one little boy, initially sent to a relative when his custodial parent suffered a psychological collapse. He began to struggle at school, and the frustrated relative sent him to another family member, thus beginning a cycle of rotation among three family members, who each believed he just needed a different school and more discipline. With each move he would attend a new school where he would begin well, but inevitably fail. Because of the moves, no one ever stopped to wonder why he was having such a hard time. Did he have a learning disability, and could the boy's feelings of abandonment be affecting his academic performance? Even when he was at one school long enough for the staff to recommend testing the child, his father refused, out of concern, he said, that his son would be labeled; instead he moved him to yet another school. Eventually he was tested and found to have significant learning disabilities, but they were never addressed. By the time he had dropped out of high school, he had missed important years in which he might have received help.

I still hear of similar stories of African Americans opening up their homes to children in and out of the family, as well as to adults or even whole families in need, and as we saw in Chapter 1 and the example of Oakland, California, there continue to be ways that African Americans provide and build community support for themselves. But I have also noticed, possibly as my own patients have become older, as our economy becomes more segregated, and the fallout from mass incarceration and the war on drugs continues to be felt, that the "village" seems to be more fragile. When Glenda lost her job in her mid-50s, and then her home to foreclosure in the wake of the 2008 crash, relationships among her many siblings had become so estranged that she could not consider asking to stay with any of them. Two brothers had prison records, and she had long felt unable to trust them not to steal from her. She, who had frequently taken in friends in need or wayward children of friends or relatives, received very few offers of assistance from her friends and none from her family, other than her adult child, who lived in another city. Both of her parents had died by that point, and there was no cushion to ease her fall. Glenda was clearly hurt by the lack of support she received, but also told me that many people she knew were anxiously struggling and seemed to feel they had nothing, either materially or emotionally, to give.

I became most aware of the role that a fragile support system can play during my work with Tracy (see Chapter 5). She reminds me frequently of her need to avoid being with people, including loved ones, in order to feel safe from her angry dissociative states, a decision that leaves her isolated. On many occasions, she has described the emotional limitations of her family members and how, because of her fears of being triggered by conflictual encounters, she needs to keep them at a distance. One sibling, bright, well-educated, and hardworking, nevertheless fell victim to drugs and alcohol. In an unfortunate coincidence, a successful nephew, whom she raised from early childhood and to whom she had had a close relationship, was severely injured at his job, only to enter into his own humiliating relationship with the workers' compensation system and their health care providers. He and Tracy are still close, and there are times when he is emotionally able to be available to her, but he can no longer consistently be so as he grapples with his own volatile moods. One young woman, also raised by Tracy, is doing very well and remains concerned about "Auntie Tracy," calling her frequently to check up on her, and often trying to talk her down from her agitated state. But she is at college across the country. Tracy's best friend, Sue, does step in quite a bit to give her all sorts of help, except when, unpredictably, she is victim of her own wildly irrational outbursts. Recently Tracy noticed that food is very important to Sue, that she becomes irrational and provocative when she is hungry, and that this reaction may be connected to Sue's childhood, during which she often went hungry. Armed with this new insight, Tracy hopes to be able to forestall upsetting upheavals with Sue by making sure her friend is kept well fed when they are together.

Probably the most complicated relationship in what might constitute Tracy's support system is her relationship with her beloved mother, who left her home in the Jim Crow South after a childhood of picking cotton. Tracy does not know much else about her mother's childhood other than her sense that it was frightening. As described earlier in the book, her parents migrated to California and worked hard to create a safe, middle-class home for their children, and seem to have succeeded. Still, as her mother has aged and faced a number of losses, her history has caught up with her. She is not frugal; she is absolutely miserly, hoarding her money and resources beyond reason. Predictably, she is not generous with her daughter, who could certainly use some help at times. After a lifetime of physical labor, her body is wracked with arthritis that she refuses to acknowledge, insisting on taking care of household tasks that should be delegated to an able-bodied person. Making matters worse, she likewise denies Tracy's physical disabilities and becomes annoyed and hurt when Tracy refuses to do one of those tasks. When Tracy complained that her mother often tries to manipulate her into spending time with her out of loneliness, even when Tracy makes clear that she is not feeling well, I tried to explore with Tracy the possibility that her mother may have other resources for companionship, such as friends or her church. But Tracy explained that her mother does not trust people outside the family: "I think it's because of growing up in the South. She don't trust anyone."

Tracy taught me another side of the vulnerabilities of her stressed social environment when she was victimized by a scam that utilized instilling fear in her for the safety of her nephew. It was clear to her that the man had to have had information about her, leading her to believe that he was someone with a connection to a person who was in her life—a relative, a friend, or a partner of either. She was particularly nervous because she had reported the incident to the police, which led her to fear retaliation. She noted, "He was a real amateur who needed the money," yet she was somewhat puzzled by her preoccupation with what happened: "I'm fine, but I'm pissed. The biggest thing is I don't know who it was."

She then told me that it was a relief to talk to me about what happened. "I can't tell friends," she explained, "because it would leak out, and people they know would go for revenge. Can't take that chance." Somewhat surprised, I asked what made her so sure that would happen. "They'd do it because they care about me," she explained. "Street stuff. And it's not a priority case for the police. And I can't tell Sue, because it would just scare her and freak her out." I said that part of the stress she was experiencing about this upsetting incident is her need for secrecy. She agreed. I told her that I was only just realizing something she had been trying to explain to me: "You are walking around in a world where others also have very short fuses." Tracy began to cry, and said, "It's their way of love, but it really happens." I replied, "Your world is dangerous because others are also traumatized and can't always manage their reactions." "Yes," she responded, "it's real. I can't let it out. I have always been the one to calm things down, but now I can't trust myself. I've always tried to be prepared, but I never prepared for this."

As you can see in Glenda's experience and, more vividly, in what I have just described of Tracy's, these women's psychological lives are significantly affected by the fragility of their respective social environments, the people and institutions that would be expected to provide support during their difficult times. Furthermore, what has undermined these potential support networks must be attributed in a great degree to racism. In Glenda's case, the history of redlining and, more recently, the targeting of African Americans for low-quality mortgages led to disproportionately high numbers of foreclosures of black-owned homes, including Glenda's. Tracy's mother's obsessive and fearful hoarding of her resources, compulsive need to work, and fearful refusal to trust anyone outside her nuclear family has limited her ability to be a source of comfort to her daughter, who nevertheless understands that these behaviors stem from her mother's childhood of deprivation and terror in the Jim Crow South.

Tracy casually mentions the low priority the crime against her is for the local police department, a pattern that began in the South, where white police left black communities to take care of themselves. (Tracy recently recalled childhood visits to her grandparents' home in which every room had a shotgun.) Perhaps if men and women in her community felt more confident that the police identified with them and took their needs for protection as seriously as they do their white fellow citizens, they would not embrace the vigilante attitude that Tracy describes. And, of course, if some of the people in her world did not experience the police as hostile and potentially lethal adversaries, they may also be more willing to leave the work of apprehending wrongdoers to them. Similarly, a community in which so many of the men have been incarcerated due to the "war on drugs" and the expansion of the correctional system is more likely to have members who have been abused in prison, denied effective treatment or rehabilitation, and stymied in getting decent jobs. In other words, such a community will be disproportionately inhabited by traumatized, possibly still drug-addicted, and unemployed men and to a lesser degree women, who are rarely able nurture themselves, never mind to offer support to anyone else. For many African Americans, then, it is a rough world indeed.

Countertransference Challenges

The current state of managed care health insurance is not always welcoming to those of us who work in a psychoanalytic or psychodynamic model, as it encourages short-term treatment. I am more at home with Carrere's (2008) description of a process that "matures and ripens a person's ability to speak about private experience," amplifying his or her "capacity for experience" and for "having all one's feelings and thoughts" (p. 401). It is a process, he continues, that, through talking to another person, "establishes the foundation for reflection and for having experiences culminating in formulations about their meaning" (p. 401). But there is one caution that emerges repeatedly in clinical literature concerning biracial psychotherapy relationships and that is the danger that the therapist's unconscious racial stereotyping presents (Leary, 2006; Smith & Tang, 2006; Sue et al., 2007; Carrere, 2008). Sue et al. go so far as to say that this stereotyping "poses the biggest challenge to the majority of White mental health professionals, who believe that they are just, unbiased, and non racist" (2007, p. 280). Leary (2000) even talks of the potential for the white therapist to retraumatize the African American patient. Referring to J. Cisz, she notes that, while there is always a danger that in the transference/countertransference relationship a therapist can repeat a traumatic interaction with a patient, most therapists can assure themselves that they played no role in the original traumatization of their clients. However, when the therapist is white and the patient black, because of the often unconscious nature of racial enactments and because of "the institutional nature of racism," the white therapist, "by virtue of her participation in the social world of which therapy is a part, may in fact, be complicit in some forms of oppression" (p. 650).

As detailed in Chapter 6, adopting a so-called "color-blind" attitude in biracial psychotherapy is both impossible and contrary to creating a productive and safe therapeutic environment. Hamer (2002) emphasizes the need to acknowledge the complexity of racial transference and countertransference: "Race matters occurring in the psychoanalytic dyad highlight the fact that the two parties have their own relationships with a consensual social reality that is often implicit, often unarticulated, and subject to revision according to a host of experiences" (p. 1233). These "implicit" and "often unarticulated" senses of the social worlds of each participant in the biracial therapy involve stereotypes that can intrude into the development of an open and emotionally safe psychodynamic setting. Leary (2006) writes: "Patient, analyst or both are confronted with a self-image that threatens self-condemnation or judgment from the other." Writing from the standpoint of being an African American analyst and citing Holmes (1999), she adds that besides disturbing "narcissistic equilibrium," the African American clinician's "effort to overcome the stereotype can disrupt . . . the therapist's ability to be resourceful" (2006, p. 86). This interference can certainly be true as well for the implicitly stereotyped African American patient, who, if he or she continues the psychotherapy, must contend with the same anxious burden of needing to "overcome the stereotype," also inhibiting his or her capacity to think and express freely within the relationship.

Leary's and Holmes' insights suggest the need to be aware of the effects of these floating stereotypes on white therapists' capacities to be fully available to their African American patients. A well-intended European American therapist may be conscientiously aware of the negative and positive stereotypes often attributed to black Americans, and hopefully aware of the particular ones specific to his or her personal history. But how does that awareness function when confronted with the reality of a unique, flesh-and-blood, African American client? Out of fear of failing to guard against a racist enactment or of being experienced as racist, the therapist may be tempted to manage the situation by obliterating or minimizing all difference. But Tummala-Narra (2015) warns therapists against "the tendency to minimize difference and universalize experience." She writes, "The therapist's ability to bear anxiety helps to facilitate the client's willingness to negotiate the multiplicity and hybridity of his or her identity and to explore shared fantasies of sameness and the other . . ." (p. 286). In some ways, to be aware of the wealth of white privilege I possess and unconsciously use every day, to loathe the system that grants me that privilege, and to have an opportunity to provide what I hope to be a helpful therapeutic service to people who have been denied that privilege has been an uncomfortable position in which to find myself as a psychotherapist. I have certainly been vulnerable to the tendencies against which Tummala-Narra warns, as well as others. I am not alone.

C.L. Thompson (1995), for instance, describes her own countertransferential challenge as a question of "how much of an activist must a patient become to demonstrate mental health" (p. 543). For me, this particular fantasy of a shared identification with an activist patient could be seductive, although it rarely emerges in my consciousness. Yet while I acknowledge that a patient's activism does not equate with mental health, and a therapist's expectation for a patient to become an activist would be intrusive and destructive, I know I inwardly cheered when Tracy, who had been very slowly inching out of her refuge of isolation, began to mention current events from the daily news. One afternoon, she walked out of Home Depot to discover a small demonstration of Black Lives Matter protesters, and decided to stay, listen, and join in. The demonstration had been called in response to the shooting of a suspected shoplifter by a security guard. Because of her fear of her anger, she left after 20 minutes in case the situation became raucous or even violent. Still, the experience felt good to her, and I interpreted her action as an affirmation of her reawakened understanding that she is not alone in the face of injustice, and that racism is real, dangerous, and worth speaking out against. And most importantly, a reminder that one can express outrage with words.

Layton (2013) reports a different kind of countertransference issue that came up for her in the treatment of a middle-aged African American woman. The patient, according to Layton, came to see her for help with an "anger problem" for which she was taking an antidepressant "so her feelings of being slighted don't lead to her getting out of control." The therapist described her discomfort with the discovery of her own wish to help her client express her anger in a way that would be more comfortable for "the white, middle-class public," and her motivation to avoid rendering the patient "the pathologized one" (p. 283). Here I think Layton was working with everything she knows about how the white world of her own class and social milieu works and its reactions to non-whites who enter it. She wanted to be able to coach her black patient, much as I wanted to facilitate Barbara's interactions with her doctors. If the therapeutic alliance is not adequately developed, failing to acknowledge and contain these impulses could be experienced as implying that the patient is acting incompetently and that white authority (the therapist) knows best. If, however, the therapist and the patient have established a discourse in which the reality of racism is acknowledged and understood, and its ramifications in the client's life can be discussed openly, this kind of interaction need not be in conflict with the therapeutic process.

A therapist's wish to use her white privilege to assist her client, in this case by mobilizing her knowledge of the ways white racism work, raises a related therapeutic question: What happens if the therapist acts on that awareness of her privilege to concretely intervene in the patient's life? We have all been in the position of writing either a letter on behalf of a client documenting the need for time off work, or a report demanded by an insurance company to enable the patient to access treatment. But there have been a few moments when I have felt a strong countertransferential urge to initiate and carry out an action in which I lend my white privilege to a non-white client in order to rectify an unjust situation in which the patient's race and class was preventing her from being heard. There was one occasion, 20 years ago, when I followed through with exactly that urge.

I was seeing Glenda under her accepted workers' compensation claim for symptoms of depression resulting from an earlier bout of job harassment. She had been doing quite well. A year or so after we'd begun to work together, however, she was fired, an act she saw as retaliatory. Her grievance protesting the firing was in the slow process of making its way to a National Labor Relations Board (NLRB) arbitration. She had become very distressed by the emotional assault of what she felt was a wrongful termination, as well as by the financial loss incurred by the significant reduction in her income. She had also been diagnosed with carpal tunnel syndrome, which was causing her additional hardship. After a few months, she was told by workers' compensation that she was to begin vocational rehabilitation, which they would arrange and for which they would pay. While this instruction may sound like something she might have welcomed, the real implications were not benign. For one thing, she was being told to train for a new job because her employer had said that she would not be able to return to her regular position, despite the fact that the issue was yet to be decided by the NLRB. Participation in the rehabilitation program, when ordered by workers' compensation, is not optional, and failure to attend appointments or, when a program was selected, attend classes, would result in complete termination of her benefits. She had no choice but to meet with a counselor selected by the insurance company, from whom she learned that the only occupational training options offered would result in jobs paying considerably less than she had been earning at her union job in which she had years of seniority. She forced herself to attend the series of meetings, fearing the consequences if she did not. However, despite informing the counselor that she had developed carpal tunnel syndrome, she was placed in a training class comprised primarily of keyboarding. She tried to comply with the class demands and somehow manage the pain.

In a fragile emotional state already, she became increasingly distraught. We began having more frequent sessions and I re-referred her to a psychiatrist who had previously prescribed her with antidepressants, to see if medications could again be of help. At the same time, I wrote a letter to her claims examiner, explaining that I thought that the pressure on Glenda was having a destructive impact on her mental state, not to mention her physical condition, and that I was deeply concerned that if it continued, she might suffer a complete collapse. I had also, with Glenda's permission, tried to speak to the counselor. Nothing helped, and Glenda was as desperate and depressed as I had ever seen her.

Her employer was the U.S. Government, and her workers' compensation was administered under the U.S. Department of Labor, so I suggested she try to involve our congressional representative. She did call the office and spoke to the appropriate person who had her fax relevant documents, but Glenda felt the woman was not responsive to her. In part, I suspect that Glenda's current state of depression may have impeded her ability to communicate effectively with the liaison, so, without thinking through much about the meaning of my doing so, I proposed that she make an appointment with the aide for the two of us, along with her union representative. At the time, I was aware of my own sense of desperation about the injustice and destructiveness of what was happening; utterly frustrated by my demonstrated ineffectiveness in petitioning her (white) claims examiner and (white) rehab counselor; and fearful that this normally resilient and self-possessed woman would, in her current state, not be taken seriously by the congressional aide. And, although I did not want to admit it, I believed that my whiteness, bolstered by my professional identification, might succeed with the congressional aide in a way that the patient's honest account of her experience, backed up by her documents, would not.

The good news was that I was right, the meeting went well, and a letter from our congressional representative did stop the vocational rehabilitation harassment in its track. But the bad news is that I was right, that the meeting went well because, to my eye, the (white) aide seemed to take the situation seriously as she focused much of her attention on me. When I tried to explore with Glenda later how the meeting had felt to her, she would only report her observation that originally, the aide "just didn't get it," but that she did seem to "get it" in our meeting. She was not willing to speculate about what had enabled the woman to shift. In reflecting back now on this event in Glenda's treatment, I believe that her reticence in commenting on the racial dynamics of the meeting and its outcome was tied to the relatively early stage of our work together. In later years, she became much more willing to introduce race and racism into her sessions when, for instance, she challenged my white ideas about child-rearing. But at this stage she, and possibly I, were not ready. Her silence on the topic did not stop my private questions and speculations. On the positive side of the emotional ledger, she may have felt cared for and validated in her experience, and relieved at the outcome. She may also have resented her temporary loss of confidence in her ability to advocate for herself and wondered how much my color played into the positive outcome of the meeting and hence may have resented me for what she saw as my assumption of my ability to communicate effectively with the aide. I cannot say that I observed any significant changes in the nature of our relationship stemming from the meeting, although, again in hindsight, my action may have contributed to the accumulative establishment of trust that has enabled us to work together through her many trials and tribulations. Did I make the right decision? I don't know. But what I am convinced of is the importance, when possible, of managing my countertransference impulses and treating them with care.

A wise colleague, an African American psychologist, alerted me to a possible countertransference challenge as he talked about a case in which he felt he had not managed to make progress with a biracial client. He lamented, "I learned that I couldn't tolerate being the bad object. I should have allowed myself to be the bad object." Carrere (2008) concurs: "Patients need us to bear the psychic frames of mind they have so carefully avoided and disavowed before they can trust doing so" (p. 405). This advice is sound, but not as easy to follow as one might wish. I have often wondered about the nature of patients' negative feelings towards me, most especially that of African American patients, since they surface so rarely, and when they do, so often quickly dive into hiding again. The discovery of the inhibitions of African American clients in relationship to their white therapists discussed in Chapter 6, the fears of upsetting them or discovering deal-breaking racism in them, resulting in the loss of a valued relationship—all these factors lead me to doubt that I am as available to my patients as my colleague and Carrere advise. I do not look forward to anyone disliking me, and despite my training and understanding the importance of working with negative transference, I wonder if I unconsciously discourage clients from revealing their bad feelings towards me. The persistent exposure to irrational negative bias faced by African Americans would lead me to predict that this psychological burden would include having some ambivalence towards their white therapists, we who can so easily live lives free from that burden. When I speak of an "irrational negative bias," I realize I am reluctant to use the word I think applies when that bias is at its worst: hate.

Hamer (2006) is less squeamish than me, as he recounts three very different vignettes in which his white patients expressed racial hatred in the context of their treatments with their African American analyst. In each case, he notes, "the racial hatred seemed to be experienced less in terms of *actions specific to persons or groups hated*, and more in terms of *who these persons or groups were*" (p. 202; original emphasis). In making this distinction, Hamer gets to the sense of the amorphous, primitive quality that defines hate. It is that irrational nature of hatred that explains the power of its toxic effects on its objects. Angry behavior can, after all, be challenged, argued about, changed, or apologized for. Focused anger, while distressing to the person who is its object, does not disempower or necessarily undermine that person's core sense of self. Being spurned for one's very identity, by contrast, chips away at a person's sense of power in the world. Because racial hatred is a shapeless mass of stereotypes that eludes real contact or connection, there is no potential for relationship. When the hatred coincides with a significant enough threat, as we saw in the case of Tracy, the immediate coping options may be reduced to fight, flight, or dissociative numbing.

Kathleen Pogue White (2002), an African American psychoanalyst, takes up experiences of being hated and hating, hoping to resolve the conundrum of how psychoanalytic treatment can help people know what they "should do with their hatred, their being hated, hating and recovering from hate" (p. 420). She tells of her own early childhood encounters with being the recipient of hostile racist projections, and the importance of her grandmother's counsel, which she translates and pares down to her "strategy of surviving being hated: see the projection, get mad, and turn the projection back" (p. 405). As we have seen so far, these steps all play a role in psychodynamic treatment with African Americans. The psychotherapist must join with the client in detailing the nature of the internalized irrational projections of a dominant culture that have been transmitted directly through encounters with the white world and indirectly within the family. The patient's anger at being hurt by these transmissions must be allowed expression and be tolerated and understood by the therapist, while the source of the hatred, once demystified, is more accurately placed where it belongs. White bemoans the lack of theoretical guidance in working with the wounds of being hated, including the response of hating in return, but the insights she offers are very useful to consider.

She insists, for instance, "that victimization is an interaction," and that if "one can't find a kernel of self-operation in a victimized condition, then despair is the correct response" (White, 2002, p. 406). White gives as an example the black professional who adjusts her manner of speech at work to blend in with her white colleagues, but suffers from the strain of doing so. The woman has made a choice. White is not asserting that black people bring on their own victimization by white society, but that there are ways in which some people incorporate being objects of racism into a psychological defensive structure and participate in its enactment. "Being hated," she writes, "can become a self-definition, safety operation, and defense against anxieties about separation and individuation" (p. 406). Essentially following White's grandmother's model, Francis (Chapter 3), for example, seemed to retreat into the assumption of being victimized racially as she tried to park her car as a means of resolving the pain of uncertainty, but also to confirm internalized feelings of being hated, and thus hateful. White states the need "to be on alert for projections from white people in general and from white people in power in particular." She cautions, "Erring on the side of wariness and vigilance is likely to save you a great deal of self-confusion and pain" (p. 405).

Yet, this form of protection does have pitfalls, as we saw not only with Francis, but more distressingly in the case of the tuberculosis outbreak in Marion, Alabama, and the woman who refused to take her medicine for high blood pressure. Ultimately, White does believe "that people can survive being hated and hating, and that the process of re-externalization of toxic projections is a necessary condition for further self-development." Reflecting on her own analysis she believes that her analyst's "capacity to bear witness" enabled her "to find a way to survive being hated and hating" (2002, p. 417). White's admonition to "see the projection, get mad, and turn the projection back" could be said to apply to all psychotherapeutic treatment, in which the therapeutic relationship can be productively mobilized to help the patient name the poison, correctly identify its source, return it, and thereby come into his or her own separate self. In a comment about the treatment of Ms. B, for example, Holmes (2006) writes that Ms. B's "own rage became more decipherable to her" and "she came to feel more real and solid." Holmes connects this shift in her patient to a new ability "to disidentify with and shed the racialized worthlessness that had defined her" (p. 228).

The division of this chapter into four sections has been, in a sense, arbitrary, in that each of the topics covered is part of a whole picture to which we keep returning: the painful gap between black and white experiences in this country. Perhaps this discussion can help therapists to engage with their African American patients so as to enable them to be seen and heard in deeper ways.

Note

1 Althea is not the only one to express ambivalence about naming racism. MSNBC television personality Melissa Harris-Perry, who is African American, went public with her belief that her (white) superiors at the station were quietly but effectively sidelining her and her program, which had typically taken on issues about racism. In an email to coworkers, Harris-Perry wrote: "I am not a token, mammy or little brown bobble head." In a follow-up interview she was reported to have said, "I don't know if there is a personal racial component. I don't think anyone is doing something mean to me because I'm a black person" (Koblin, February 27, 2016). Ms. Harris-Perry's program was, in fact, cancelled two days after the above email went public (Koblin, February 29, 2016).

References

Boulanger, G. (2004). Lot's wife, Cary Grant, and the American dream: Psychoanalysis with immigrants. *Contemporary Psychoanalysis*, 40 (3): 353–372.

Boulanger, G. (2014). Reversing a lifetime of betrayal. Paper given at Division 39 meeting in New York City, NY.

Carrere, R.A. (2008). Reflections on psychoanalysis conducted as a talking cure. *Contemporary Psychoanalysis*, 4: 400–418.

Grier, W.H. & Cobbs, P.M. (1968/1992). *Black rage*. New York: Basic Books.

Hamer, F.M. (2002). Guards at the gate: Race, resistance and psychic reality. *Journal of the American Psychoanalytic Association*, 50: 1219–1237.

Hamer, F.M. (2006). Racism as a transference state: Episodes of racial hostility in the psychoanalytic context. *Psychoanalytic Quarterly*, 75: 197–214.

Holmes, D. (1999). Race and countertransference: Two "blind spots" in psychoanalytic perception. *Journal of Applied Psychoanalytic Studies*, 1 (4): 319–332.

Holmes, D.E. (2006). The wrecking effects of race and social class on self and success. *Psychoanalytic Quarterly*, 75: 215–235.

Koblin, J. (February 27, 2016). Host says MSNBC silenced her show. *New York Times*, Business Day section.

Koblin, J. (February 29, 2016). MSNBC cancels show after tension with host. *New York Times*, Business Day section.

Layton, L. (2013). Dialectical constructivism in historical context: Expertise and the subject of late modernity. *Psychoanalytic Dialogues*, 23: 271–286.

Leary, K. (2000). Racial enactments in dynamic treatment. *Psychoanalytic Dialogues*, 10: 639–653.

Leary, K. (2006). The John Bowlby memorial lecture 2005: How race is lived in the consulting room. In White, K. (Ed.), *Unmasking race, culture, and attachment in the psychoanalytic space* (pp. 75–89). London: Karnac Books.

McDonald, J.A. (2006). Potential influence of racism and skin tone on early personality formation. *The Psychoanalytic Review*, 93: 93–116.

Meares, R. & Graham, P. (2008). Recognition and the duality of the self. *International Journal of Psychoanalytic Self Psychology*, 3: 432–446.

Rankine, C. (2014). *Citizen: An American lyric*. Minneapolis, MN: Graywolf Press.

Smith, B.L. & Tang, N.M. (2006). Different differences: Revelation and disclosure of social identity in the psychoanalytic situation. *Psychoanalytic Quarterly, 75*: 295–321.

Sue, D.W., Capodilupo, C.M., Torino, G.C., Bucceri, J.M., Holder, A.M.B., Nadal, K.L., & Esquilin, M. (2007). Racial microaggressions in everyday life: Implications for clinical practice. *American Psychology, 62* (4): 271–286.

Thompson, C.L. (1995). Self-definition by opposition: A consequence of minority status. *Psychoanalytic Psychology, 12*: 533–545.

Tummala-Narra, P. (2015). Cultural competence as a core emphasis of psychoanalytic psychotherapy. *Psychoanalytic Psychology, 32* (2): 275–292.

Vaughans, K.C. (2014). Disavowed fragments of the intergenerational transmission of trauma from slavery among African Americans. In Vaughans, K.C. & Spielberg, W. (Eds.), *The psychology of black boys and adolescents*, Vol. 2 (pp. 563–575). Santa Barbara, CA: Praeger.

White, K.P. (2002). Surviving hating and being hated: Some personal thoughts about racism from a psychoanalytic perspective. *Contemporary Psychoanalysis, 38*: 401–422.

8 Reparations

There is a word that has a long history in psychoanalysis, and an even longer history in the post-Civil War American lexicon. In these final pages, it feels fitting to consider the concept of "reparation." For psychoanalytically oriented psychotherapists, "reparation" has typically referred to unconscious processes through which those who suffer with guilt attempt to repair harm they believe they have done to others. Outside the mental health field, "reparations" is a term that has had a very specific meaning in American history, as it refers to the proposition that African Americans be granted compensation for the financial, educational, professional, legislative, health care and other losses/thefts that they have suffered as a result of slavery and its long aftermath. In other words, the latter use of the word represents a concrete, large-scale application of a process that psychoanalysis looks at within the interpersonal and intrapsychic worlds of individuals in treatment. Can the insights of psychoanalytic thinking about reparation be of use in considering the meaning of reparations in the pursuit of justice and equality? I believe they can.

The project of this book has been to encourage the use of everything at our disposal—psychodynamic theories and observations, the works of historians, novelists, and journalists, and occasionally the visual arts—to understand and attempt to repair some of the psychological injuries of injustice that affect the lives of the individual African Americans with whom you and I live and work. This process has implicitly meant employing psychoanalytic ideas about reparation and trying to understand what is needed for a practitioner to establish a psychotherapeutic relationship that enables the patient to achieve a degree of healing from the effects of those injuries. The distinction between the private, interpersonal world of the individual and his or her family and therapist and the social and political environment is a false one, as I hope that by now is clear. The clinical focus in this book is consistent with the movement for concrete reparations, as reparation is fundamental to achieving justice, and justice is fundamental to achieving a more psychologically healthy national community, in which individuals such as my patients, and all of us, can breathe and relate to those around us in a safer and more honest way. At this point, I am first going to give a brief overview of the history of the reparations movement.

The Call for Reparations

A number of African Americans have long voiced their calls for various forms of reparations or compensation from the U.S. governmental authorities, first for almost 250 years of unpaid labor during slavery, and then for the subsequent 150 years of legal and illegal financial, educational, and legislative theft. In 1963, Martin Luther King, Jr., called for "significant compensation for slavery, segregation, and continuing anti-black discrimination," supporting the "principle of compensation for stolen wages." Six years later, James Forman interrupted a church service in New York to demand reparations, including "creation of banks, universities, and training centers for African Americans." In 1972, the National Black Political Convention called for the U.S. president to establish a majority black commission to "determine a procedure for calculating an appropriate reparations payment in terms of land, capital and cash and for exploring the ways in which the Black community prefers to have this payment implemented" (Feagin, 2004, p. 68). The National Coalition of Blacks for Reparations in America, or N'COBRA, was formed in 1987, and in 1993 the NAACP officially endorsed the call for reparations (Coates, 2014, p. 22).

In fact the call for reparations had begun much earlier. One freed slave, Belinda Royall, filed one of the first, rare, successful suits for reparation. Kidnapped as a child from Ghana and enslaved for 50 years, she was freed in 1783, at which time her master abandoned his property and took flight in the turmoil of the Revolutionary War. She petitioned the Commonwealth of Massachusetts for reparative compensation for her labor and enslavement. She was awarded 15 pounds and 12 shillings (Coates, 2014, pp. 19–20). According to Litwack (1980), as the Civil War concluded, many freedmen expected that with Emancipation that they would be compensated for their years of unpaid labor and grasped at the possibility of 40-acre allotments as a means of transitioning to freedom. Within two years after the end of the war, it became clear they would likely be bitterly disappointed (pp. 399–402).

For the most part, the call for reparations for the millions of descendants of slaves has fallen on deaf, if not hostile, white ears. In 1993, early in the 103rd Congress, Rep. John Conyers of Michigan introduced H.R. 40, the Commission to Study Reparation Proposals for African Americans Act. He selected the number 40 in honor of those 40 acres. The commission would, in part, also aim to "educate the public, especially the white public on the racist realities of United States history" (Feagin, 2004, p. 70). H.R. 40 was referred to the Judiciary Committee, which immediately referred it to the Subcommittee on the Constitution and Civil Justice. There it died and thus never even came to a vote. Conyers has reintroduced H.R. 40 ten times, for succeeding congressional sessions, with identical results (p. 70). Conyers' bill calls only for the establishment of a commission to *study* the issue, and in more than 20 years it has not made it out of committee. In July 2008, the U.S. Senate and House of Representatives apologized for slavery and for subsequent discriminatory laws, but the resolution explicitly stated that this apology cannot be used as a basis for claims for restitution or reparations (Thompson, 2009).

Because of the obvious white skittishness about the topic of reparations for African Americans, there has been little public discussion of the meaning and scope of the monetary losses to African Americans. To begin with the value solely of stolen labor over 250 years of slavery, not only did slave labor build both the White House and the Capitol (Coates, 2014, p. 52), but from the late 1600s into the 1800s, slaves produced "*the majority* of major agricultural exports in the Western-dominated world trade" (Feagin, 2004, p. 52; original emphasis). Moreover, "Without the often profitable enterprises around African and African American enslavement, it is unclear how or when the United States would have developed as a modern industrial nation" (p. 52). Profits from slavery, then, were not just a southern phenomenon. Feagin cites historical economist James Marketti, who, in 1983, calculated the dollar value of labor stolen through slavery, including interest, to estimate that African American individuals and families lost from $2.1 to $4.7 trillion. An updated figure, of course, would be much higher (p. 53).

As we know, Emancipation did not end the unfair economic burden of being black. Coates (2014), in making his case for reparations, points out that even the New Deal, "much like the democracy that produced it, rested on the foundation of Jim Crow." Social security and unemployment insurance "excluded farm workers and domestics—jobs heavily occupied by blacks," leaving 65 percent of African Americans ineligible nationally, and 70–80 percent of African Americans in the South ineligible (p. 32). The NAACP described the safety net created by the New Deal, which had represented such a significant turning point for American society, as "a sieve with holes just big enough for the majority of Negroes to fall through" (p. 33). Similarly, after World War II, blacks were effectively locked out of the G.I. Bill's housing benefits (p. 33). All these *legal* exclusions prevented vast numbers of African Americans from accumulating the kind of capital resources to own and maintain property to pass on to their children, to send children to college, to survive economic misfortunes, or basically to do what they observed white Americans of the mid-twentieth century doing to "get ahead." Marketti estimated the monetary cost to African Americans of legalized denial of "access to land, credit, political power, and education" from the end of slavery, 1865, until 1968, when legal segregation ended, at $1.6 trillion in 1983, and would now be "several trillion dollars" (Feagin, 2004, p. 54). "Fifteen generations of white head-starts and advantage in income and other assets," including perpetual income gaps, have resulted in a huge wealth gap (p. 76). Coates cites the Pew Research Center as putting the ratio of white household wealth at "roughly 20 times as much as black households," and concludes that, "Effectively, the black family in America is working without a safety net" (p. 16).

After Glenda had been fired from her job, she expressed guilt one day over her inability to buy a car for her daughter, who was in graduate school in a city in which a car was close to a necessity. When I indicated to her that her daughter, a very bright young woman, was sure to understand her mother's situation, Glenda fired back at me, "I want to be able to help my children just the way you do yours." Since she did not know whether or not I had children, it was clear she was referring to my class as a professional, my white advantage, or both. I felt chastened by her reminder, which pulled me back from my ill-advised attempt to assuage her guilt at not being able to help her daughter and to focus on her sadness and anger at the injustices that put her in that position. We have seen how Tracy's difficulties in coping with her hardships were exacerbated by the emotional struggles of her family members and friends whose own traumas and setbacks had left her potential support system too emotionally fragile to hold her distress. And we saw that Glenda also lived among stressed family members and others in her life. Her situation vividly demonstrated to me how her family's lack of economic resources left her with no potential for help during a hard time, no familial or community safety net. While her parents had been able to buy a home for themselves and their children, by the time of their deaths, the property was worthless and Glenda was in the process of losing her own home, a victim of unemployment and the predatory lending that characterized the 2008 housing crash and which had, given the revelations that eventually came out about the mortgage business of the time, almost certainly targeted her as an African American woman. No one in her family was in a position financially or psychologically to step in to help her out.

Glenda's family's story illustrates the vital role housing has played in establishing and perpetuating the wealth gap between African Americans and whites, and in impeding the development of black economic stability and progress. You may recall from Chapter 1 that battling housing discrimination in Oakland and throughout California was a high priority for African American activists well into the 1960s. Coates (2014) provides a case study of this phenomenon by describing in some detail the relatively typical mechanisms and history of discriminatory housing practices in post-war Chicago. Redlining was a practice whereby home loans were denied to non-whites of many varieties, but especially African Americans, preserving certain areas for whites only. For property to be insured by the government-sponsored Home Owners' Loan Corporation it *had to be* covered by a clause in the deed (a restrictive covenant) barring the sale of the property to a non-white person. Redlining was not a secretive practice; it was completely supported by the federal government to insure that "millions of dollars flowed from tax coffers into segregated white neighborhoods." The purported purpose was to preserve property values. Coates describes what happened in 1951 when an African American family moved into an apartment building in Cicero, a suburb of Chicago. Thousands of whites threw bricks and firebombs and set fire to the building. The Cook County grand jury did not charge the rioters, but "indicted the family's NAACP attorney, the apartment's white owner, and the owner's attorney and rental agent, charging them with conspiring to lower property values" (p. 36).

Furthermore, when African Americans did manage to buy homes, they were not offered mortgages like those given to white borrowers, but instead were subject to a "contract" system that gave the borrowers no protection from losing their properties. As Coates points out, those policies "placed black America's most energetic, ambitious, and thrifty countrymen beyond the pale of society and marked them as rightful targets for legal theft." He speculates on the message this situation sent to African American children, "watching your elders play by all the rules only to have their possessions tossed out in the street and to have their most sacred possession — their home — taken from them" (2014, p. 50). Redlining and white flight "destroyed the possibility of investment wherever black people lived" (p. 39). It was not until 1968, with the passage of the Fair Housing Act, that this practice was outlawed. "By then," Coates writes, "the damage was done—and reports of redlining by banks have continued" (pp. 35–36).

Chicago's black homeowners fought back. In 1968, they formed the Contract Buyers League. Its members knocked on the doors of neighbors of the wealthy speculators and informed "them of the details of the contract lending trade"; withheld their installments, putting the money instead into an escrow account; and sued the sellers, "accusing them of buying properties and reselling in such a manner 'to reap from members of the Negro race large and unjust profits.'" Citing the 13th and 14th Amendments, they demanded return of money paid at 6 percent interest, subtracting a "fair, non-discriminatory" rental price for the time inhabitants occupied the homes (Coates, 2014, pp. 12–13). In 1976, the group lost a jury trial, after which the foreman of the jury was quoted as saying that he hoped the verdict would put to rest "the mess Earl Warren made with *Brown v. Board of Education* and all that nonsense" (p. 19).

This account has only skimmed the surface of the financial costs of 400 years of being black in America. Feagin estimates that "the sum total of the worth of all the black labor stolen by whites through the means of legal slavery, legal segregation, and contemporary racial discrimination is truly staggering ... perhaps in the range of $5–24 trillion" (2004, p. 55). Shocking as these numbers are, Coates (2014) highlights an obvious but very important meaning of these losses for the African American people and their communities: "Whereas individual poverty deprives one of the ability to furnish basic needs, concentrated poverty extends out from the wallet out to the surrounding institutions—the schools, the street, the community center, the policing" (pp. 5–6). We have not even touched on the costs of generations of deliberately inferior educational opportunities; discrimination in hiring, training, and union membership; inadequate health care; discriminatory policing; and the kinds of mental health stresses and burdens that I have described in preceding chapters.

From slavery to redlining, the practices described above were fully legal and were policies of the U.S. Government at the time of their implementation. The federal government, representing all of us, has made no move to take responsibility for its history, despite the fact that there are precedents for doing just that. Since 1953, Germany (initially only West Germany) has paid out many billions of dollars in compensation to claims by victims of the Nazis, and new claims continue to be processed. Significantly, since the 1990s, victims of forced labor have been able to file claims for compensation for their enslavement

(Shoah Resource Center, www.yadvashem.org). A 2014 poll (Swanson) showed that a majority of Americans (55 percent) favored Germany's reparations program, and when the U.S. Government eventually provided monetary compensation for Japanese Americans interned during World War II, the same poll revealed that 37 percent of Americans support that decision, with, it should be noted, 41 percent opposed.

Among African Americans, 59 percent believe that descendants of slaves should be compensated financially, but a tiny 6 percent of whites support that position. A somewhat larger 19 percent of whites supported the idea of "special education and job training programs for the slaves' descendants," versus 63 percent of blacks. According to the same poll, most white Americans (51 percent) believe that slavery is "not a factor at all" in the lower average wealth of black Americans, while, on the contrary, 48 percent of African Americans believe slavery has played a significant role in their lower economic status (Swanson, 2014).

In a 2001 poll on the same subject, with similar results, one respondent, a white Illinois man, expressed what may be a common rationale for shoving aside calls for reparations:

> Reparation for something that was done a hundred years ago? It just doesn't seem fair to tax people today for somebody else's stupidity a hundred years ago . . . [Slavery] was a horrible thing. But where would it start and where would it end?
>
> (Washburn & Garrett, 2001)

To this man, as to the majority of Americans who believe that slavery played no role in the wealth gap between black and white Americans, "something that was done a hundred years ago" is best left in history books. Furthermore, why should he, a twenty-first-century taxpayer, have to pay for a "somebody else's stupidity"?

This stark contrast of positions on the question of reparations between black and white Americans is not, I believe, simply a matter of money and taxes. The costs of the military budget, the space program, and foreign aid rarely meet such adamant resistance by taxpayers as does the potential cost of reparations. Considering the question pragmatically, one veteran of the Confederacy intelligently and futilely advocated reparations "as a potential economic stimulus for the South" (Coates, 2014, p. 22), an argument that made considerable sense considering the relative poverty of much of the South after the Civil War. Nor do all African Americans who support reparations expect to gain much by way of personal wealth from them. For example, one 85-year-old African American woman from Chicago who supported the idea of reparations thought the government should fund projects "that would benefit the people as a race" (Washburn & Garrett, 2001). At the heart of the resistance to reparations is not, I believe, the money to be repaid, as much as it is the fact that to accept the appropriateness of reparations is to acknowledge and take responsibility for the wrongs that were and are being done. If it agreed to consider reparations, the U.S. Government would be adding substance to the 2008 Congressional apology to the country's African American population for slavery and, most likely, for the subsequent government-sponsored harm done to the economic lives of its black citizens. To begin to study reparations, as would be required with the passage of H.R. 40, would necessitate looking into the details of this country's dark history, a process that runs counter to American insistence on looking forward, pressing the reset button, and forgetting. Furthermore, acknowledgment, apology, and reparation presuppose an admission of guilt. In these factors lie the resistance to reparations from white America and, conversely, the powerful, positive meaning such a move would have for African Americans.

Just as demands for reparation began with the end of the Civil War, so too did defensive avoidance of the topic within white society. In *Long Overdue: The Politics of Racial Reparations* (2007), Henry describes the establishment of white America's approach to dealing with slavery's injuries: "White Americans in the North chose to heal the wounds with White Americans in the South," a process in which were "forged a number of unifying myths to make it safe to remember the Civil War," and to not remember its relevance to African Americans. (p. 6). Researchers for the Equal Justice Initiative (E.J.I., 2015), for instance, discovered an "astonishing absence of any effort to acknowledge, discuss, or address" the history of lynching in communities where lynching had taken place, while monuments and markers continue to "memorialize the Civil War, the Confederacy, and historical events during which local power was violently reclaimed by white Southerners" (p. 5). Significantly, we are just now (starting around 2015) seeing public, concerted, heavily contested, and only partly successful demands to confront the "unifying myths" of the Confederacy either by removing Confederate flags from state buildings, or by "remembering" the real histories of defenders of slavery and racism and removing their names and statues from city parks, street signs, schools, and college campuses.

Nigerian critic, poet, and journalist Chinweizu Ibekwe, speaking at the 1993 Pan-African Conference on Reparations in Nigeria, makes the case for the psychological importance of acknowledgment of the justice of reparations to both Africans and members of the African diaspora:

> More important than any monies to be received ... is the opportunity the reparations campaign offers us for the rehabilitation of black people ... our minds, our material condition, our collective reputation, our cultures, our memories, our self-respect, our religions, our political traditions and our family institutions; but first and foremost for the rehabilitation of our minds ... [The] most important part of reparation is our self-repair.
>
> (Feagin, 2004, p. 80)

Continuing to leave our national history in an ambiguous limbo without honest reckoning denies the victims, survivors, and descendants of slavery and

Jim Crow an opportunity for that "self-repair," demonstrating to them that white Americans are reluctant to endure the discomfort and cost of examining and repairing a relationship so badly damaged by greed and racism. This country was founded on two original sins—the genocide of the native populations by the European settlers, and slavery—so the motivation to develop an ahistorical stance towards considering the socio-political lives of its people is no mystery.

In terms of African American history, it is noteworthy that the United States Holocaust Memorial Museum was opened in 1988 in the heart of the Capital a little more than 40 years after the end of World War II; yet the first National Museum of African American History did not open until September 2016, nearly 400 years after the first African slaves arrived in this country. By November of the same year, the importance of the museum's opening was made touchingly clear in a brief report on National Public Radio. Already visited by more than 300,000 people, its associate director, Beverly Morgan-Welch, told a reporter, "The normal dwell time [length of visits] for most museums has an hour and 45 minutes to two hours. Our dwell time can go to six." She added, "I've heard people standing and talking to each other and saying this feels like home" (Shah, 2016). Responses of a few visitors to the museum are shared on the museum website, and demonstrate how significant its opening has been for African Americans who have managed to obtain passes to see the museum. Azeez O., a young visitor from New Jersey:

> Um, wow (pause) I can't even put it into a lot of really big words. I mean it's just amazing just to see the fact that so many African Americans—the impact that we had on this country . . . it's mind-blowing. I had an idea of it before but to actually see it, and see the displays and representation of African American culture is just . . . it's like—I can't even put it into words . . .

An older man from Evanston, Illinois, named Charles N., who describes himself as a reader and thus familiar with much of what was represented in the museum, nevertheless said, "It's really nice to see everything pulled together . . . as you go through and see everything—it's not so much that we deserve this, we are due this . . ." (2017, https://nmaahc.si.edu/blog/visitor-voices-nmaahc).

Henry offers a thoughtful understanding of how American history and ideology have prevented the process of acknowledgment that would precede reparations. "Reparations," he writes, "including an apology for slavery, challenge the notion of American democracy and implicitly, the very foundation of 'American exceptionalism.'" He adds that "any challenge" to our notion of being "'chosen people' falls outside the confines of public discourse" (2007, p. 28). Coates (2014) suggests that discussion about reparations may be "frightening not simply because we might lack the ability to pay. The idea of reparations threatens something much deeper—America's heritage, history, and standing in the world" (p. 52). Similarly, Henry writes, "White opposition to an apology for slavery is a refusal to concede the higher ground" (2007, p. 176). White resistance, then, to reparations can only really be understood as a psychological phenomenon. By the same token, an honest and credible discussion and implementation of reparations for African Americans would also have profound psychological significance.

Psychoanalytic Reflections

As it happens, psychoanalytic theory has had plenty to say about reparation, some of which is helpful in understanding this disjunction between black demand and white refusal, and in fleshing out the comments of Henry and Coates cited above. Klein, Winnicott, and others opened the doors to examining the intrapsychic mechanisms of guilt and reparation in the mother/child dyad, and in their elaborations are ways to think about the challenge to white American society that the reparations movement presents. From a psychoanalytic point of view, the link between assumption of guilt and the need to repair is explicit, albeit not necessarily conscious. In order to make any true progress in achieving justice for African Americans, and repairing the troubled relationship between our country's ideals and its tainted history of racism, we may have to understand something about the nature of guilt. Melanie Klein most famously situated the origins of guilt in the minds of infants as they negotiate their alternating libidinal and aggressive responses to their mothers' breasts. Klein postulated that babies experience anxiety about their aggression, and that the anxiety represents a struggle with guilt, itself such an uncomfortable feeling, undergirded by fears of annihilation, that the infant is moved to try to fix his or her imagined ruptured relationship with the mother—to make reparations. In her article "A Contribution to the Theory of Anxiety and Guilt", Klein emphasizes that

> . . . the primary object against which the destructive impulses are directed is the object of the libido, and that it is therefore the interaction between aggression and libido—ultimately the fusion as well as the polarity between the two instincts—which causes anxiety and guilt.
> (Klein, 1948, p. 123)

The "essence of guilt," she writes, lies in the "feeling that the harm done to the loved object is caused by the subject's aggressive impulses" (p. 120).

To Klein, it seems obvious and logical that impulses towards making reparation arise in response to guilt, and in relationship to a loved object. Because of that libidinal attachment, the infant is particularly motivated to make reparations. Ogden (1989), along with others, dispenses with Klein's assignment of the emergence of guilt and the wish to repair to a stage in infancy, but instead describes the dual phenomena as part of an ongoing "depressive mode" that coexists with other modes throughout one's lifetime. He adds a significant elaboration to the evolution of guilt: "As one becomes capable of experiencing oneself as a subject, one at the same time (via projection and identification) becomes capable of experiencing one's 'objects' as also being subjects" (p. 12). The importance of this development in being able to feel guilt is that

> ... only in the context of the experience of *subjective others* does the experience of guilt become a potential human experience. Guilt ... has no meaning in the absence of the capacity for concern for other people as subjects. Guilt is a specific sort of pain that one bears *over time* in response to real or imagined harm that one has done to someone about whom one cares.
> (Ogden, 1989, pp. 13–14; original emphasis)

The ability to experience others as subjects—to be able to empathize and to imagine oneself in the others' shoes—is a necessary precursor to feeling guilt and a desire to make reparation.

Carveth (2006), in fact, demands "that we reserve the term *guilt* for pangs of conscience *that lead to reparation*, as distinct from pangs that substitute for reparation, and stop confusing it with the unconscious patterns of self-torment and self-sabotage that Freud described" (p. 188; emphasis added). Bonovitz (2009) distinguishes so-called "White guilt," a "defense against seeing the other in relation to one's self," from a real guilt that compels the person to "not only acknowledge the hate and violence perpetrated by Whites onto Blacks and one's own participation in this but also to recognize the person who stands in the thick cloud of historical residue" (p. 452). As Ogden (1989) says, reparation that comes from guilt as delineated by Carveth "does not undo what one has done." Rather it represents an attempt by a person "to make up for what he has done, in his subsequent relationships with others and himself" (p. 14). In other words, history is not annulled, mystified, or erased, but is integrated into the relationship as the reparation unfolds. Ogden adds that a person who is in the state of "whole object relations" and thus capable of experiencing guilt and the desire to repair, "is rooted in a history that one creates through interpreting one's past" (p. 13). He writes, "New experience is added to old, but new experience does not undo or negate the past" (p. 12).

The impulse to make reparations, therefore, begins with an experience of anxiety and guilt related to a belief of not having lived up to one's ideals and of having hurt another person. This injury takes place within a history that injurer and injured share and acknowledge. Furthermore, the injured person is understood to be a full human being with feelings and a subjectivity similar to one's own. It is not difficult to extrapolate these ideas to make sense of the resistance to history, guilt, and reparation that characterize our national ethos. In Chapter 7, I talked about the observations of Cheng (2001) and Straker (2004) of the complexities of American whiteness. Both noted that whiteness as an American construct that debases and exploits non-white people repeatedly betrays its own founding ideals of democracy and humanitarianism. Awareness of this self-betrayal seems destined to produce the anxiety from which would emerge guilt and the wish to repair, yet, as we observe, that shift has not taken place in the body politic of this country. White America in its institutional form has yet to come to terms with the realities of 400 years of its history. The evidence of the Equal Justice Initiative regarding lynching, the twenty-first-century battles over flying the Confederate flag, resistance to removing Andrew Jackson from the $20 bill, and so on seem to affirm that failure. The fact that the most recent movement among African Americans for justice is called "Black Lives Matter" demonstrates that African Americans believe and are willing to declare that their subjectivities have not been recognized by white America, and that to white Americans their lives do not matter. Instead, the white anxiety that surely must exist seems to remain frozen in long-standing denial, and hence there has been a failure to internalize the psychic underpinnings of mature guilt, as laid out by Ogden: the historical rootedness of one's perceptions of oneself and of the harm done to another, and the ability to see the full personhood of the object of one's aggression. Benjamin (2016) might suggest that white Americans are operating under the sway of a fantasy that "only one can live," or that white Americans can survive only if they/we "shut out others' despair."

In talking about the situation of the inevitable experience of failure by the caregiver towards the child, Benjamin stipulates that reparation requires that "the caregiver acknowledges a violation of expectancies" and re-establishes "coherence." Through the caregiver's acts of "responsiveness and correction" emerges a new, mutual kind of relatedness, which Benjamin calls "a moral third," in which both caregiver and child can grieve together, the connection "need not be severed," and it is understood that "both deserve to live." In this scenario, the "tragic world" of devastation and dissociation, an apt description of racially torn America, is juxtaposed with a "lawful world," and out of a confrontation between these split worlds is a process of "coordinated expectancies" and "mutual adaptation," moving towards the restoration of "interrupted fittedness." There is, of course, a huge incongruence between the idea of restorative reparation that Benjamin is here describing, in which an original "fittedness" is "interrupted," and a process that aims to repair a relationship for which there never was an idyllic golden age. The emphasis in the political movement for reparations is, appropriately, on repairing injuries inflicted by one group on another from the outset of their relationship. Nevertheless, I think there are very significant lessons to be learned here. Benjamin's words are particularly germane when she claims that the outcome of a successful reparation establishes a mutual understanding that "both deserve to live," and that the relationship of injured and injurer is not forever doomed to being one of winner/loser, or more dramatically, one in which only one group can survive, so that repairing the injured will mean psychological or real death to the injurer. Institutionally, white America continues to live in the prison of that expectation that only one can live. Reparation in a clinical setting, according to Benjamin, occurs when the therapist can acknowledge and respect the patient's needs and demonstrates a willingness to adapt without resorting to self-protection. We can assume the same requirements would be needed for success in an American program of reparations.

This failure to face institutional responsibility is, I believe, psychologically damaging, not only to African Americans, but also to the multiple cultures and communities that comprise this country. Carveth (2006) writes, "The enlarged capacity to experience and bear guilt (i.e., to love and thereby have conscience) that is a mark of civilization reflects the healing, not the deepening, of our cultural malaise" (p. 176).

Nuts and Bolts

In the absence of the establishment of Representative Conyers' commission, some have proceeded to put forth their own ideas about what reparations might actually look like. Feagin (2004) suggests that, even without a national program on the immediate horizon, state legislative action is a possible avenue for achieving limited relief until national action is taken. For example, in 1994, a survivor of the 1923 destruction of a small African American town in Florida and the massacre of its residents by white mobs, involving the overt collusion of law enforcement, went to the Florida legislature to seek redress. The Rosewood Compensation Act allotted each affected black family $25,000, plus up to $150,000 for documented losses. While the state did acknowledge its role in failing to prevent the massacre and funded the compensation, no apology was given to the Rosewood survivors (p. 72). Nevertheless, Feagin focuses his attention on ideas for a national program of reparation, one that "can and should be seen as dealing not with slavery alone but with the entire history of racism in the United States and its exercise abroad" (p. 77). He argues that the scale of reparative projects must be huge enough to make a dent in the wealth gap, ultimately in the trillions, or "at least as large a commitment as the federal government commitment to national defense," and, he adds, it "would need to last for a long time," possibly several generations (p. 78).

Some scholars have proposed two structures whereby reparations could be implemented. In one format, "potential black beneficiaries" would elect representatives to establish a "private trust organization" to be "administered by elected trustees and financed by United States government funds, perhaps for a specifically limited period." Trust funds would be allocated to programs "for the educational, economic, and political empowerment of African Americans." An alternative arrangement would see the creation of a national trust fund administered by African Americans and would resemble the Small Business Administration, with a board of governors who would report to Congress (Feagin, 2004, p. 76). An area of dispute about the implementation of reparations concerns the option of paying out individual compensation, such as happened in the Rosewood case, as opposed to collective reparations, as suggested earlier by the 85-year-old Chicago woman who advocated programs "that would benefit the people as a race." As we saw above, white support for reparations in general is minuscule, but even within that group, support for individual payments is about half that of collective compensation. While Feagin directs his attention to institutional reparations, he does point out that "white Americans have been able to do as they please with their accumulated wealth, and they have gained from long term racial discrimination targeting African Americans" (p. 75). Henry points out that individual payments raise the problem of the variation in the "individual harm suffered by African Americans." He writes, "It therefore is both morally and politically more compelling to argue that development banks and educational trust funds should be set up for those most economically and educationally disadvantaged" (p. 177). N'COBRA, on the other hand, calls for funding both individual compensation and programs for "institutional asset-building in black communities" (p. 74).

A version of this debate is being played out currently in Alabama. You will recall the ugly history of the Tuskegee syphilis study, in which hundreds of impoverished African American men were the unwitting subjects of experiments designed to observe the course of syphilis, despite the fact that these men could have been treated and cured of it. In July 2017, the Associated Press (2017) reported: "More than 6,000 heirs of the roughly 600 men involved in the study received settlement payments through the decades," but apparently a "relatively small" amount of money remains, and the question is, how should that money be distributed? Lillie Tyson Head, president of the Voices of our Fathers Legacy Foundation, wants the money given to descendants, money that "could help pay for college scholarships," and a "memorial garden" that the descendants' group wants to create. However, the Tuskegee Human and Civil Rights Multicultural Center, "which includes an exhibit about the syphilis study and a memorial to the men," has applied for the money. As of this writing, the case has not been decided (Associated Press, 2017).

Feagin offers a list of suggestions for how the government should allocate funding: "*large-scale* job training," "first rate public schools and housing," "seed capital to build small businesses," and "a huge investment fund that would be used to create many new job-creating enterprises" (2004, p. 75; original emphasis). Bryan Stevenson of the Equal Justice Initiative appeared on *The New Yorker Radio Hour* in 2016, where he proposed reparations that included automatic voter registration for every African American at the age of 18, enabling him or her to vote anywhere in the U.S., and half-price tuition at state colleges and universities. The possibilities are endless, and a Conyers-like commission would have its work cut out in exploring and considering the many options and priorities.

Whatever form reparations ultimately take, the process of acknowledging their rightful place in American history should not be put off any longer. Given what we have seen of American history, any move towards reparations will no doubt generate a white backlash, but that reality does not mean that such a program would not be the right thing to do. The theft of black labor and economic resources and the failure to appropriately repair that theft have played major roles in many of the psychological problems that I have outlined throughout this book. But just as important would be the refreshing psychological effects of facing the truth, painful as it is, on our national culture and all members of the American family. The psychoanalyst Janice Gump (2010) wrote, "To a large extent, conditions enabling the integration of slavery's traumas have been absent" (p. 46). I believe it is exactly that failure to allow and process true guilt and make appropriate reparations that account for that absence. It is possible, as Coates (2014) suggests, "that wrestling publicly with these questions matters as much as—if not more than—the specific answers that might be produced" (p. 60).

In spite of it all, African Americans have continued to make their way, living their lives, and contributing to their communities and to the national culture as a whole. Since slavery, they have always created strategies for protecting themselves, their children, and their communities from the injuries of bondage, violence, and discrimination, and for constructing avenues for living meaningful lives. As I hope has been clear throughout this project, African Americans are far from passive victims, and our towns and cities all have evidence of the ingenuity, drive, and community spirit that have, since their arrival in North America, characterized their adaptation to the challenges of their lives. It is my hope that a combination of increased training of young African American psychotherapists, and the development of a deeper attention to the role of historical context in psychology by all therapists, will expand the availability of quality psychodynamic treatment for our African American patients.

Barbara suggested one day what an honest reckoning would mean to her. She was complaining that recent African immigrants with whom she has had some limited contact seem insensitive and condescending to her and other African Americans. In a seeming non sequitur, she blurted out, "We got a half black president, and I know reparations are not going to happen, but can't we have an apology?" I asked about the connection in her mind between her observations of the immigrants and the futility of reparations. Barbara replied, "They look down on us, saying we're lazy, but they know the humiliating things that happened to us." For her, an apology by the federal government would say to her and to the world that her people have dignity and deserve respect.

Perhaps one February, when Black History Month rolls around again, Barbara and others will be able to celebrate not only concrete improvements in the lives of African Americans, but also a greater sense of confidence that their history has been acknowledged and their right to apology and recompense has been recognized. At the same time, their white fellow citizens will be in the process of coming to terms with the injustice inherent in the national culture slavery created and come to realize that sharing what this country has to offer will benefit everyone.

References

Associated Press (July 15, 2017). Families of Tuskegee syphilis study victims seek leftover settlement fund. *New York Times*.
Benjamin, J. (2016). More than one can live. Annual Lecture, Northern California Society for Psychoanalytic Psychology, Oakland, CA, May 21.
Bonovitz, C. (2009). To see or not to see: Blinded by guilt: Reply to commentary. *Psychoanalytic Dialogues*, 19: 450–453.
Carveth, D.L. (2006). Self-punishment as guilt evasion: Theoretical issues. *Canadian Journal of Psychoanalysis*, 14: 176–198.
Cheng, A.A. (2001). *The melancholy of race: Psychoanalysis, assimilation, and hidden grief*. Oxford: Oxford University Press.
Coates, T. (May 21, 2014). The case for reparations. www.theatlantic.com/magazine/archive/2014/06/the-case-for-reparations/361631/
E.J.I. (Equal Justice Initiative) (2015). Lynching in America: Confronting the legacy of racial terror. www.eji.org/lynchinginamerica (accessed November 1, 2017).
Feagin, J.R. (2004). Documenting the costs of slavery, segregation, and contemporary racism: Why reparations are in order for African Americans. *Harvard Blackletter Law Journal 20*: 49–81.
Gump, J.P. (2010). Reality matters: The shadow of trauma on African-American subjectivity. *Psychoanalytic Psychology*, 27 (1): 42–54.
Henry, C.P. (2007). *Long overdue: The politics of racial reparations*. New York & London: New York University Press.
Klein, M. (1948). A contribution to the theory of anxiety and guilt. *International Journal of Psychoanalysis*, 29: 114–123.
Litwack, L.F. (1980). *Been in the storm so long: The aftermath of slavery*. New York: Vintage Books.
Ogden, T.H. (1989). *The primitive edge of experience*. Northvale, NJ & London: Jason Aronson Inc.
Shah, P. (November 3, 2016). At African-American Museum, visit "dwell time" is off the charts. National Public Radio.
Shoah Resource Center, www.yadvashem.org (accessed November 1, 2017).
Straker, G. (2004). Race for cover: Castrated whiteness, perverse consequences. *Psychoanalytic Dialogues*, 14: 405–422.
Swanson, E. (June 2, 2014). Americans can't even stomach an apology for slavery, much less reparations. *HuffPostPolitics*, www.huffingtonpost.com/2014/06/02reparations-poll_n_54321.html (accessed November 1, 2017).
Thompson, K. (June 19, 2009). Senate backs apology for slavery. *Washington Post*.
Washburn, G. & Garrett, C. (May 20, 2001). Races differ on reparations: Very few whites, most blacks want slavery redress. *Chicago Tribune*, articles.chicagotribune.com/2001-05-20/news/0105200360_1_reparations-whites-slavery (accessed November 1, 2017).

Index

Note: Since the major subject of this book is African Americans, entries under this keyword have been kept to a minimum and readers are advised to search under more specific terms.

13th Amendment 52, 181
14th Amendment 52, 181

A., Dr. 138, 139, 144–145, 148n1
affirmative action 1, 50, 71n2; Althea 33, 48, 70
African American children, acquisition of racial awareness 77–82
African American family relationships 29–30, 35, 56, 135, 158–159; gaps in support 164–168
African American men: "hostility towards black women" 107; legacy of trauma and psychological damage 28–29; murder rates 29
African American Museum and Library at Oakland 16
African American patients: attitudes to white psychotherapists 127–139
African American psychotherapists 9, 132, 138, 139, 144–145, 148n1, 148n2; transference/countertransference issues 172–174
African influence-based names 38–39
Afro-American Association 13
aggression 98; *see also* anger, repression of
Alexander, M. 53, 66
Althea: affirmative action program 33, 48, 70; anger 100, 103–105, 162; attitude to white medical and mental health professionals 127, 133–134, 135, 137, 139, 146; black idleness myth 58–59; concealment of intelligence and abilities 30–31, 33, 34–35, 48; confusing experiences of racism 153–155, 156, 157–158; family history of slavery 24, 28; maternal deprivation 47–48, 93–94; and Obama 46–47, 48; and police violence 64; presumption of criminality 89; profile 19; racism experiences 69–70; response to racial injustice 160–162; skin color 47, 93–94, 95, 135, 157; and the "white backlash" 50
Altman, N. 4
anger, repression of 98–100, 158; Althea 100, 103–105; "black rage" 105–107; Loretta 101, 102; physical consequences 100–101; Tracy 101–102, 107–124; workplace 102–103
Ardoin, Amede 62
Armstrong, Louis 91
Asian Americans, behavior towards African Americans 154–155
assassination fears, Barack Obama 48–49
author profile 7–8

"bad nigger" figure 107
Baker, Peter 49
Bakke, Allan 50, 71n2
Baldwin, James 85–86
Ball, Charles 42
Ball, Edward 67
Barbara 159; attitude to white medical and mental health professionals 130, 131, 140, 141, 156–157, 170; Christianity 40–41; and Obama 49; presumption of criminality 87–88, 90; profile 19; racial mythology 82–85;

reparations 190; response to racial injustice 159; shame regarding slavery 21–23, 37, 82–83
Bechet, Sidney 43
Beneath the Underdog (Mingus) 80–81
Benjamin, J. 187–188
Bennett, J.O. 135
Bernard, John 43
Berry, Halle 93
Between the World and Me (Coates) 44, 64, 86
Bible stories 41–42
black churches, Oakland, California 16
Black Codes 61
black foremen/slave drivers 32
Black History Month 21, 190
black idleness myth 56, 57; and workaholism 57–60
Black Lives Matter movement 67, 70–71, 106, 170, 187
Black Panther Party 12, 13–14, 20, 65, 68–69
Black Power movement 13, 35, 38–39
Black Psychoanalysts Speak (White) 105
Black Rage (Grier and Cobbs) 106–107
"black rage" 105–107; *see also* anger, repression of
"blaming the victim" 36
Blinder, A. 131
blood pressure, physical consequences of repressed anger on 100–101
blues, the (music) 91–92
Bluest Eye, The (Morrison) 107
body, physical consequences of repressed anger on 100–101
Bonovitz, C. 186
Bonovitz, J. 141
Boston, school busing 50
Boulanger, G. 4, 5, 55, 110, 113, 115, 155–156, 158
Bowen, Keith 61–62
Boyd, Cheryl 48
Brotherhood of Sleeping Car Porters 10
Brown, Michael 29
Brown, P.L. 16
Brown, William Wells 74
Brown versus the Board of Education 71n3, 181
Burkard, A. 143
Bush, George 66, 67
Butler, Paul 66

Cain and Abel Bible story 41
cakewalk 43–44

capital punishment 65
Carrere, R.A. 168, 172–173
Carveth, D.L. 186, 188
Charleston, South Carolina: black church murders, June 2015 102
Cheng, Anne Anlin 36, 82, 141–142, 186
Cheryl: profile 19; skin tone, reluctance to acknowledge racism 147–148
Chicago, housing discrimination 180–181
child abuse 29–30, 55
children *see* African American children
Christianity 39–41
Cisz, J. 168
Citizen: An American Lyric (Rankine) 71n1, 85
Civil Rights Movement 13, 21, 50, 68, 79, 134; and cultural roots 38–39
Cleaver, Eldridge 14
Clinton, Bill 67; apology for Tuskegee syphilis study 129, 130
Clinton, Hillary 48
Coates, Ta-Nehesi 44, 64, 73, 86, 179, 180–181, 184, 190
Cobb, Jelani 48
Cobbs, Price 106–107, 152, 153
COINTELPRO (Counter Intelligence Program), F.B.I. 13
color blindness 89, 96n1, 143–144, 169
"colored people" 91
Commission to Study Reparation Proposals for African Americans Act (H.R. 40) 178, 183, 188
Commonwealth of Massachusetts 178
Confederacy: commemoration of 22, 183, 187; defeat of 21, 46, 51
containment 115, 116–117
Contract Buyers League, Chicago 181
Conyers, John 178, 188
corporal punishment of children 29–30
corruption, Reconstruction era 52
countertransference 7, 9, 126, 128, 151, 168–175
"crabs in a bucket" 34–36
crack cocaine: and mass incarceration 66, 165; Oakland, California 14
criminal justice system 65, 66–67; black women 66; mass incarceration 66, 165, 168
criminality, presumption of 86–90
cultural roots: African influences on 38–39; Civil Rights Movement 38–39; slaves' preservation of 37–38

dance, African American 43–44
Daniel, J.H. 138, 148
Dator, J.H. 102–103
Davoine, F. 4
De Gruy, J. 27, 34
Death in Life: Survivors of Hiroshima (Lifton) 4
Dellums, C.L. 12
Dellums, Ron 12, 16
depression, under diagnosed in African Americans 136
desegregation of public schools 1, 50, 71n3
Diala, C.C. 128
Dimen, M. 4, 5
Django Unchained 163
Dorner, Christopher 104–105, 162, 163
double consciousness 33, 82
Double-V campaign 11
Du Bois, W.E.B. 33, 43, 54–55, 78, 81–82
Dwayne 136–137; profile 19

education, role in Althea's life 34, 70; during Reconstruction 52
Eisenhower, Dwight D. 83, 84
Emancipation 1, 22, 51–57, 178, 179; ambiguity of 75–76; former slaves' family relationships 25, 27; freedmen's responses to 51–53, 54–55, 74
EMDR (eye movement desensitization and reprocessing) 111, 116, 120
employment discrimination: Oakland, California 12
Equal Justice Initiative 61, 183, 187, 189
Erikson, Erik 4
eye movement desensitization and reprocessing (EMDR) 111, 116, 120

Faimberg, H. 4
Fair Employment Practices Law, 1959, California 12
Fair Housing Act, 1963 12, 106, 181
Fairbairn, W.R.D. 98, 99
F.B.I., COINTELPRO (Counter Intelligence Program) 13
Feagin, J.R. 102, 179, 183, 188, 189
fear 64, 86; and anger 98, 99; Tracy 59–60, 62–63, 64
Flood, Elizabeth 10
Florida 62, 188
folk tales 32, 42–43
forgetting 108, 116–117

Forman, James 178
Francis 14, 151; profile 20; racism experiences 68–69, 154; transference/countertransference issues 174
freedmen: responses to Emancipation 51–53, 54–55, 74; trauma and psychological damage 74
Freedmen's Bureau 51–52, 53, 54–55
Freud, S. 186
Frye, Marquette 106
Fugitive Slave Law 28

G.I. Bill 179
Garrett, C. 182
Gaudilliere, J. 4
Geertz, Clifford 3
Genovese, Eugene D. 44n2
Germany: reparations for Nazi victims 181–182; *see also* Holocaust survivors/victims
Glenda 179–180; child abuse 29–30; confusing experiences of racism 152; "crabs in a bucket" 34; gaps in support 165–166, 167, 180; and Obama 48; profile 20; racial awareness 78, 80, 85; response to racial injustice 162–163; transference/countertransference issues 171–172
Graham, P. 158
Grand, S. 4
Grant, Oscar 29
Gray, Freddie 64
Great Migration 7, 62, 80, 155, 166
Grier, William 106–107, 152, 153
guilt 185–188
Gullah 44n3
Gump, J.P. 5, 23, 38, 190
Guntrip, H. 98, 99
Gutman, Herbert 36, 44n2

Hamer, F.M. 5, 77, 82, 93, 147, 148, 169, 173
Harnden, T. 48
Harris-Lacewell, Melissa 48
Harris-Perry, Melissa 175n1
hate crimes 50; *see also* "white backlash"
Hayes, Rutherford B. 52
Head, Lillie Tyson 189
health, consequences of repressed anger on 100–101
Hemings, Sally 54
Henry, C.P. 183, 184–185, 189
High Cotton (Pinckney) 81
Hill, Anita 6

Hiroshima and Nagasaki nuclear attacks survivors 4
history, influence on psyche 3–5, 46
History Beyond Trauma (Davoine and Gaudilliere) 4
Holmes, D.E. 5, 69, 80, 84, 159, 169, 174
Holocaust survivors/victims 134–135, 164; fear of not being believed 55–56; German compensation to 181–182; legacy of trauma and psychological damage 4, 23, 74
Home Owners' Loan Corporation 180
Horne, Lena 21, 92
house slaves 31–32
housing discrimination: Chicago 180–181; Oakland, California 12, 106
H.R. 40 (Commission to Study Reparation Proposals for African Americans Act) 178, 183, 188
humor, African American 43, 44
Hurricane Katrina 4

Ibekwe, Chinweizu 183
identity, black 73–77; acquisition of racial awareness 77–82; cultural roots 38–39; skin color and shading 90–96
immigration, psychic impact of 4
Immortal Life of Henrietta Lacks, The (Skloot) 131
Incidents in the Life of a Slave Girl. Written by Herself (Jacobs) 25
injustice 5; experiences of 151, 159–164
intergenerational transmission of trauma 3, 4–5, 23–24, 46
intermarriage, fear of in Reconstruction era 53–54
Invisible Man, The (Ellison) 82
Irish Americans 139
isolation 113

Jackson, Andrew 187
Jackson, L.C. 138
Jackson, Martin 31
Jacobs, Harriet 25, 27–28, 31, 51, 53
Japanese Americans, compensation for wartime internment 182
Jefferson, Thomas 22, 53–54
Jews/Jewishness 8, 133, 134–135
Jim Crow 8, 22, 44, 60, 66, 84, 88, 102, 153, 154, 155, 156, 168, 179, 184
Johnson, Lyndon 12, 13
Jonah 113
Josephs, L. 139–140, 143

Juneteenth (June 19, 1865 commemoration) 51
justice, desire for 160; Dorner 104–105

King, George G. 76
King, Martin Luther Jr. 48, 83, 178
Klein, Melanie 185
Knox, S. 143, 145–146
Krieger, N. 100–101
Krystal, Henry 4, 23, 55–56
Ku Klux Klan 52
Kugelmass, H. 127–128
Kwanzaa 39

labor unions 10
L.A.P.D. 104–105
Layton, L. 158, 170
Leary, K. 5, 82, 88, 89, 139, 141, 143, 147, 169
Lee, Barbara 16
Levine, Lawrence 21, 32, 37, 44n2, 91–92
Lewis, John 48
life expectancy of African Americans 101
Lifton, Robert Jay 4
Limbaugh, Rush 46, 47, 71n1
Litwack, L.F. 25, 26, 29, 31, 32, 44n2, 51, 53, 54, 55, 56, 61, 178
Long Overdue: The Politics of Racial Reparations (Henry) 183
Loretta: anger 101, 102; attitude to white medical and mental health professionals 131, 132, 134–135, 139; presumption of criminality 86–87, 88–89; profile 20; response to racial injustice 162, 163–164; and the "white backlash" 50
Lot's wife 155, 156
lynching 61–62, 183, 187; violent legacy of 62–65

Marion, Alabama, tuberculosis outbreak 130–131, 132, 174
Marketti, James 179
Martin, Jonathan 102–103
Martin, Trayvon 29, 122, 162, 163
mass incarceration 66, 165, 168
Massive Psychic Trauma (Krystal) 4
"matrifocal" family structure 35–36
McDonald, J.A. 134, 159
Meares, R. 158
melancholia 142
Miami Dolphins 102–103

microaggressions 88–90, 105
military, segregation in 11
Miller, A.E. 139–140, 143
Mingus, Charles 80–81, 92
minstrelsy 76
"miscegenation" 53–54
misrecognition 88–89
Morgan-Welch, Beverly 184
Morrison, Toni 107
Moses (biblical character) 41
Moses (slave) 32–33
Moynihan, Daniel, 1965 report 35–36
Muhammed, Elijah 41
music, African American 1, 11, 43, 91–92

NAACP 11, 178, 179
National Black Coalition Convention 178
National Coalition of Blacks for Reparations in America (N'COBRA) 178, 189
National Museum of African American History 184
Naval Ammunition Depot, Port Chicago 11
Nazaryan, A. 15
Nazism 8; reparations for victims 181–182; see also Holocaust survivors/victims
N'COBRA (National Coalition of Blacks for Reparations in America) 178, 189
"Negro Family, The: The Case for National Action" (U.S. Department of Labor/Moynihan) 35–36
Negro Motorist Green Book, The 60
"Negroes" 91
New Deal 179
New Jim Crow, The (Alexander) 66
news events, and trauma 5–6
Newton, Huey 13, 14, 65

Oakland, California: African American history in 9–16; black churches 16; crack cocaine epidemic 14; crime rate 15; employment losses 12, 14; housing 12, 14, 15; military installations 11–12; politics 16; population structure 10, 11, 12, 15; public schools 15–16; "white flight" 12, 15
Obama, Barack 5, 46–47, 50, 68, 73, 86; assassination fears 48–49, 64; as "half-black" 49

Obama, Michelle 48, 49, 64
Office of African American Male Achievement, Oakland 16
Ogden, T.H. 185–186, 187
Other, the 142–143

Pan-African Conference on Reparations 183
Papanikolas, Z. 43–44
paranoia 153
patient profiles 6–7
Patriot groups 49
penicillin 129–130
Peskin, H. 117, 118
Pettigrew, T.F. 35
Pettigrew, William 32–33
Pew Research Center 179
Pierce, Chester M. 88
Pinckney, Darryl 81
Pinckney, Clementa 73, 86
Pittman, L. 26–27
police, and African Americans 13, 29, 64, 66, 67, 106
politics, in psychotherapy 9, 119–120
Port Chicago 50, 11
"post-racial" America 68
Post Traumatic Slave Syndrome (De Gruy) 27
"posttraumatic life" 117, 118
posttraumatic stress disorder *see* PTSD (posttraumatic stress disorder)
Powell, Colin 68
Powell, D.R. 148n1
Profile of the Negro American, A (Pettigrew) 35
Proposition 14 12, 106
prostitution 66
PTSD (posttraumatic stress disorder) 7; Dwayne 136–137; Holocaust survivors 23; Tracy 63, 113, 123; Vietnam war veterans 115
public schools: desegregation of 1, 50, 71n3; Oakland, California 15–16
Pullman, George 10

Quintana, S.M. 79

race 73, 82
racial melancholia 142
racial microaggressions 88–90, 105
racial misrecognition 88–89
racial profiling 5, 70, 101, 111
racial stereotypes 73, 90; and white psychotherapists 135–136, 168–169

racism 143; acquisition of racial awareness 77–82; and anger 99–100; and black identity 73–77; experiences of 85–86, 151–159; impact on African American psyche 24; presumption of criminality 86–90; racist mythology 82–85; skin color and shading 90–96
railways, African American employment in 10
Rankine, Claudia 71n1, 85, 151
Reagan, Ronald 50
Reconstruction era 52–55
redlining 180, 181
"Redskins," Washington, D.C.'s football team 90, 96n2
Reinhardt, Mark 76
religion 39–41
reparations 52, 178; German compensation for Holocaust survivors/victims 181–182; H.R. 40 (Commission to Study Reparation Proposals for African Americans Act) 178, 183, 188; history of, for African Americans 178–185; practicalities 188–190; psychoanalytical perspective 178, 185–188, 190; U.S. compensation for wartime internment of Japanese Americans 182
resistance 37–44
riots, Watts, Los Angeles, 1965 106
Rock, Chris 86
Rogin, Michael 76, 141, 142
Rosenblatt, P.C. 107
Rosewood Compensation Act 188
Route 66 60
Royall, Belinda 178
Rumford, Byron 12
Rumford Fair Housing Act, 1963 12, 106, 181
Rushdy, Adam 21
Ryan, William 36

schizophrenia, over-diagnosis of African Americans 136
school busing 50
Seale, Bobby 13
Secret Service, and Obama 49
Self, Robert 10, 13
self-esteem, and racial identity 79–80
"sexual assault," lynching for 61–62
sexual harassment 5–6
sexual mingling, fear of in Reconstruction era 53–54
Shay, J. 115

shop personnel, suspicion of African Americans 67, 70, 89–90, 101, 120
Sickle Cell Anemia Research Foundation 13
Sidney, S. 100–101
Silicon Valley 15
skin color and shading 90–96, 134; Althea 47, 93–94, 95, 135, 157
Skloot, Rebecca 131
slave owners 22; responses to Emancipation 51, 53, 74; self-deception about slaves' feelings towards them 75
slave patrols 67
slavery 1; black foremen/slave drivers 32; economic value of unpaid labor 179, 181; experiences of living as property 24–30; legacy of trauma and psychological damage 4, 21–24, 55, 74; scale of 44n1; U.S. Senate and House of Representatives apology 178, 183; *see also* Emancipation; reparations
slaves: art forms and survival 42–44; concealment of intelligence and abilities 31–33; "crabs in a bucket" 34–36; family relationships 25–30, 35–36; as property 24–30; relationships with masters 31–33; resistance, survival, and creativity 37–44; responses to Emancipation 51–53, 74, 75; sexual abuse of 25; spirituality 39–42; trauma and psychological damage 4, 21–24, 55, 74
Small Business Administration 188
Souls of Black Folk, The (Du Bois) 33, 72
South: black church murders, June 2015 102; commemoration of Confederacy 22, 183, 187; migration to California from 7, 58, 68, 80, 155, 166; *see also* Jim Crow
Southern Poverty Law Center (S.P.L.C.) 49
Spielberg, Warren 56, 160
spirituality 39–41
spirituals 43; *see also* music, African American
S.P.L.C. (Southern Poverty Law Center) 49
Spock, Dr. Benjamin 30
S.S. *E.A. Bryan* explosion 11
Starobin, R.S. 32–33
Steele, C.M. 90
stereotypes *see* racial stereotypes

Stern, Julia 142
Stevenson, Bryan 189
story-telling 42–43, 44
Straker, G. 141, 142–143, 186
stress, physical consequences of 100–101
Suchet, M. 5, 23
Sue, D.W. 89, 136, 138, 143–144, 168
support, gaps in provision 151, 164–168
syphilis, Tuskegee syphilis study 129–130, 131, 189

Texas 51
Thomas, Clarence 6
Thompson, C.L. 59, 93, 158, 170
Thompson, V.L.S. 127, 128, 132, 135–136, 138–139, 144, 145
Tilden, Samuel J. 52
torture victim's fear of not being believed 55
Tracy 159; anger 101–102, 107–124, 137; attitude to white medical and mental health professionals 132, 147; fear 59–60, 62–63, 64; gaps in support 164–165, 166–168, 180; origins of trauma 109–115; profile 20; racism experiences 5, 70; transference/countertransference issues 170, 173; workaholism 57–58, 59–60, 107, 109
transference 7, 126, 133; *see also* countertransference
trauma: effects of 5; persistence of 46
trickster tales 42–43
Truman, Harry, Executive Order 9066 11
Trump, Donald 50
tuberculosis, Marion, Alabama, outbreak 130–131, 132, 174
Tucker, Donald 49
Tummala-Narra, P. 126, 169
Turner, Nat 51
Tuskegee Human and Civil Rights Multicultural Center 189
Tuskegee syphilis study 129–130, 131, 189

United States Holocaust Memorial Museum 184
Urban League, Oakland, California 11

vagrancy and vagrancy laws 56–57, 59, 67
validation 115, 117–118, 144
Vaughans, K.C. 5, 26, 29, 52, 56, 64, 160
Vera Institute of Justice 66
Vietnam War veterans 4, 115

violence 61; Black Panther Party 13; lynching and its legacy 61–65; post-lynching period 65–70
Voices of our Fathers Legacy Foundation 189
Voting Rights Act, 1964 1, 106
voting rights of African Americans 1, 61, 106

Wagner, A.M. 77
Walker, Kara 76–77
"War on Drugs" 66, 165, 168
War on Poverty 13
Washburn, G. 182
Washington, Booker T. 55
Waters, Ethel 91
Watts, Los Angeles, 1965 riots 106
White, Kathleen Pogue 99, 105, 173–174
"white backlash" 49–51; and the criminal justice system 66–67; Reconstruction era 53–54, 56–57
"white flight" 12, 15, 181
white psychotherapists 1–2, 6, 68, 126–127; African American attitudes to 127–139; author profile 7–8; countertransference issues 151, 168–175; discussion of racial difference with patients 144–148; and racial stereotypes 135–136, 168–169; whiteness 139–144
whiteness 139–144, 186–187
Wilkerson, I. 62
Williams, Serena 46, 47, 71n1, 85, 151
Williams, Venus 46, 47
Winfrey, Oprah 68
Winigrad, B. 105
"without legal employment" status 57
Woods, Mario 123
work songs 43; *see also* music, African American
workaholism: and black idleness myth 57–60; Tracy 57–58, 59–60, 107, 109
workplaces, repression of anger 102–103
World Trade Center attacks, and trauma 5
Wounded by Reality: Understanding and Treating Adult Onset Trauma (Boulanger) 5

"yellow" 91–92

Zimmerman, George 162, 163, 164